Nightmare Fuel

THE SCIENCE OF HORROR FILMS

NINA NESSETH

NIGHTFIRE

A Tom Doherty Associates Book

New York

CONTENTS

Nightmare
Fuel

INTRODUCTION

"*Do you like scary movies?*"

That's what the voice says on the other end of the line in the iconic opening of *Scream* (1996, dir. Wes Craven). What would your answer have been? I would have said yes. Chances are, you picked up this book because you'd say yes too. Hopefully, you are also practical enough to lock your doors before finding yourself in Casey's (Drew Barrymore) situation, where a killer can just let themselves in without you noticing.

How did you feel the first time you watched that scene? Were you frustrated that Casey whiffed an easy piece of horror trivia? Confident that you would have gotten it right had you been in her shoes? Were you shocked that easily the most famous person on the movie poster was dead before the title card?

Were you scared?

If you felt any of those feelings, rest assured that you're not the only one. It's by design that you felt exactly the way you did.

Think about the last horror movie that you watched in theatres. Was it scary? It's interesting, isn't it, that whenever someone hears that you've seen a scary movie, their first question isn't *Was it good?* Instead, it's *Was it scary?*

The long history of horror movies proves that people like to be scared for entertainment (only further reinforced by the success of haunts and horror video games). A good chunk of people who claim to be horror-averse more likely just hate one style or type of horror. In my experience, all it takes is a conversation to reveal that someone who says they hate horror really means that they hate monster movies, but they actually love the entire *Final Destination* franchise. Or they hate splatter, gore, and body horror, but love a good haunted house or possession story. Horror is a genre as broad as the range of human fears, and it takes as many shapes. In the same way, horror fans come in many forms, from all-around aficionados to adoring fans of a single scary flavor. What binds us all is our love of the scare.

THE TROUBLE WITH DEFINING HORROR

Horror films have been around since the beginning of cinema and have a firm toehold in theatres today. With directors who are often forced to shoot around tiny budgets, horror has been a source of creative filmmaking—influencing practical and digital special effects, camera techniques, sound, editing, and narrative storytelling—across all genres. Despite this lush history, the horror genre is often dismissed as trash. And if a horror movie *does* break into the right critical circles and win awards, it is suddenly distanced from the genre. That's what happened with *Jaws* (1977, dir. Steven Spielberg) and *The Silence of the Lambs* (1991, dir. Jonathan Demme). Even *The Exorcist* (1976, dir. William Friedkin), oft called the best horror film of all time, was never meant to be a *horror* film, according to its director. Is a little polishing all it really takes to relabel would-be horrors as prestige dramas? I could never wrap my brain around the inflexible thinking that (usually non-horror) filmmakers and critics grant to horror, as if it weren't the genre that is most likely to break its own rules.

Not that we genre fans are much better when it comes to putting horror into boxes.

Let's get real with each other: horror fans are notoriously picky about what gets to qualify as horror. Many people agree that 1960 was a great year for horror, with the introduction of classics such as *Black Sunday* (dir. Mario Bava), *Peeping Tom* (dir. Michael Powell), and of course, Hitchcock's *Psycho*. But even given its undeniable influence on the genre, there are some who don't think *Psycho* merits a space in the horror category because Norman Bates, despite his monstrous actions, does not fit some critics' definitions of what makes a monster . . . because he isn't supernatural in any way. (Noël Carroll, for instance, requires his monsters to be in "violation of the natural order" as determined by contemporary science. By this definition, if we strip away movie context, Norman Bates doesn't have the right traits to make him a monster—but Superman does.) And there's recently been an uptick in what some are calling *elevated horror*, whose bigger budgets and broader critical appeal make us question the borders of the genre. These films, such as *Get Out* (2017, dir. Jordan Peele), *Hereditary* (2018, dir. Ari Aster), *It Follows* (2014, dir. David Robert Mitchell), and *The Witch* (2015, dir. Robert Eggers), bring scares while appealing to highbrow sensibilities in their execution. Do they have any more merit as horror than budget scares? Not necessarily. I like to think of them as yet another shape that the horror film can take.

Do slashers fit your personal definition of horror? How

about horror sci-fi? Or psychological thrillers? Does a movie need to have just a few horror elements to qualify, or does it have to tick every box on a trope checklist?

I get it, I really do: horror is a sprawling genre, with a sometimes-overwhelming number of subgenres. Drawing lines feels personal. I *get it*, but I won't gatekeep. You might see some examples in this book that you don't personally consider horror, but maybe someone else does. I've chosen horror moments that I think are great and that illustrate an argument.

That said, I think there are some essential facts of horror that we can all agree upon. Horror is often defined by its intent to scare, or, at the barest minimum, make audiences uncomfortable. But, more so than any other film genre, it is special in that it *promises* to deliver on that emotional response. It promises to make you feel fear, and a horror movie's success hinges on the delivery of that promise. Sure, some dramas aim to make you feel sad or inspired, and comedies are hoping to tickle your funny bone, but you can still enjoy dramas that don't make you cry and comedies where some of the jokes don't quite hit your personal brand of humor. But you won't hear many people leaving a theatre saying, *Wow those scares didn't land, but it sure was a great movie!* If a horror movie isn't scary, then what's the point?

The truth is that so much orchestration goes into those scares. Horror taps into its audiences' psychology and biology, and it uses these systems to inform the moments that give us the creeps. In return, as an audience, we collaborate with horror films to create tension and build our own fear. Horror demands that we are complicit. And our complicity, our participation with horror as a genre, has built up in us very specific expectations of what we're going to see when we sit down to watch a horror film.

John Carpenter nailed it when he said, "That's what

people want to see. They want to see the same movie again." In this case he was talking about sequels, but I think the sentiment translates well to the entire genre. Andrew Britton describes this phenomenon in more elaborate terms with reference to the Linda Blair–led slasher *Hell Night* (1981, dir. Tom DeSimone):

> [E]very spectator knew exactly what the film was going to do at every point, even down to the order in which it would dispose of its various characters, and the screening was accompanied by something in the nature of a running commentary in which each dramatic move was excitedly broadcast some minutes before it was actually made. *The film's total predictability did not create boredom or disappointment. On the contrary, the predictability was clearly the main source of pleasure, and the only occasion for disappointment would have been a modulation of that formula, not the repetition of it.* [The emphasis is mine.]

I'm fascinated.

The best scary movies are the ones that make you nervous about walking on staircases or turning out the lights. They're the movies that have you peeping through your fingers at the screen and keep you up at night afterward.

I want to dissect every way horror films affect us: how the people who craft scares leverage science against their audiences; how we engage horror with our brains and bodies; and why we constantly come back for more scares when, logically, we should avoid the scenarios that we see on-screen, not happily expose ourselves to them.

While working on this book I had the happy opportunity to sit down and talk with people from all around the horror film community—horror film scholars and historians, directors, composers, and film editors—to pick apart their perspectives on the genre as creators and as consumers. One common thread appeared in nearly all of my conversations: creating horror involves elements of empathy, sympathy, and identification. The recognition that we feel while watching horror, itself a cognitive phenomenon of our brain firing chemical signals, was built out of the emotional storytelling of its creators.

I want to dig into the hows and whys of all of the bits and pieces that make horror work. What makes movies get under our skin? What makes the most effective monsters and scares? What essential roles do sounds and visuals play? Why do some films age well while others become, well, *quaint* over time?

As a horror fan myself, this investigation has deepened my appreciation for the tropes that pop up with regularity in this genre. As a scientist, it has helped me explain to myself why I'm so freaked out by what is "just" an image on a screen.

So, I'll ask you again: *Do you like scary movies?*

Have you ever wondered why?

CHAPTER 1

THIS IS YOUR BRAIN
ON HORROR

Nothing annoys me more than hearing people describe watching movies as a "brainless" activity—as if it involves somehow turning off your brain's circuitry and relying solely on your eyeballs to coast through the movie's run time. Plot twist: your brain is very much involved, engaged, and making the experience for you. Nothing makes this engagement more apparent than watching horror movies, where the filmmakers are crafting scares with your brain's and body's most likely reactions in mind.

Let's start with a scene that appears in almost every horror flick ever made. Our protagonist is home alone at night, and the house is dark. They hear sounds they can't explain, so they investigate. They go into a dark hallway and see a door at the end, slightly ajar. The room beyond is hidden by darkness. Is there something on the other side of the door? As the protagonist slowly makes their way forward, it's so quiet that you can hear every breath and floorboard creak. The movie score is starting to creep up in volume. Your eyes scan every shadow and black corner of the hallway in case something might be hiding there, but it's still too dark to be sure. We see something like apprehension on the protagonist's face as they reach for the doorknob and *jump back suddenly!* to a musical sting as a cat streaks out of the room.

Of course! It was the cat making those strange sounds—because cats are nocturnal weirdos that get bored and race around the house at night, knocking things off of shelves and doing whatever it is that cats do. The protagonist is relieved, laughing off their paranoia as they bend down to scoop up their pet. But in the next shot, they stand up, cat in their arms, and we see that a monster has appeared right behind them.

There's a lot to unpack in this scene. The elements of fear, horror, and shock are all there, and are definitely being experienced by the character on-screen. When it comes to you as a moviegoer, your mileage may vary in terms of how much you experience each while you watch the scene play out.

When we look at what gives any good horror movie its true horror vibe, we end up with two distinct elements: terror and horror. We often use these terms interchangeably, but they are very different. Terror is where tension lives. It's that awful, creepy-crawly feeling, the anxiety and anticipation that builds toward a horrifying event or realization—basically, it's the heebie-jeebies. Horror is how we *react* once that event actually occurs. We can thank Ann Radcliffe, mother of Gothic literature, for those definitions.

To tweak Radcliffe's vocabulary a little bit, I'm going to roll terror and all of the other pre-horror emotions into one and call it fear. We *know* fear. We experience fear all of the time as a mechanism to protect us from a Bad Thing that might happen.

Horror is the result of the Bad Thing happening.

It's not surprising to know that fear is a useful tool. It keeps us alive. If you're feeling fear in a dangerous situation, you're more likely to problem-solve, try to put space between yourself and that situation, or be more cautious and avoid getting into that dangerous situation in the first place.

Fear is such a useful tool that some fears stick around for generations. A great example of an evolved fear is a common one: fear of the dark. Tool use and technology have created a world where humans have no natural predators, but if we turn the clocks far enough back on our history, we quickly find that we weren't always at the top of the food chain. A theory for why humans are afraid of the dark stems from this history: many predators, like large wild cats, prefer to attack at nighttime. This also happens to be when human eyesight is at its worst. Fundamentally, we lack a shiny layer of tissue at the back of our eyeballs called the *tapetum lucidum*, which reflects light and allows for better night vision. It's also why many animals have glowing eyes in photos taken with a flash, whereas humans are prone instead to "red eye," thanks to light bouncing off our blood vessel–rich retinas. Humans who were more fearful of the dark were more likely to stay somewhere safe during the night to avoid predation; whereas fearless humans might have been more likely to do something reckless, like venturing out at night with limited vision.

This fear may not be especially *useful* today, with our lack of predators and abundance of light, but it seems to have been conserved over generations. A small 2012 study performed by Colleen Carney at Ryerson University in Toronto subjected a group of good and poor sleepers to random bursts of white noise while they were either in a well-lit room or in the dark. In general, greater startle responses were recorded in the dark than in full light, and poor sleepers reported much more discomfort than their peers who have few problems snoozing. Discomfort is an important, if subjective, descriptor here: while it's pretty common to hear people say that they're afraid of the dark, it's not typically a *screaming* sort of fear. What's most commonly reported is a sense of uneasiness and foreboding when surrounded by darkness.

Filmmakers use this uneasy feeling to their advantage, often using dark color palettes and even darker corners to mask all sorts of ghouls, killers, demons, and other threats at the edges of the frame. If you've ever found yourself scanning the blackest parts of the screen for even a hint of something nefarious, it's this evolved fear, coupled expertly with your basic understanding of horror movie tropes, at work.

The first thing to remember is that fear lives in your brain. We can experience more than one type of fear, and there is evidence for more than one kind of fear pathway in the brain. Many of them (but not all!) are grouped together in what's known as the limbic system. There isn't perfect consensus on which brain parts get to be included in the limbic system, but in general these areas are thought to be where the bulk of our emotions are processed.

Let's go back to our horror protagonist, who's just heard a strange noise. The limbic structures that we're concerned with in this scenario include the amygdala, the hypothalamus, and the hippocampus.

The *amygdala* is an almond-shaped structure buried deep in each of the temporal lobes of your brain. The amygdalae are key to decoding many emotional responses, including the famed fight-or-flight response. It's also linked to storing and processing fear-related information and fear memories. In 1994, researcher Ralph Adolphs and his team investigated disorders that caused lesions that affected the amygdala. What they found was that these people tended to have a tougher time recognizing and interpreting fearful expressions on other people's faces. Interestingly, this same study found that the recognition of other emotions, like happiness, surprise, sadness, anger, and disgust, wasn't affected. The amygdala is generally accepted as the primary brain center for fear processing, but even the amygdala might send signals along different circuits depending on whether the input is related to fear of pain, versus fear of a predator, versus fear of an attack by another human, and so on.

The *hippocampus* also plays a role in storing and retrieving memories, not to mention providing context to content. It is named for its shape, which looks like a seahorse's curled-up tail (or, as I prefer to think of it, a jellyroll). The hippocampus and amygdala are the parts that will, consciously or unconsciously, compare the strange noise to memory and help our protagonist decide whether it might belong to a threat.

The *hypothalamus* is the link between your brain and your body's hormones. It controls functions like thirst, appetite, fatigue, and more by producing signaling hormones that trigger other parts of the brain and body to release whatever other hormones are needed to suit a task—kind of like a hormonal relay system. The amygdala may be responsible for the famed fight-or-flight response, but it's the hypothalamus that sends the signal to the amygdala that *activates* that response.

These three limbic structures aren't the only parts of the brain in play in our protagonist's scenario. As they make their way down the hallway, our protagonist tries to keep their fear in check before it gets the better of them. The *ventrolateral prefrontal cortex* (VLPFC) is your brain's go-to region for willpower or self-control. Trying to get a handle on curbing your feelings of fear or some other emotion? The VLPFC will help you out by inhibiting other regions like the amygdala. Meanwhile, the *ventromedial prefrontal cortex* (vmPFC) is actively taking stock of how much control you have over a situation and helps shape your stress response.

When the cat jumps out and startles our protagonist, this new input bypasses the limbic system completely and goes straight to reflex mode. The *brainstem* is responsible here; it skips a lot of the processing work that happens in the crinkly folds of the cerebral cortex. It's responsible for a lot of automatic functions that you really shouldn't have to think about, like breathing or keeping your heart beating or reflexively protecting yourself from something jumping out at you.

And then, of course, our protagonist has a monster to contend with.

THREAT

Every horror film worth its salt has some sort of threat, whether real or imagined. *A Nightmare on Elm Street* (1984, dir. Wes Craven) has Freddy Krueger. *Friday the 13th* (1980, dir. Sean S. Cunningham) has Jason Voorhees (well, *technically* Jason Voorhees's mom). *The Blair Witch Project* (1999, dirs. Eduardo Sánchez and Daniel Myrick) has, well, the Blair Witch. Luckily, human brains have built-in systems for dealing with threats. If we take the same scenario from the opening of this chapter, here's the gist of what's happening: from the very start of that scene, your brain is telling you that a threat might be present. Even if you logically *know* that you're just watching a movie, your body is preparing for that threat, you know, *just in case it's real*. As a viewer with your butt safely in a seat and outside of the action onscreen, you can recognize a scary situation and build up your own anticipation, which is half the fun of watching horror.

If you were in the protagonist's shoes, though, you might actually feel afraid, and that's not unusual. It would actually be *useful* for you to feel fear! After all, fear is a tool your brain uses to prepare you and your body to deal with a threat. If you aren't feeling afraid yet, you are at the very least in an enhanced sensory state—vigilant, even. Your "thinking" brain takes a back seat to your senses. Everything you see, hear, smell, taste, or touch becomes crucial to identifying if potential threats are nearby.

The good news is, we're *really good* at picking up on potential threats. Oft-cited research such as that done by Sandra Soares at the University of Aveiro has found that threatening images—such as images of snakes—can trigger a threat response even when the images are flashed so quickly that the viewer might not be consciously aware that they saw the threat at all. This is in line with what's known as the Snake Detection Theory, demonstrated in research where participants (even infants!) could more readily point out snakes in images than flowers. This particular theory goes on to suggest that humans have evolved to selectively fear threats like snakes, much in the same way that humans have evolved to fear the dark, as a way to avoid the risks associated with something that we might not see until it's too late. Snakebites might not be a major threat these days, but the evolved adaptation—the ability to visually pick out potential threats—can still be useful.

It's worth mentioning that threat detection isn't limited to snakes. In general, threats like guns or spiders are also quickly spied and recognized by humans. People who can pick up on threats quickly are more likely to survive. In part, you can thank your amygdala for putting you on high alert. The amygdala is wickedly sensitive to anything novel.

Humans are also extra receptive to things appearing in

our peripheral vision. In fact, we may even be faster at re-acting to threats that appear in our peripheral vision than to threats that appear right front of our faces. In one study, researchers measured brain area activation to images of fearful and neutral faces presented either in the peripheral or central visual fields, and they found that participants showed responses in their frontal lobes and deep right tem-poral lobes (including the amygdala) as early as 80 milli-seconds after the fearful faces were shown in the peripheral vision. Compare that to fearful faces presented centrally: in this case, activity was sparked along a more classical *visual* pathway instead of in areas more directly tied to interpret-ing fear. Not only that, but this interpretation took nearly twice as long, about 140 to 190 milliseconds. We are not only processing stuff appearing in our peripheral vision be-fore we're really conscious of what we're seeing, but we're also more readily processing it as a threat.

Once the threat we're fearing makes its appearance, we have a few ways in which we're programmed to respond. You've probably heard of the fight-or-flight response before, a response famous for taking over your brain and body and getting you out of sticky situations, but *fighting* and *fleeing* aren't the only Fs that help us deal with stress—and they aren't even necessarily the first go-tos.

A few other Fs are often cited as common responses to threat: *freeze*, à la deer-in-headlights; *fright*, a.k.a. "playing possum"; and *friend* (also sometimes *flirt* or *fawn*), as in trying your darndest to engage and de-escalate the threat. Taken together, the Fs are sometimes referred to as the de-fense cascade model (although *friend* is often dropped).

The Fs explain a lot of the reactions we see in horror film characters. Sometimes it seems like a character on-screen is doing something incredibly stupid that you'd never do if you were in their situation, but even real people behave in sometimes unexpected ways when their brains are hijacked by fear.

Freeze

In the home invasion slasher *You're Next* (2011, dir. Adam Wingard), Erin (Sharni Vinson) finds herself in a position where she can't easily run away or fight. She is trapped at her boyfriend's family's isolated house with no cell service, no living neighbors, and an injured leg, *and* she's facing more than one armed would-be assassin. She is a clear-headed and decisive woman, well prepared by her childhood on a survivalist compound, but that doesn't mean she isn't afraid. By finding places to hide, she is able to not only uncover information about her attackers' identities and motives, but to take stock of her surroundings, keep track of the threat, and plan ways to defend herself.

Tackling threats head-on or running away aren't always the best courses of action when you're in danger. Sometimes your best bet is to freeze, as if you're trying to escape the *T. rex* from *Jurassic Park* (but not as if you're trying to escape a regular *T. rex*, since all evidence points to these extinct predators actually having had good binocular vision whether you're standing still or running for dear life, on top of having a super-keen sense of smell).

Freezing on the spot is also known as attentive immobility, and it's often an instinctual first phase in a fear response. It's triggered by the periaqueductal gray area of the brain when the noticed threat is interpreted, usually subconsciously, as not immediately pressing. The periaqueductal gray is gray matter that surrounds the cerebral aqueduct, a passage containing cerebrospinal fluid that protects the brain. This area is strongly linked to processing pain, and works closely with the amygdala in situations involving triggering fear responses, especially freezing, and in encoding fear memories.

Standing stock-still out in plain sight of your threat can have unexpected advantages. The whole goal of attentive immobility is in the name: your focus is on paying attention and gathering information about the threat while it's still far enough away that you're not in immediate danger (and to keep it as far away as possible). You may not be moving, but you're far from passive. You're in a state where you can track the threat's movements and switch to fight mode or run away if it comes too close. As evidenced by a slew of horror movie death scenes, immediately running away instead of gathering more information can be a terrible choice when the risk of being noticed, overtaken, and attacked from behind are high and likely.

Of course, it's ideal if you can freeze in a hiding spot, given that this way you can observe a potential attacker without them observing you right back. Horror movies often show a character hiding, usually around a corner or in a closet, a hand clasped over their mouth, trying to be as quiet as possible and bracing for the moment when they might be found out. In *You're Next*, Erin hides in a basement stairwell, where she can listen unseen to the masked attackers as they argue and reveal details about their motives and potential weaknesses. As horror tropes go, when hiding characters are found out, it's usually because an unplanned sound signals their location. In Erin's case, her cell phone briefly gets service at the worst possible moment and she gets an alert that an emergency text message she sent out earlier was received.

In nature, deer get a lot of flak for instinctively freezing in the threat of oncoming traffic, but when fawns freeze in the underbrush when they sense a predator, the benefit is clear. Darting out suddenly to flee might give them a small advantage while the predator responds to the suddenness of the flight, just as Erin emerging suddenly from her hiding spot gives her the advantage of a surprise attack.

If the fear that freezes you is overwhelming, though, this whole process can fall apart by tipping your brain over into hypervigilance. Hypervigilance is when the attention response is amplified to the point where you're scanning your environment randomly and rapidly, and you can't think clearly enough about your options for survival.

There is another reflex related to attentive immobility, known as the orienting reflex, which kicks in before you've even decided there is something to be afraid of. The response was first described in *Reflexes of the Brain*, by Russian psychologist Ivan Sechenov, way back in 1863, but the term for it was coined later by Ivan Pavlov (the very same Pavlov who conditioned dogs to salivate when a bell was rung). The orienting reflex is what makes you go *What was that?* when something changes in the world around you and immediately yanks your attention to whatever it was you heard or saw or otherwise sensed. Once your attention is focused, you can decide how to respond (and if the stimulus is intense enough, your defense responses will be activated). It sounds similar to the freeze response, but the main difference is that the orienting reflex is prone to habituation, where the freeze response is much more resistant. This is the reason you can get used to the creaks and groans that your house makes, but you wouldn't easily stop getting freaked out by gunshots outside your window.

A lot of formal features in films—of any genre, not just horror—trigger our orienting reflex and grab our attention. Features as simple as cuts, zooms, edits, and sudden noises are enough to set off our *What was that?* detectors, even if we're not aware that it's happening. Of course, in other movies, these features are innocuous. In horror films, these techniques are often cleverly deployed not only to grab our attention, but to warn us of the possibility of threat.

Now your body is primed to either run really fast or get scrappy.

Fight

Laurie Strode (Jamie Lee Curtis) tried running away from Michael Myers—now she's forced to fight him to protect not only herself, but the kids she's babysitting in *Halloween* (1978, dir. John Carpenter). Toward the end of the film, Laurie shuts herself in a close-to-empty closet in a desperate attempt to hide, but the killer soon finds her. You can pinpoint the moment when fear takes over and she reaches for anything that will help her fight back. Her hands find a coat hanger, which she unwinds and stabs into Michael's eye the moment he breaks through the closet door. When he drops his knife, she snatches it up without hesitation and stabs him in the chest. Only once he hits the ground does the fight seem to drain away from her, as she stumbles over to the bedroom exit to catch her breath against the doorframe.

At this point, we're beyond the feeling that there *might* be a threat; the threat is present and you have to deal with it. Your brain must make a quick choice between telling you to run away or to face the threat and fight. Unless your plan is to stay in a hiding spot (if that's where you're frozen), the shift between freeze and either fight or flight will take seconds, if not milliseconds. You've taken in as much information as you can, which the thalamus in your brain processes to send signals off to the necessary areas, including the amygdala. The amygdala triggers the hypothalamus, which directs a cascade of chemicals and hormones to flood through the brain and body. This wash of hormones signals another part of the brain, the pituitary gland, to produce a hormone called ACTH (adrenocorticotropic hormone), which in turn signals the adrenal glands on your kidneys to produce the hormones epinephrine and norepinephrine (a.k.a. adrenaline and noradrenaline).

Epinephrine and norepinephrine get your heart racing, and direct blood flow away from less crucial parts of your body, like your skin, to prepare your muscles for action. It may seem redundant to have both epinephrine and norepinephrine do the same thing, but it's better to have a backup plan (or hormone) than to not, right? Once that initial surge of epinephrine subsides, the hypothalamus initiates phase two of the stress response, which regroups the hypothalamus, the pituitary gland, and the adrenal glands—also referred to as the HPA axis—with the end goal of releasing cortisol, a stress hormone. Cortisol works to increase blood sugar levels and give you an extra boost of energy; it also curbs other functions that aren't big contributors to your immediate survival, like digesting food.

This is your sympathetic nervous system in action. Your sympathetic nervous system is one part of your autonomic nervous system, which manages involuntary processes that keep you alive. The sympathetic nervous system's main role is fight-or-flight arousal. The other part of the autonomic nervous system, the *para*sympathetic nervous system, takes care of activity when the body is safe and at rest ("feed and breed" and "rest and digest" sound like ideal living compared with "fight or flight"). Cortisol is what keeps the gas pedal pressed down on the sympathetic nervous system during a threat response, keeping the body on high alert. The parasympathetic nervous system takes over once cortisol levels drop after the threat passes.

People in fight mode are capable of all sorts of blind violence once their conscious, "thinking" brain has given over control to the periaqueductal gray. They will use any weapon and inflict any injury they can. This is true across species: insects will bite, sting, and release toxic secretions; birds will peck and scratch; mammals will fight tooth and claw (and hoof and horn)—and humans will punch and kick and stab at eyeballs with coat hangers. This impulsive, purely reactive fighting can save your life, but it can also be mindless and difficult to control. It's not unusual for the fight to go on long after the threat has ended.

Flight

Even in a state of pure terror, Sally Hardesty (Marilyn Burns) knows better than to try to square off against a chain saw in the original *Texas Chain Saw Massacre* (1974, dir. Tobe Hooper), especially when said chain saw is wielded by someone much larger and physically stronger. After she sees her boyfriend get sawed through, her mind flips into escape mode. She may not be able to fight back effectively against Leatherface, or any of her other attackers in the film, and she's too scared to plan a clever escape, but she can easily outrun her threats. In the end, running is what saves her.

In many cases, the best option is to run away. By putting as much distance as possible between you and a threat, you're getting yourself out of range of a physical attack and, ideally, removing yourself to a safer spot where you won't get killed by a man with a chain saw.

Your brain and body prepare you for flight in the same way that they prepare you to fight: the difference is mostly context. If you have a potential escape route, and if your threat is closing in, your brain yields control to the periaqueductal gray, and the adrenaline that's flooding your body and prepping your muscles will send you running.

Researchers have been able to simulate flight brain activity in lab settings with a Pac-Man-like game (which is much easier and more ethical than, say, wielding a knife and chasing participants around a building). When the participants were caught by a predator in-game, they received mild electric shocks. The participants' functional magnetic resonance imaging (fMRI) scans saw activity in the prefrontal cortex when the predator was a safe distance away, which means that the participants were taking stock of the situation. When the predator got nearer, metabolism shifted over to the periaqueductal gray, triggering flight.

It's important to remember that adrenaline gives you a boost; it doesn't give you superpowers. Despite the stories you hear of mothers getting adrenaline rushes that let them lift cars off their trapped children and demonstrate Incredible Hulk–like superstrength, this isn't something we have empirical evidence for. What's more likely is that something in the cocktail of hormones surging through your body is causing an analgesic effect, blunting the strain and screaming pain that you would usually feel when pushing your body to its limits. Another benefit of adrenaline is better eyesight, thanks to your pupils dilating to let in more light. In these moments, nothing is more important than trying to survive.

But how long can the fight-or-flight rush really carry you? We understand the pathways of the adrenaline rush, but research has done little in the way of quantifying it. In horror movies, victims seem like they might run forever until they're done in by tripping over a stray branch. In real life, every person has a different capacity for intense physical activity—like running for your life—and there will also be slight variations in how fast each person's body breaks down or metabolizes adrenaline. What we do know is that adrenaline recruits more muscle fibers and the nerves that control them than are normally used at once, and it is the rare extreme fight-or-flight situation where all of these motor units would be called into action. So, whatever your personal capacity, you can be confident that your body will try its darndest to get you out of a life-or-death situation until you reach the point of physical exhaustion.

Post-threat, this boost of hormones usually tapers off quickly enough, and that's the ideal scenario. In cases where people experience chronic stress, these hormones (cortisol in particular) can take their toll on the body. In the crush of fight or flight, most of your body processes are disrupted in some way to divert your energy into survival mode. As you can imagine, a long-term disruption can be super damaging to all areas of your health. Long-term stress manifests symptoms ranging from sleep problems like insomnia and mental health disorders such as anxiety and depression, to digestive issues, heart conditions, and cognitive impairment.

Fright

In *Martyrs* (2008, dir. Pascal Laugier), we follow Anna (Morjana Alaoui) as she tries to help her childhood friend Lucie (Mylène Jampanoï), who escaped an abusive cult as a child and has made it her mission to find and murder her former abusers. Anna is captured by this very same cult, whose leader, known only as Mademoiselle, believes that trauma can make susceptible people see beyond the curtain of death. Anna endures extreme torture in the name of transcendence, which culminates in her skin being flayed. Despite the massive trauma inflicted upon her, Anna is alive at the end of the film, but she appears to be catatonic.

On the surface, fright might sound a lot like freeze, but it is a distinct fear response, a state also known as tonic immobility or quiescence or "playing possum" (although the colloquial use of the phrase "playing possum" implies that the victim is *willfully* faking death—tonic immobility is most certainly an *involuntary* fear response). Where freezing is an initial response that can help you stay unnoticed and plan an escape when a threat is detected, tonic immobility is more likely to occur once an attack is already under way and your senses are overwhelmed with fear.

We commonly see this response in animals. When a rabbit is clamped in a fox's jaws, it might appear already dead, but really its parasympathetic nervous system has just kicked into overdrive in a last-ditch attempt to stave off further attack or injury. The body goes limp and lies still. Heart rate slows, and the eyes may remain open or closed, but the animal is unresponsive to its surroundings.

In *Martyrs*, the film seems to interpret Anna's final state as one of enlightenment as sought by the cult; she is senseless to everything else. It's suggested that, after so much torment, she is simply beyond fear. Before her flaying, Anna even hallucinates a conversation with now-dead Lucie, who marvels that Anna isn't scared anymore. Another interpretation is that Anna's body is making a last-ditch effort to protect against the torture that she knows she can't escape.

For a human to experience tonic immobility, they would have to be subject to an overwhelmingly threatening and life-risking situation where escape is blocked. There is evidence for tonic immobility in humans, and it has been suggested as an underlying cause for "rape paralysis" reported by victims of sexual assault. The symptoms are undeniably similar: an inability to move, scream, or call out, numbness and insensitivity to pain, and feeling cold—all without a loss of consciousness.

In order to study tonic immobility in humans, researchers in Brazil attempted to trigger the response and measure it as objectively as possible. To do this, they assembled a small group of participants who had experienced a traumatic event in the past, some who now lived with symptoms of post-traumatic stress disorder (PTSD) and some who didn't have these symptoms. All participants were then asked to describe their traumatic experience in meticulous detail. The research team recorded the script of their description and made a recording of the script using a professional speaker with a neutral tone. Finally, they were asked to listen to the recording. It's worth mentioning that the participants knew that this was the plan and that there was a possibility that they would trigger symptoms of PTSD through this experiment; they also knew that they had the power to end their part in the experiment at any time.

What the researchers found was that listening to the recording was a pretty reliable tool for inducing a tonic immobility–like response, and that the response was higher in participants living with PTSD. One notable difference: reliving the events sped up the participants' hearts, where tonic immobility in real circumstances tends to slow the heart rate down, but this study concluded that this was enough evidence for tonic immobility in humans.

There is an evolutionary basis for tonic immobility. Even though it might seem logical to prey on something that's staying still (and therefore easier to catch), many predators will only strike to kill prey that is moving. In an extreme example, some hawks might actually starve to death if they aren't fed moving prey, because they interpret unmoving prey as dead—and therefore inedible—meat. If prey isn't moving, a predator might become distracted, relax its attention, or instead direct their attack to something else that *is* moving. In *Martyrs*, Anna's immobility isn't such an effective protective tool because what's threatening her is a human who sees her as means to a philosophical, metaphysical end and not as a tasty treat.

Friend

Michelle (Mary Elizabeth Winstead) doesn't remember how she got into the bunker in *10 Cloverfield Lane* (2016, dir. Dan Trachtenberg). She remembers trying to leave town, another car sideswiping hers, and then . . . waking up in a hermetically sealed shelter underground. Howard (John Goodman) claims that he saved her, and that the world outside the bunker has become toxic and uninhabitable. Michelle senses that there's more to Howard not letting her leave than just her safety, but he's already shown himself to have a hair-trigger temper. Her only option for survival is to play her part in a simulacrum of friendship so that she can buy herself enough time to plan and execute an elaborate escape.

What's sometimes referred to as the *fawn response* isn't included in the defensive fear cascade model because it isn't a typical automatic response to a threat. Rather, this is a learned behavior, and one that is super context-specific. *Fawning* works to stave off an attack by appealing to the attacker. Of course, that means the threat is something that *can* be appealed to or appeased. It wouldn't make sense to try to appeal to a supernatural monster that, for all you know, doesn't deal in human emotions, let alone compassion or bargaining. The threat in this case is almost always human, and the situation is almost always one where the victim is trapped—often for a long period of time, such as in an abusive relationship.

Michelle in *10 Cloverfield Lane* and Casey Cooke (Anya

Taylor-Joy) in *Split* (2016, dir. M. Night Shyamalan) are both good examples of horror situations where their human, or human-ish, captors can be reasoned with. Michelle learns quickly that hostility gets her nowhere with her abductor, and that anything but playing house with Howard—eating meals together, playing board games, watching movies, and letting him infantilize her—will earn threats of death by shooting or by immersion in a barrel of perchloric acid. In *Split*, Casey is the only one of the three abducted girls who manages to engage in meaningful conversation with her captor(s) (James McAvoy). She quickly learns which of his personalities are willing to negotiate, which may demonstrate compassion, and at least one that can be tricked by feigning friendship.

Stockholm syndrome might be considered a cousin to this response, although there is enough mystery surrounding it that it might be more accurately described as a phenomenon than a syndrome. A syndrome describes a collection of symptoms, where Stockholm syndrome is typically characterized by one specific behavior: the victim forms a sympathetic alliance with their captor. There isn't enough diagnostic information for Stockholm syndrome to qualify for a spot in the DSM-V, the officially recognized manual of psychological conditions and disorders. The phenomenon is named (by the media rather than medical experts, which might explain the inaccurate use of the word "syndrome") for an incident in 1973 in which four hostages from a bank robbery in Stockholm, Sweden, refused to testify against their captors in court.

Neither Michelle's nor Casey's experiences would seem to qualify as Stockholm syndrome scenarios. While both can at times be sympathetic toward their captors, they never ally with them. Contrast their situations with that of Cheryl Dempsey (Stacy Chbosky) in *The Poughkeepsie Tapes* (2007, dir. John Erick Dowdle). Cheryl was the teenaged victim of serial killer Edward Carver (Ben Messmer) who was tortured and abused but ultimately kept alive by her captor as a slave. What probably started as a fawn response to keep herself alive transformed into a dependent relationship. Even after Cheryl was discovered and rescued, she would defend her kidnapper and insist that he loved her.

It's amazing to think that humans have such varied built-in systems for dealing with threats and that this variety gets put to such good use in horror movies. Things get even more interesting when on-screen threats cross the liminal space between film and viewer to trigger these built-in threat responses in the audience.

JUMP SCARE

If you've seen a horror movie, you've experienced the jump scare. For many of us, it doesn't feel like a true horror movie experience if we haven't jumped in our seat at least once, even if the scare itself feels cheap and predictable. And, not to put down the jump scare, but it *is* cheap. The technique bypasses logic completely and goes straight for your reflexes—that's why your body jolts even when you know the scare is coming.

C. Robert Cargill, one of the screenwriters for *Sinister* (2012, dir. Scott Derrickson), once said, "A good jump scare is like a magic trick," but if you're the one jumping in your seat, it doesn't feel too magical at all.

The reflex itself is known as the startle response, and it happens in two distinct phases that occur so fast they feel like one blended reaction: in the first phase, your heart rate spikes, you gasp, you blink, and your hands extend; in the second phase, your muscles tense, your hands clench, and your eyes are open again. Your body is bracing itself for an unexpected physical attack. In fact, it is the same physical response that most people would have if someone came up behind them and whacked them on the back.

Despite a solid understanding of what is happening in the body during a startle response, there's some disagreement about how it might have evolved in mammals (humans included). The startle reflex is thought to have evolved to protect your body and limit damage from sudden predator attacks, especially attacks from behind—that much researchers agree on. But the full-body reaction is part of what leaves us scratching our heads a little: Is it meant to draw our limbs up to protect our soft and squishy organs from damage? Are we unconsciously going through the motions needed to jump out of the way if necessary? Is it just an all-systems interruption to force us to pay attention to a potential threat? The answer can be any of these ideas, or maybe some combination of all of them. It is also thought that the face-scrunching blink that happens when most people startle is a reflex to protect the eyes from damage. That is, it's not just your closed eyelids being enlisted to protect: your grimace crinkles your nose and stretches muscles around your mouth and eyes to pull every reasonable part of your face, from your cheeks to your brow, toward your eyes to offer more cover.

Although it feels like a jump scare is bypassing your brain, researchers have been able to propose a likely neural path for the signal that triggers the startle response in mammals. A key cluster of neurons in this pathway is known as the caudal pontine reticular nucleus (PnC), part of the reticular formation in the brainstem. For context, the reticular formation is an intricate and complex collection of neurons and connective tracts throughout the brainstem that are major players when it comes to alertness and consciousness. The PnC is specifically thought to integrate information from afferent nerve cells bringing auditory (sudden loud noise!), balance (sudden head movements or unexpected falls), and tactile information (*Aaah! Something touched me!*) from outside the body, and then send out signals activating interneurons and motor neurons in the brainstem and spinal cord to contract muscle groups in the head, neck, and limbs into the signature startle pose.

In the movie theatre, the startle is a harmless reflex, but outside in the real world, it can have major consequences. Special attention has been paid to researching how people behave during a startle event to understand this response in pilots and to prevent incidents in flight. As you can imagine, the wrong response during an unexpected event can be catastrophic if you're responsible for safely flying an aircraft. So much of flying may be automated now, but in situations when the pilot has to respond quickly to the unexpected, a clear head and quick judgment are crucial. Research here often differentiates between startle (like a lightning strike) and surprise (like a technical failure) situations. In this context, startle situations are just like jump scares: a sudden and unexpected stimulus, like an explosive bang or a bright flash of light. Surprise situations are situations where something happens that doesn't match up with what was expected.

That said, surprise and startle are not mutually exclusive. In a 2016 simulator study by Wayne Martin and his team, pilots were asked to fly a missed approach. A missed approach is a maneuver undertaken by a pilot anytime it is judged that a successful landing cannot be made. Many factors can qualify for an approach to be discontinued, from the runway being obstructed, to landing clearance not being received, to the aircraft not being in the right position to touch down safely in the designated zone on the runway. In some cases, an unexpected fire alarm and loud explosion noise was sounded while the pilots were flying. The sounds shouldn't have changed how the pilots flew their task, but the study found that more than a third of the pilots were delayed in initiating the missed approach when the sounds were played.

Outside of a simulation, a startle can translate to a bad snap decision even in seasoned pilots. The biggest issue is that the startle gets processed along a divided pathway—the speedier one speeds right through the thalamus to the amygdala and sends that familiar cascade of stress hormones flowing; the slower one gets processed in the cortex, or the "thinking" part of the brain. Stress conditions affect our working memory, making our brains feel fuzzy and dumb so that anything beyond a simple choice might feel impossible. Stress also makes our fine motors less finely tuned—like we see in films when someone is being chased and suddenly can't seem to do the simple task of putting a key into a lock without fumbling and dropping the keys on the ground. That, combined with startle information reaching your cortex at a delay, means that these situations can turn hairy fast, whether you're flying a plane or trying to start your car for a quick getaway from a murderer.

For horror movie audiences, jump scares serve double duty by releasing some of the tension that's been building throughout the film while also signaling to your body to release some adrenaline into your bloodstream. Tension is a credit to film technique and should be built up and released more than once as a horror plot unravels. It's also key to a good jump scare, also known as a *fear-potentiated startle*. Basically, the more anxious you are feeling, the bigger the startle you're likely to experience (and yes, people with anxiety do tend to have a more sensitive startle with a bigger response).

A great example of tension-building, even when you can actively predict that a jump scare is coming, is the initial scare sequence from *Lights Out* (2016, dir. David F. Sandberg). The sequence is recycled from the 2013 short film that inspired the feature: a light is turned off over a seemingly empty space to reveal a threatening figure silhouetted in the dim light. The lights are turned back on, and the figure is gone. The character who witnesses this phenomenon investigates it by turning the lights on and off repeatedly. The lights go out: the figure is there, in the exact same position; the lights come on: they're gone. Tension ramps because we recognize the threat and know that a Bad Thing must surely happen soon.

The lights are flipped off, then on, then off, then on, and the figure is suddenly close enough to touch, having somehow crossed twenty feet in a fraction a second. And even though you know it's coming—actually, *because* you know it's coming—it is super effective. According to psychologist Dr. Glenn D. Walters, when it comes to horror films, the allure of the genre can be boiled down to three main ingredients, and the first two ingredients are tension and unrealness (the third ingredient is relevance). When you are anticipating the startle, through a combination of the film's buildup and your complicity as a moviegoer aware that you are watching a horror movie, that's tension and unrealness in action.

Are there exceptions to the rule that the best jump scares are of the fear-potentiated startle flavor? Absolutely. You can have a jump scare that comes out of nowhere, while the audience is relaxed and unsuspecting, but it's a lot harder to pull off in a way that's effective and scary. I can think of one movie that pulls off an amazing cold jump scare, and that, of course, is *The Exorcist III* (1990, dir. William Peter Blatty).

Often referred to as the Nurse Station Scene, it features an extended take down a long hospital hallway. Most of the action happens in the extreme background of the scene and out of focus, and to call it "action" is a stretch. A man stands at a nurse's station while the nurse looks over charts. There is a smaller jump scare setup, wherein the nurse investigates strange sounds emerging from a patient's room. The investigation is cut like the setup for a classic jump scare, with a close-up of the nurse's hand slowly opening the door to find that the strange crackling sound is nothing other than the sound of ice melting in a glass of water, eerily amplified in the hospital's quiet. As the nurse relaxes into this realization, a patient sits up and yells at her, causing her to scream and us, the audience, to jump.

This scare cleverly releases tension and tricks us into thinking that we've had our scare for the scene. The sequence doesn't build anticipation in the same way that the *Lights Out* sequence does, cueing us with repetition. Instead, this scene slowly builds tension with a long stretch of mundane moments. In a way, *The Exorcist III*'s jump scare is like waiting for a bus at a bus stop, where the longer you wait, the more you expect that something is going to arrive soon. The challenge with *The Exorcist III* is that there's no clue as to what that something will be.

After the initial jump scare with the yelling patient, we return to the long hallway shot and the nurse returns to her station. Security guards mill around, in and out of view. When the nurse decides to check on a strange sound from another room, we break completely from the pattern established by her first investigation. There are no tension-building close-ups revealing the contents of the room. Instead, we stay at the far end of the hallway and we watch her disappear into the room and return, apparently having found nothing of note. She locks up and turns her back on the room. Just as she walks away, a demon impossibly walks straight through the just-closed, just-locked door and marches behind the nurse ready to cut into the back of her neck with a giant pair of shears. The demon's appearance is also coupled with the only non-diegetic sound of the entire scene—a loud musical sting—which signals that this is the big scare that we've been building toward. And boy, is it scary.

Of course, not all people have the same startle sensitivity. We know that anxiety can be a factor, but a combination of genetics, culture, and nurture can also influence whether you're the sort of person who jumps and screams when startled, or who just gives a little jolt and gasp. Ever feel like you jump out of your skin more readily than your friends? I can't say that I'm a confirmed hyper-startler, but I am known to startle and scream in my own home if my wife is standing somewhere I'm not expecting . . . and at work my coworkers tend to loudly announce themselves when they approach my office so I don't jump (which somehow makes it worse). The sensitivity of your startle reflex doesn't directly dictate whether you will like scares more or less. That said, if you're good at reappraising the arousal that comes from a good startle as enjoyment, then there could be a correlation. I know that I definitely appreciate a jump scare that sets my heart racing a lot more when I'm actually looking to be scared.

Researchers from the University of Bonn in Germany once identified gene variants that might be responsible for some people being hyper-startlers. Their study involved testing ninety-six women for a variant form of the COMT gene (COMT stands for a catabolic enzyme named catechol-O-methyltransferase—an enzyme that breaks down dopamine in the brain and weakens its signal). The

COMT gene has been linked to the ability to keep emotions in check. COMT's two forms, called alleles, are Val158 and Met158. More or less half of the population carries one copy of each allele. So, they would have one copy each of Val158 and Met158. Everyone else is divided between carrying either two copies of Val158 or two copies of Met158. Met158 is considered the variant form of the COMT gene.

The researchers showed these women images that were pleasant (like cute puppies or babies), neutral (like hair dryers), and frightening (like weapons or injured people at crime scenes), and a loud, white noise–like sound called a startle probe was randomly played. The intensity of their startle responses was measured via electrodes attached to their eye muscles. The idea is that when you're startled, these muscles contract to make you blink. They found that women who had two copies of the Met158 variant of the COMT gene tended to show a more sensitive startle when scary images were showing, whereas women who had only one copy of the variant were able to keep their startle more in check.

Other people can have such a sensitive startle response that it becomes a pathology, known as *hyperekplexia*—a term that translates to "excess surprise." This is an extremely rare genetic condition linked to mutations on the glycine receptor gene (GLRA1). The mutation affects the brainstem and spinal cord, lowering the threshold of what might trigger a startle, but also immediately following the startle "jump" with body stiffness, sometimes so severe that the affected person will fall to the floor. If this reminds you of those videos of "fainting goats" that tend to make the rounds on the internet every so often, it's because the condition is very similar. (The fainting goats' condition, called congenital myotonia, is actually a separate disorder that can also be found in humans.) The difference between a person with hyperekplexia and a person with a standard startle response is that while most people will startle once and then experience a diminished response with each subsequent startle, especially if they happen close together, a hyperekplexic person will have just as big a startle every single time.

In real scenarios, your brain might get the chance to sift through the sensory information you've taken in and bring logic back into the mix:

- That door slammed on its own upstairs because you left a window open.
- That weird shadow is a pile of laundry that you dumped onto a chair.
- Bogeymen don't really exist.
- It was just a cat. You can relax.

But you don't feel very relaxed, do you?

False alarms can backfire. If your senses are tipping you off to a potential threat but no threat appears, a few things can happen: one, your threat alarms are less likely to go off the next time the same thing happens (this is specifically referred to as the False Alarm Effect or habituation); two, the next time the same warning occurs, you ignore it; and three, you might have a completely counterproductive response, where you end up responding in a way that is less useful and protective than you would have if you had received no warning at all.

But horror films don't give you much of a chance to reason. Everything is a setup. And we know that everything is a setup. The rules in horror movie worlds usually don't follow the same rules as the real world. Bogeymen can and do exist—and they're out to get you. False alarms are a great device in horror films for granting a temporary break in tension and make for a more interesting viewing experience if executed well (at least physiologically; the plot might still suck). But these reprieves never last long before we get ramped back up into horror mode.

SCARE SPOTLIGHT:
CAT PEOPLE (1942, DIR. JACQUES TOURNEUR)

Alice (played by Jane Randolph) has good reason to be nervous—she's been flirting with her married coworker Oliver (Kent Smith), and Oliver's wife, Irena (Simone Simon), has taken notice. This would be a tricky situation for the average person, but Irena may or may not be able to transform into a panther. After a dinner date with Oliver, Alice chooses to walk home alone in the dark, refusing Oliver's company because "[she's] not afraid," but the audience knows that Irena is following close behind. After a few blocks of walking through silent, empty streets, Alice gets the sense that someone is stalking her. She picks up her pace, straining to hear if the only sounds are her footsteps and not the echoes of someone else's following behind. Finally she stops, clutching a lamppost and looking around to see if she can spy who (or what) is making her feel watched.

We hear the low growl and hiss of what could be a threatening wildcat about to pounce. We, along with Alice, brace for Irena to attack in full panther mode. Instead, the sound turns out to be a bus's air brakes as it pulls up to a stop.

Not all jump scare culprits are real threats, but when it comes to sudden startles, your body is doing its best to keep you alive. It will always respond first and evaluate the threat later. When the scare turns out to be harmless, the technique is known as a Lewton Bus, referring to producer Val Lewton's hand in this scene from *Cat People*. It is characterized specifically by a slow buildup of tension that feels like it will definitely lead to the reveal of a threat, only to catch the audience totally off guard by something completely nonthreatening.

Val Lewton was hired by RKO Pictures while it was in a slump: *Citizen Kane*, these days often referred to as the best film of all time, was actually a flop when it was first released in 1941. RKO needed to make money fast and, taking inspiration from competitor Universal Studios' successful monster movies, they hired Lewton to lead a unit dedicated to horror. B-horror, that is. Since Lewton wasn't granted much of a budget, he had to find clever ways to get moviegoers onto the edge of their seats that didn't demand elaborate effects. If you ever find yourself tired of scares that lean too hard on CG and special effects, then Val Lewton films might be just the breath of fresh air you need.

Lewton may not have had much money to develop his films, but he had plenty of imagination, and firmly believed that he could disturb audiences through the unseen. *Cat People* features his most famous jump scare, but Lewton included (and continued to refine) startle effects in all nine of his horror films with RKO Pictures.

So if jump scares are such a reliable way to activate our startle reflex and get our hearts racing, why do they feel so *cheap*?

The issue might be that recent horror films are simply relying too much on jump scares *because* they are a reflex and can be achieved so easily. Interestingly, *Where's the Jump?*, an internet archive of jump scares in film and television series, keeps a list of the films with the highest tally of jump scare moments. Of the seventy or so "High Jump Scare Movies" on their list, only about six are films released before the year 2000 (and none is from earlier than 1981). I love a good startle as much as the next fan, but the sharp uptick in their use makes me wonder what more creative scares we might be missing.

While jump scares have been having their (very long) moment for the past few decades, there's one more emotional horror staple that had its heyday when practical effects were favored that I personally think is due for a proper resurgence: the gross-out.

DISGUST

Disgust is a distinct emotion from fear but no less a horror staple, whether it's in the form of blood-and-gore splatterpunk or moral disgust at a specific situation or person's behavior.

Once something gross has been brought to your attention, instead of triggering a fast sympathetic nervous system response like a threat would—assuming there's no obvious threat present—a different response is processed. A main function of disgust is thought to have evolved to help us avoid disease, so it tracks that the reasonable responses to something disgusting are aversion, avoidance, and, well, wanting to vomit. A lot of universal disgusts, like human feces or pus-filled open sores, have clear ties to disease prevention. Others are less obvious, like body disfigurement or stepping on a juicy slug with your bare foot.

Like other emotions, including fear, the insula seems to be heavily implicated in processing disgust and recognizing when others are grossed out. The insula is a brain region that seems to be deeply involved in pathways that describe our experiences with emotional and bodily self-awareness. More than one lesion study has looked at cases where there was injury to the insula and has noted that these injuries affected the ability to recognize expressions of disgust on others' faces. This is important: the ability to recognize disgust in others is a protective strategy. If you see that someone else is disgusted, it might mean they have come into contact with something that increases their risk of developing sickness or disease. If you have come into contact with that same something, you might be at risk too.

Wanting to hurl could very well protect you; if the threat is potentially inside you, then feeling sick is a smart response—like a behavioral extension of your immune system. When you see something disgusting, like moldy food, our brain sends a signal to urge you to vomit (or at least make us feel queasy) just in case you ate that moldy food and need to purge your body of dangerous spores. The same goes for when you see someone else vomiting. Were you exposed to what is making this person barf? It's hard to tell, so you might as well barf too, just in case. The brain has a dedicated vomit center, the area postrema, that is primarily in charge of monitoring your blood for substances that might be toxic (like too much alcohol) and signaling to your body that it needs to vomit when toxins cross into dangerous levels. Anything that can be interpreted as potential poisoning symptoms might trigger the vomit response, even the dizziness you feel when you're experiencing motion sickness.

Of course, not all disgust is born of disease prevention. A lot of what people find disgusting is learned, either culturally or by learned association. The Exploratorium in San Francisco has a great exhibit where a drinking fountain is mounted inside a toilet. The drinking water is perfectly safe and clean, but many visitors have a hard time bringing themselves to drink from it because they can't get past the association of toilets with urine and feces. Similarly, many people balk at the idea of eating insects, while in many parts of the world insects are part of a normal diet. Cultural disgust can be malleable and change over time; over recent years, Western countries have become more tolerant of the idea of insects as dietary protein (and you may even be able to find cricket flour at your local grocery store!).

These negative associations can serve up some memorable imagery in horror films. Take this gross-out moment from *Suspiria* (1977, dir. Dario Argento): ballet dancer Suzy Bannion (Jessica Harper) is in her boarding room, brushing her hair before dinner. Something catches in her comb. It's a maggot. She notices more maggots. Then the screams begin: maggots are dripping from the ceiling across the entire dormitory. You don't need me to tell you what makes this scene disgusting: maggots are associated with rot and dead bodies. Their presence means that there's something putrefying somewhere unseen. In context, this is not only gross and unhygienic, it's threatening.

Confession time: I am personally super susceptible to gross-outs in horror films, especially when it comes to gore and body horror. Any reference to cannibalism will make me hesitate to watch a movie, even though some of my favorites end up being movies centered around people eating other people—here's looking at you, *Raw* (2016, dir. Julia Ducournau). I find it particularly funny because in real life, it's quite the opposite: I've grown molds and bacterial colonies on petri dishes, which smell really bad. I have done all sorts of animal organ dissections, replete with nasty sights, sounds, and smells, and these don't faze me at all. But give me a gross moment in a horror movie, where I *know* that I'm watching a movie and that it's not real, and my stomach starts to churn.

While I was working on this book, I did a mini-marathon

of David Cronenberg films, which are infamous for their body horror and seem to be constructed specifically to inspire disgust. His films *Shivers* (1975), *Rabid* (1977), *The Brood* (1979), *Videodrome* (1983), and *The Fly* (1986) all feature some form of oozing sores, pulsing nodules, or new body orifices that have no business bursting through human flesh. Skin, hair, and fingernails are prone to sloughing away, and when it comes to effluvia, there are buckets of every goop and fluid the body can produce, and some the body definitely shouldn't be producing. None of this bothered me while I was watching the movies. But a day after my marathon, I was eating a lunch coated in a sauce that was just the right amount of viscous. My brain conjured a memory of the Brundlefly (as played by Jeff Goldblum) vomiting strange corrosive juices onto his food. And I had to put my fork down.

There's no reason for me to make a connection between the gross image of a fictional man-fly hybrid to the food I was eating and the potential that I might be eating something harmful, but my brain did the work forming those connections and making me feel disgust, just in case. It was probably helped by memories of my university student years, when I had the unfortunate tendency to boil and eat hot dogs that were *kinda* gray, or to strain the lumps out of spoiled milk for my coffee. When I ate these questionable (and undeniably gross) foods, I did tend to get sick, so in a sort of backward way my brain was trying to protect me by conjuring feelings of disgust—just in case my association between a slimy sauce and a slimy Cronenberg monster meant that my food might make me feel sick. For what it's worth, I did eat my lunch and I was fine.

Research has also suggested that pairing disgusting images with a fear message (in the case of most horror movies, the message is: "This will kill you!") will actually enhance the effectiveness of that fear message. So, if you see something that you know is scary and it also looks gross, you'll feel more aversion and want to avoid it even more than if it was just scary and not also gross. This is the reason why a lot of countries, including Canada and the U.K., include large graphic images along with the health warnings on cigarette packages. A warning that smoking might cause oral cancers is much more persuasive when you have to look at a giant, full-color image of a tumor-riddled human tongue every time you reach for a pack of cigarettes.

Okay, so I've walked you through the reactions that the human brain and body can have when it encounters something scary, threatening, or just plain gross and just how powerful those reactions can be. Some are pretty common reactions to have in everyday life, and the less-common ones can be found easily on-screen. How does all of this translate to the experience of watching horror films?

FEAR AT THE MOVIES

When you're in a movie theatre, or sitting at home on a couch watching a horror film, you're not going to run away or start kicking and punching your friend next to you. You may be glued to your seat, but you're not *paralyzed* with fear. It's not like you actually believe that you're in a threatening situation. So what's really going on in the brain? While we understand how our brain and body respond to fear and threats, our reactions to what we see *on film* seem to be a bit different.

Maybe we're not experiencing true fear at all.

In 2009, researcher Thomas Straube and his team at the Friedrich Schiller University of Jena watched brains watching horror movies. They observed forty test subjects with functional magnetic resonance imaging (fMRI) to see which areas of their brain showed increased activity while watching threatening scenes from *Aliens* (1986), *The Shining* (1980), *The Silence of the Lambs* (1991), and *The Others* (2001) versus neutral scenes from the same movies where nothing scary happens.

Instead of seeing the amygdalae getting fired up during the scariest scenes, the fMRI scans instead revealed activity in:

- the visual cortex (the area of the brain responsible for processing information about what you see);
- the insular cortex or insula (a deep brain structure that is, as we recall, tied to a ton of cognitive functions, such as self-awareness, perception, emotion, and empathy, and, weirdly, sense of smell);
- the thalamus (an area that works as a hub for processing sensory information and then sending it to different parts of the cerebral cortex); and
- the dorsal-medial prefrontal cortex (an area of your brain that, on top of being associated with planning, attention, and problem-solving, is involved in creating your sense of self, or *me*-ness, and understanding information pertaining to people who aren't you, including integrating other people's perspectives).

What this study suggests is that, despite the clear threats on-screen, we might not be activating *real* fear experiences.

Based on the lack of amygdala action observed in this study, Straube also reasoned that the amygdala might be more implicated in sudden, unexpected threats, and not so much the sustained tension that is built in (and expected from!) horror movies. In terms of the areas of the brain that *were* being activated, though, it seems less like the participants were responding to a threat with fear and more like they were paying attention to the victims' predicaments and trying to find a way out of danger *with* them (remember: empathy and sympathy have just as big a role to play in horror as identification does). It could be that horror movies are actually providing mental training for when we might be in danger in the real world. This is all speculative, of course, and sounds a heck of a lot like the plot to a movie like *Scream,* where characters survive based on their understanding of horror movie tropes and the rules of engaging horror movie threats.

It might be more accurate to say that when you're watching horror, your body doesn't go specifically into a state of *fear* but instead goes into a state of *arousal.* A lot of emotions can throw you into a high arousal state: fear, of course, but also excitement, anger, and more (and yes, sexual arousal counts too). These states get the sympathetic nervous system fired up in the same way, so it comes down to the brain to interpret the arousal and output how you're feeling about it. When your body is in *any* state of arousal, you are primed for a strong physical reaction.

Ever get really spooked during a movie and then start laughing? That's your limbic system and prefrontal cortex reinterpreting the situation and deciding that you're still safely in a movie theatre watching a movie. If we revisit the original *Texas Chain Saw Massacre*'s ending, we get a great example of what's called excitation-transfer theory in action. Sally is in the back of a pickup truck driving away from her attacker, who is still in the middle of the road, brandishing his chain saw. She is crusted with blood and her eyes are wide. She has spent the night in an intense state of fear arousal and has barely stopped screaming the entire time. But you can see the moment where she recognizes she's finally safe, even though her body is still on high alert; her screams transform into terrified laughter.

Excitation-transfer theory is also implicated in why it's so satisfying to see a monster or villain get defeated at the end of a movie. We're already aroused by the horror that we watched for the bulk of the film, but in the moments when the good guys win, we're not scared anymore—so that arousal can get funneled into the experience of another emotion (in this case, the "Heck yeah!" emotion).

SCARE SPOTLIGHT:
HEREDITARY (2018, DIR. ARI ASTER)

To describe the relationship between Annie Graham (Toni Collette) and her mother as "fraught" would be a bit of an understatement. Following her mother's death, Annie starts to uncover secrets about her mother's hold on her family that spiral into one nightmarish situation after another. The movie is relentlessly dark and rattling.

A24, the studio that distributed *Hereditary*, had twenty moviegoers wear Apple Watches during a promotional viewing to record their heart rates over the course of the movie. What they found was that heart rates rarely fell below 100 beats per minute (bpm) beyond the opening sequence and end credits, and that there were significant spikes, to 130 bpm around the half-hour mark, 140 bpm an hour in, and a startling 164 bpm in the final act. For comparison's sake, an average resting heart rate for an adult falls within the 60 to 80 bpm range.

Headlines blared that *Hereditary* was scientifically proven to be an incredibly scary, if not *the scariest*, horror movie.

It's a cool experiment, but this is hardly rigorous science. Twenty people does not a good research sample size make, and although heart rate is not a terrible way to infer stress and fear, especially given that the highest peaks do coincide with specific (and effective!) scares in the film, you can't say that fear is the only factor for the increased heart rates—just being at the movie theatre and excited to see a movie would be enough to pitch your heart rate above its resting state.

That said, this study should be repeated with fancier tools (like fMRI scans paired with heart rate and other arousal measures), a larger number of participants, and a range of horror movies. Inquiring minds want to see brains in action during slashers versus creature features and more, not to mention how *Hereditary* stacks up against other films.

Another popular theory for why we get so immersed in horror scenarios involves what are known as mirror neurons. Mirror neurons were first described in the '90s by a research team at the University of Parma in Italy. Their experiment involved inserting electrodes into the brains of macaque monkeys so that they could record cellular activity as the monkeys either performed specific tasks with their hands, such as gripping and holding objects, or watched the experimenters performing these same tasks. What they observed was that some areas of the brain related to specific movement would light up with activity in the monkeys' scans regardless of whether they were watching someone else perform a task or if they were performing it themselves.

It was suggested that these neurons, which were firing in a way that mirrored observed actions as if the observer were executing them, might not only fire for motor functions, but for sensory functions, too. These firing neurons could be the basis not only for imitative learning (literally *monkey see, monkey do*), but for empathy.

Cue massive hype in the world of neuroscience.

By blurring the lines between *seeing* and *doing*, mirror neurons opened the door to a plausible explanation for how we can glean intentions and feel empathy for others. So, it was decided that mirror neurons must be behind many human experiences. Mirror neurons are why spectators feel like they're part of the action when watching sports! Mirror neurons are why we feel our bodies want to move when we're watching dancers perform! Mirror neurons are why we feel fear when we see someone screaming on a movie screen! Mirror neurons are why some people cringe and even experience pain when they see someone being attacked and stabbed in a slasher flick!

One neuroscientist, Vilyanur Ramachandran, has gone so far as to describe mirror neurons as the basis for human culture. It's a cool theory, but before we put all of our eggs into the mirror neurons basket, we have to consider that the experimental research data so far has turned up mixed results, especially when it comes to *human* mirror neurons. Most of the data that we have has come from monkeys, like the macaques in the first mirror neuron study, because it's more than a little invasive to stick electrodes into people's brains in the name of science. What data we do have for human subjects have, for the most part, been measured using fMRI scans, and at least one study instead recorded participants' motor-evoked potentials, tiny muscle twitches that signal a muscle is ready to move, while they watched the experimenters pick up and hold objects. These experiments are enough to provide evidence in support of mirror neurons in humans, but they aren't as specific as the macaque studies to identify individual cells.

Mirror neurons might have a role to play in how we identify with horror movie victims who are running for their lives in terror—or, in rare cases, identify with the killer—but until we have more evidence, we have to take this theory with a grain of salt.

Speaking of grains of salt: an interesting thing to note about fear studies in general is that a lot of them take place in lab or research settings, and—if the study is ethical—the participants are aware that part of their experiment will include an induction of fear. Furthermore, a lot of different emotions are processed by neurons in similar locations of the brain, so it can be hard to differentiate images for positive versus negative emotions on an fMRI scan, let alone emotions that are decidedly more similar, such as disgust versus fear. Finally, when you know you're in a lab, you're pretty confident that nothing bad is *really* going to happen to you (despite the library of scary flicks that feature human experimentation as nightmare fuel). After all, the researchers have limits to how much they can simulate a threat. With that knowledge in place, some of the responses that we measure might be merely approximations of fear responses that we'd experience in real situations, and in some cases might be altogether different responses. At the very least, we have a starting point to build from. We understand what stimuli might make people jump and what might make their hearts race; they're no more in a true threat situation in a movie theatre than they are when they're in a research lab. The context makes everything unreal.

Where movie-watching is concerned, this is where our complicity as viewers comes back into frame to push back against these unreal situations. We've spent this chapter exploring how the brain can respond to horror and different kinds of threats. Those responses come into play while we watch movies as part of our immersion in the viewing experience. Scripted scenarios and editing tricks work because we prime ourselves to expect them.

Thinking back to Glenn Walters's recipe for horror, we've dissected tension and teased apart unrealness. That leaves us with the final ingredient. To get to the guts of relevance, we'll have to dig into some history.

IN CONVERSATION WITH
JAMIE KIRKPATRICK

Jamie Kirkpatrick is a film editor whose genre credits include We Summon the Darkness *(2019, dir. Marc Meyers) and* My Friend Dahmer *(2017, dir. Marc Meyers).*

How many horror features would you say that you have to edit to call yourself a "horror editor"?

While I don't think of myself as a horror editor—I work on lots of different stuff—it just so happens that I grew up kind of really immersed in that world. I've always been fascinated by it. It's funny, I rarely go see horror films in the theatre. Mostly it's because I'm a wuss. I don't enjoy being scared in a movie theatre. I just find it too stressful. I drop my popcorn. I'm embarrassed that I'm putting my hands up to my face when there are people, strangers, sitting next to me.

As someone who has edited many different genres, is there anything unique to editing for horror?

I don't think there's any other genre where the genre itself kind of dictates a certain style of editing.

Maybe the one exception is physical action, like fight scenes. Horror comes with, for a lack of a better word, a lot of baggage. And another way to say that would be: there are tropes. There are expectations that anybody who is a fan of horror has going in. They're not necessarily all active expectations. You're predisposed to expect certain things when you go to a horror film, and that's because those things have become tropes over years, if not decades, of movies. Here's a simple example: a character is walking through a dark location, so we expect something or someone to jump out at them at some point. Sometimes the filmmakers will embrace that expectation, and we will receive that expected moment, or sometimes they will subvert it, and the moment will never happen, but you are nonetheless left all scrunched up and freaked out.

So, when I'm editing horror, that's when the question becomes: What's scarier? Is it scarier to see how freaked out the character is in the close-up? Or is it scarier to be in her shoes, looking through her eyes?

One of the fun things about horror editing, specifically, is that discovery. Every scene is different, and every film is different based on, you know, whatever has come before in that particular movie or, in some cases, what you know is going to come after in that movie.

What's come before can be a complicated question when it comes to horror.

Right? The term "horror" encompasses so many different things for so many different people. One of the things I'm fascinated about in the genre is how many subgenres of horror there are. Like, very distinct, super-distinct, subgenres. I think it's fascinating that people, creators, who were drawn to horror, you could ask every single one of them about the initial impulse that led them to write their scripts, and I guarantee you, they will go, well, I wanted to do a haunted house movie. Or, I wanted to do a possessed kid movie. Or, I wanted to do a slasher film.

And you're like: those are all horror. Those are all different kinds of horror movies, but they're also, horror aside, completely different kinds of movies.

How much of the process, then, is plugging into a horror trope recipe and how much of it is really understanding what's going to happen to the audience when they watch the final scene?

I am often asked "What makes a good editor?" As I've gotten a little bit older and done more projects, I've realized it literally comes down to one thing and it's empathy. They are able to put themselves into the minds of their characters. When you can do that, you can be secure in the knowledge that when you're working on something and feeling a certain way while watching the scene, the audience will also feel that way. With a horror movie, it's watching a whole audience of people jump at the exact moment you were hoping they'd jump.

I think it's so rare that people realize how manufactured those moments are. Like truly manufactured.

I hope you'll forgive my metaphors and similes, but jump scares are the well liquor of a bar. It's just there to get you drunk and it will work every time. If that's all you care about and you just want vodka and soda, that's fine! But there's no subtlety to them. Jump scares can be done in slightly different ways; you can dress them up. But when you boil them down they're all the same. Whereas, what I think of as quiet scares or tension scares, that's top-shelf whiskey. Where it takes a lot to get to that place. It's not about the end result so much; it's about how you come away from the film like, oh my god, that one scene just like got to me.

What would you say is a good example of "quiet horror"?

I would say that *The Shining* is a great example. Kubrick was a master of his craft in terms of knowing specifically how to use the visual medium to make something scary.

The best example in the whole movie is Danny on the tricycle. That's an example of a constructed moment built from something not inherently scary.

It's that pattern of POV hallway shot: empty hallway.

Reverse on the kid's expression: happy.

Back to the hallway shot. Over the shoulder of the kid going down the hallway: empty hallway.

Turning the corner: empty hallway.

It's two or three repetitions of this pattern, and the sequence is *just* long enough that you drop your guard. You start to remember when you were a kid on a bike. The freedom of that! To roam around a hotel—how awesome is that! And then of course at that moment Danny rounds the corner one last time and you get the over-the-shoulder shot of the twins just standing there. Again, there's nothing inherently scary about two girls standing in a hallway. They're not bloody (yet). But it's so unexpected and there's a cognitive dissonance with seeing people who should not be in that place.

It's one of the scariest moments in the movie and it's all editing. It's 100 percent editing.

CHAPTER 2

A BRIEF HISTORY
OF HORROR

Movies are never created in vacuums. By virtue of being pieced together by real people based on how they view the world around them, films are destined (or doomed) to, consciously or subconsciously, reflect the filmmakers' relationships to society and culture. As Wes Craven famously said in the 1991 documentary *Fear in the Dark* (dir. Dominic Murphy): "Horror films don't create fear. They release it."

While some films are absolutely intentional explorations of social issues, from Sophia Takal's take on *Black Christmas* (2019), which overtly explores rape culture, to Jordan Peele's *Us* (2019), which takes on American privilege and marginalization, many filmmakers are unconscious of the way their films are holding up a mirror to the anxieties gripping society at the time when their film is being made. In his foreword to the book *Subversive Horror Cinema: Countercultural Messages of Films from Frankenstein to the Present* (2014), director Jeff Lieberman describes his surprise when audiences unearthed social and political commentary within his creepy-crawly horror *Squirm* (1976), about killer earthworms: "critics found some very profound subtexts which

I myself wasn't aware of. Nature getting revenge on man for his disrespect of ecology. The symbolism of man's mortality and his inevitable fate of becoming worm food. . . . This could all very well be true, but if it is, it was not done purposely on my part." And George Romero has famously commented that *Night of the Living Dead* (1968) was never intended to be a discussion about race.

The nuances of creating versus releasing fear can be lost a little when you're writing an entire book dedicated to picking apart how horror moments are carefully crafted to get certain synapses in your brain to fire. But there's something compelling about the idea that, consciously or not, horror is reflecting the fears of a public consciousness. It has always had this role. There's a reason why some older horrors don't resonate as sociocultural norms have shifted over time while other films, the ones that tap into evergreen fears, tend to persist.

Let's test this theory by taking a quick tour of horror movie history, from the first on-screen terrors to today. This is by no means a deep dive; to do horror history justice, we'd want to dedicate an entire book to it. Instead, we will look at tentpole trends in horror, sometimes referred to as *horror cycles,* and look at whether the horrors represented in those cycles echo the horrors happening in the real world at the time.

SILENT SCARES: THE FIRST HORRORS
(ca. 1890s–EARLY 1920s)

What scared us? War, Change, Communism

At its very beginning, film was an extremely limited medium where storytelling is concerned. The Lumière Brothers' Cinématographe, one of the earliest movie cameras, was hand-cranked and could record a whopping 16 frames per second. For reference, the contemporary standard frame rate is 24 frames per second, while some films, notably Peter Jackson's *The Hobbit* trilogy, have experimented with higher frame rates (holding at 48 fps). The human eyeball only begins to perceive the illusion of smooth and seamless movement from still images at roughly 18 frames per second, so while 16 frames per second does produce a sense of movement, it looks pretty jerky and jittery.

Early cameras also couldn't hold much film, which meant that once the first moviemakers started crafting stories instead of just documenting real life, they had to be economical with their narratives. (Although, in the age of social media, thanks to extreme short-form media apps like Vine and TikTok, we've since mastered the art of telling complete and compelling stories in as little as six seconds.)

The arrival of film as a medium for the masses coincided with the shift from the Victorian era into Modernism, as the nineteenth century hinged over into the twentieth. This change in sensibility was concerned with a commitment to new beginnings and a rejection of the past. Outside of the art sphere, the world and society were also swiftly changing in the years leading up to World War I. In the decades after the industrial revolution, technological, scientific, and engineering advances persisted, transforming homes and society again and again.

While not the first film, let alone a horror film, *L'Arrivée d'un train en gare de La Ciotat* (1896, dirs. Auguste and Louis Lumière), known in English as *The Arrival of the Train*, is the film that we most often refer to when we are trying to paint a picture of how audiences experienced movies at the dawn of cinema—whether that picture is an accurate one or not. The fifty-second-long scene shows a train arriving at a station. The common myth attached to this film was that audiences were so naive to the film experience that when they first watched the image of a train pulling up toward the camera, they thought the train would burst through the screen. And so the audience responded accordingly, screaming and pressing toward the back of the auditorium. Of course, historians doubt that audiences who saw *L'Arrivée d'un train en gare de La Ciotat* were so panicked by the sight of a grainy and silent black-and-white train approaching them, and there are no surviving accounts of its first showings in Paris to shed light upon the truth. According to Martin Loiperdinger, a film scholar at the University of Trier in Germany, there likewise exist no police reports or newspaper articles about the incident. It's unlikely that such a huge cinematic impression would leave zero paper trail in this way.

That said, the rumor about a celluloid train freaking out moviegoers is about as old as the movie itself. Maybe what we're really talking about when we talk about *L'Arrivée d'un train en gare de La Ciotat* is the birth of the movie marketing gimmick.

A lot of the earliest horror films feel more like experimental uses of technique and technology than narrative ambitions. One trend that does seem clear from the earliest horrors, though, is that Faustian stories were popular. We saw Faustian tales in popular literature around this time too. Faust is said to have been based on a real figure—Dr. Johann Georg Faust—a German alchemist, magician, and accused blasphemer whose life straddled the fifteenth and sixteenth centuries. The legend that grew out of his life would become the "deal with the Devil" trope. Playwright Christopher Marlowe popularized the story in Europe in the late 1500s with his play *The Tragical History of Doctor Faustus* (although the most influential adaptation of the legend would come a few hundred years later in the form of a poem by Goethe). The play presents Doctor Faustus as an ambitious man who calls upon the Devil for knowledge and power. The Devil sends Mephistopheles as a proxy, who agrees to grant Faustus powers, for a time, in exchange for his soul. In Marlowe's versions (there are two), Faustus squanders his powers and is dragged to hell at the end. Other adaptations have given the all-powerful Faustus the opportunity to repent and save his soul.

There's something about the Faustian tale that seems to have appealed to the earliest filmmakers. It could simply be the fact that the story of Faust and Mephistopheles is a familiar one that had already persisted for centuries, but the more likely explanation is that horror stories were already reflecting societal fears. With themes exploring politics, morality, and whether ambitions of transcendence should be punished, it's no surprise that Faustian parables experienced a resurgence around the turn of the twentieth century, into a fug of moral crisis and uncertainty. Tensions were mounting across Europe in the years leading up to World War I and the Balkan wars. In general, there was a fear that things had gone off track—a feeling that would only be exacerbated by World War I.

Le manoir du diable (1896, dir. Georges Méliès) is one such Faustian story, and it is credited as the first-ever horror movie, mostly thanks to the presence of horror staples, like the Devil, a transforming bat, and ghostlike figures. The movie itself doesn't feel like it was built with the intent to scare, despite seeming to be a vampire narrative of some sort. In fact, most of the earliest horror films were more aligned with what we'd describe as horror comedies.

In 1897, a shorter, but strikingly similar film called *Le château hanté* (in English, *The Haunted Castle*) was released. It was also directed by Georges Méliès, but it tends to be mis-attributed to his contemporary George Albert (G. A.) Smith and is often considered to be a lost film because of this mis-attribution (sadly, most of the horror films from this era are considered to be lost films). While the term "lost film" makes it sound like someone accidentally misplaced a film reel somewhere, a huge factor in why so many of the oldest films are lost to the annals of time is because the film stock used to create the film was extremely unstable. Depending on the care with which nitrate-based film stock (made with a com-pound called nitrocellulose) was stored, it could last for one hundred years or more, or it could degrade into a powdery, highly flammable residue that might spontaneously combust. Chemistry aside, perhaps the biggest reason for so many lost films isn't accidental destruction, but intentional destruction. With a few exceptions, early American film studios didn't necessarily see the value in archiving film reels. Rather than saving shelf space for their works, reels were simply junked when they were no longer being circulated.

While he didn't direct *The Haunted Castle*, G. A. Smith did serve up some spooky fare of his own in the late 1890s, in-cluding *X-Ray Fiend* (1897) and *Photographing a Ghost* (1898). The latter is often considered to be the film that birthed the paranormal investigation subgenre.

While most Faustian tales of this era ended with Faust being dragged to hell, *Faust et Méphistophélès* (1903, dir. Alice Guy), quite possibly the first horror movie directed by a woman, grants *Faust* an apparently happy ending, saved from eternal damnation and reunited with his love Marguerite.

Similar to the Faustian legend, adaptations of Mary Shelley's *Frankenstein* were also popular among the earliest horror filmmakers. The short 1910 version of *Frankenstein* (dir. J. Searle Dawley), from Edison Studios (which also gave us one of the first Faustian films), was probably the first of these. In a thematic vein similar to that tapped into by Faustian stories, *Frankenstein* explores human progress and fears associated with expanded knowledge and the dangers of ambitious pursuits.

In other parts of the world, early filmmakers were also drawn to what might be considered horror narratives. In Japan, a film manufacturing company called Konishi Honten (which would, 130 years after its founding in 1873, merge with the more well-known camera and tech company Minolta) released two films written by Ejiro Hatta: *Shinin No Sosei*, or *Resurrection of a Corpse* (1898), and *Bake Jizo*, or *Jizo the Spook* (1898), which are both now considered to be lost films. *Shinin No Sosei* allegedly told the story of a man who comes back from the dead after finding himself freed from a dropped coffin. There's no preserved description of *Bake Jizo*, but in Japanese legend, Jizo is a deity who acts as a guardian to children, especially children who have died before their parents.

This is a stab in the dark, given the sheer lack of information on these films and overall dearth of records on Japanese film from this era, but reports that the actors in *Shinin No Sosei* were Konishi Honten employees seems to suggest that these might have been early demonstrations of film techniques by a camera company. The presence of death and spirits in these first films isn't surprising. While a Western lens readily interprets images of undead men and ghostly guardians as horror tropes, it's hard to say without seeing the films whether the spirits featured in them were evil or not. Japanese culture has a very different relationship with spirits than other parts of the world. They're not so much enemies to be defeated as material beings that coexist alongside humans. Generally speaking, this era in East Asia was seeing dominance shifting for the first time from China to Japan, as Japan was experiencing huge growth and industrialization as part of the Meiji Era Restoration. Cultural anxieties relating to these major changes would be more apparent in the horror films that followed in decades to come. As if holding fast to tradition, until well into the 1920s many Japanese films leaned into performance techniques developed for traditional stage entertainment and storytelling, such as Nō and Kabuki, rather than evolving a new visual language for film.

While the first few decades of film saw the medium getting its footing as a storytelling tool, horror films soon began developing the visual tropes that would continue to resonate for the next hundred years and counting. Growth of the film industry into the 1920s also spelled a demand for longer horror films that could more fully explore themes of fear.

THE NOT-SO-GOLDEN AGE
(1920s–1930s)

What scared us? Economic Crisis, Political Turmoil

The end of World War I saw the rise of German Expressionism. The burdens of postwar losses, economic crisis, and political extremism left German filmmakers exploring their medium as a form of bold artistic and stylistic pursuit as well as a means for elaborating narratives much darker than those being built by their Hollywood counterparts. The shadowy atmosphere and exploration of themes such as madness and betrayal associated with German Expressionist cinema are often considered to be what birthed the aesthetics of the cinematic subgenres of film noir and gothic horror as we understand them today. Memorable horror films from this era are *The Cabinet of Dr. Caligari* (1920, dir. Robert Wiene), *Nosferatu* (1922, dir. Friedrich Wilhelm Murnau), and *M* (1931, dir. Fritz Lang). Eventually, Hollywood would pick up threads of German Expressionism overseas with films like *The Phantom of the Opera* (1925, dir. Rupert Julian).

The harshness of Expressionism aside, the Roaring Twenties saw Americans enjoying relative comfort during postwar economic expansion, but as the decade wore on, the tides of good fortune began to turn.

In 1929, the stock market collapsed completely and the United States saw a cataclysmic economic downturn. Families lost their jobs and homes. Around the same time, droughts destroyed houses and agricultural opportunities, ushering in the Dust Bowl era of the Great Depression. In the United States, movies with fantastic and fabulist elements became a favorite way to escape the weight of the Great Depression, and horror movies were no exception to this rule.

While some horror films certainly were found unsatisfying at the time—largely because they lacked those fantastical elements and dealt with darker and uneasy themes, like the ones explored in *Freaks* (1932, dir. Tod Browning)—what did suit audiences' desires for fantasy were the movies that Universal Pictures presented as their first forays into the horror genre with their classic gothic monsters. The first on the scene were *The Hunchback of No-*

tre Dame (1923, dir. Wallace Worsley) and *The Phantom of the Opera*, although these days, they aren't the films that people tend to recall first when the words "Universal" and "monster" are spoken together in the same breath. The Universal Classic Monster A-Team generally includes Boris Karloff's monster in *Frankenstein* (1931, dir. James Whale) and *The Mummy* (1932, dir. Karl Freund), Bela Lugosi's *Dracula* (1931, dirs. Tod Browning and Karl Freund)—and sometimes Claude Rains's *The Invisible Man* (1933, dir. James Whale) gets to join too. Later, the team was rounded out with Lon Chaney's *The Wolf Man* (1941, dir. George Waggner) and Ricou Browning and Ben Chapman's jointly uncredited roles as the Gill Man from *The Creature from the Black Lagoon* (1954, dir. Jack Arnold).

These iconic monsters were often depicted in ways that walked the fine line of showing a monster as a threatening, inhuman "Other" and as a sympathetic, often lonely creature that acknowledges the human condition. As Stephen King describes it in *Danse Macabre*, there's "something so sad, so miserable there that our hearts actually go out to the creature even as [we] are shrinking away from it in fear and disgust." In this way, the monsters become convenient and recognizable stand-ins for audience anxieties, displacing them just enough outside of the human sphere that they can be experienced from a safe fantasy vantage point.

This distancing through fantasy likely served as a useful tool as oversight of the film industry became stricter. By 1922, outside forces were pushing back against Hollywood. At the local level, religious leaders would make up morality rules and would hack up movie reels until they were deemed fit for audiences to consume. In 1930, former postmaster general Will Hays developed a set of thirty-six production rules and recommendations for conserving wholesome content in film. These rules had a wide scope, basically strangling depictions of anything that might be deemed to lower the morality of the audience or place the audience in a position where they might feel sympathetic toward evil, crime, or sin. This meant that religious figures could not be ridiculed or otherwise treated comedically, characters couldn't be shown nude (or even dancing suggestively), and topics like sex, passion, crime, and violence were off the table. The Hays Code was supposed to be a voluntary system, but Hays's political influence allowed him to set up this new production code system in such a way that, if filmmakers wanted their movies to actually be shown in theatres, they'd have to toe the line of propriety.

Other parts of the world saw similar restrictions. The British Board of Film Censors (BBFC) introduced an "H" rating (for "horrific") in 1933 and openly discouraged the production of films that would befit an H rating. Meanwhile in Japan, the film industry had been policed by tight regulations as early as 1917, to control against obscenity—a term that refused to be pinned down by a concrete definition. Unsurprisingly, the result of this sort of control meant that fewer horror movies tended to be produced for wide release . . . at least until studios realized that they were losing out on profits and picked up the horror thread anew.

ENTER THE ATOM (1940s–1950s)

What scared us? Thermonuclear Weapons, Communism (Again)

Post-Hiroshima and post-Nagasaki fear of nuclear radiation and how it could affect us suffused society in the '50s. In 1950, President Truman made the controversial decision to supercharge research into nuclear weapons, adding fuel to the nuclear arms race between the United States and the Soviet Union, the development of the hydrogen bomb, and schoolchildren everywhere practicing how to hide under their desks in case of a nuclear attack, guided to "duck and cover" by a cartoon turtle.

The term "Doomsday Clock" was coined around this era as a metaphor to describe how close humanity has come to nuclear annihilation. By 1953, the clock had been revised to state that humanity was "two minutes till midnight"— that is to say: approaching the end.

This fear ushered in a new era of movie monsters: the radioactive mutants. *Them!* (1954, dir. Gordon Douglas) is one of the first and most well known of these features, in which a colony of giant ants are discovered, apparently mutated from the first nuclear tests at the Trinity site in New Mexico. Dr. Medford (played by Edmund Gwenn), the entomologist who helps to destroy the killer ants, directly cites the real horror of the film when he observes, "When Man entered the Atomic Age, he opened the door to a new world. What we may eventually find in that new world, nobody can predict." Unsurprisingly, what followed was a wave of "big bug" copycat films, like the humongous stop-motion scorpion of *The Black Scorpion* (1957, dir. Edward Ludwig), the hundred-foot-tall tarantula of *Tarantula!* (1955, dir. Jack Arnold), and other non-arthropod mutant monsters.

In other parts of the world, similar threats resonated. In 1954, the first *Godzilla* (dir. Ishirō Honda) film was released in Japan (later to be reedited and introduced to North America as *Godzilla, King of the Monsters* in 1956). A later release, *Matango* (1963, dir. Ishirō Honda), or *Attack of the Mushroom People*, was almost banned when it was first released in Japan. The victims portrayed in the film are abandoned on an island where the local flora and fauna seem to have been mutated by nuclear waste. When they eat the monstrous (and monstrously addictive) mushrooms native to the island, they find themselves transforming into mutant mushroom people. What was so controversial about this film was that it was apparently felt that these transforming mushroom people appeared strikingly similar to victims of atomic bombings in Japan. Director Ishirō Honda has also commented that *Matango* reflects other relevant fears of the time, including drug use and addiction (not unlike drug-related fears that were unfolding in Britain and the United States around the same time, as heroin use began to climb).

Not everyone was afraid of radiation, though. Despite the horrors of the atomic bomb, excitement was still running high about the potential powers of radiation. This led to a lot of ill-advised personal products, from a conceptual nuclear-powered car (the Ford Nucleon) to actual uranium sand houses, which were briefly popular cure-all spaces where you could book an appointment to rest your feet in some mildly radioactive uranium sand.

One of the weirder fads to come out of the Atomic Age was a hobby known as gamma gardening, which took hold both in parts of Europe and the United States. It's unclear where the rumor started, but reports popped up around 1947 alleging that plants that grew in the atom-blasted soil in and around Nagasaki were larger and yielded more than regular crops. It wasn't long before government experiments enlisted farmers in the United States to observe the effects of radiation on crops—essentially to understand just how messed up agriculture would become if an important crop-growing region got nuked, and also to see if radiation could in fact create useful mutations. The Giant Insect movies of the 1950s tended to draw a straight line between the idea of radiation causing mutations and its worst-case scenarios.

The giant locusts of *Beginning of the End* (1957, dir. Bert I. Gordon) were even born thanks to regular locusts chowing down on beachball-sized tomatoes and strawberries grown in an experimental gamma gardening laboratory.

Tied to fears of radiation were fears about communism. FBI director J. Edgar Hoover was famously quick to equate any form of protest with communism, and Wisconsin senator Joe McCarthy, who is well known for his fear tactics during this era, terrorized others (especially Hollywood) with hair-trigger accusations of subversion or treason without much, if any, evidence. McCarthyism fostered an environment in which paranoia and mistrust flourished.

The resultant fear that people you see every day might secretly be enemies is reflected in horrors of this era—notably *Invasion of the Body Snatchers* (1956, dir. Don Siegel). Alien invasion movies had their moment in the 1950s as the totalitarian takeovers presented in films like *The War of the Worlds* (1953, dir. Byron Haskin) and *The Thing from Another World* (1951, dir. Christian Nyby) resonated with moviegoers worried about Soviet occupation.

One such alien invasion movie, *The Blob* (1958, dirs. Irvin S. Yeaworth, Jr., and Russell S. Doughten, Jr., uncredited), has seen its red, amorphous, all-consuming alien interpreted as a metaphor for the Red Scare. In an interview, producer Jack Harris dismissed the association as "hogwash." According to Harris, Yeaworth saw the Blob as a parable "about God's wrath upon evildoers." I'm not exactly sure who Yeaworth envisions were evildoers in *The Blob,* unless he's referring to punishing teen sexuality, given that the entity was discovered by some youngsters (played by Steve McQueen and Aneta Corsaut, who were twenty-eight and twenty-five, respectively, and look it) who had been on a romantic venture to the local lovers' lane.

From nuclear bugs to extraterrestrial monstrosities, some of the forms that fears took in the 1940s and 1950s were really *out there*. Once you center a movie around a giant radioactive killer eyeball with tentacles—hi, *The Trollenberg Terror* (1958, dir. Quentin Lawrence)!—how do you top that? It was almost inevitable that horror would recalibrate by pulling back from the cosmic horrors with a return to the familiar.

HELL IS OTHER PEOPLE (1960s)

What scared us? Social Turmoil, Changing Values

Two key movies appeared on the scene in 1960 to mark the shift from creature features to the unknowable terrors held within the minds of other humans. Those movies were *Psycho* (1960, dir. Alfred Hitchcock) and *Peeping Tom* (1960, dir. Michael Powell).

While both films depicted serial killers of sorts—*Psycho*, adapted from the novel of the same name by Robert Bloch, drew inspiration from killer Ed Gein's crimes in the late 1950s, the same man who would later inspire Leatherface in *The Texas Chain Saw Massacre*—the now-household term "serial killer" had yet to become familiar in the way it would in the decades to come, as more families would begin to have TV sets in their homes where they could watch the news of national and international crimes unfold.

Psycho's Norman Bates (Anthony Perkins) seemed an awkward but polite young man, hardly a threatening figure until he shocked audiences by dispatching with the film's heroine within the first hour of the film. *Peeping Tom*'s Mark

Lewis (Carl Boehm) is another average-looking, shy young man who hides murderous voyeurism (born of a lifetime of systematic psychological abuse and conditioning at his father's hands). With the world recovering from one war and moving into another, the reality of horrors taking human form on-screen was poignant to audiences. This is a fear that seems to reappear more often than others throughout decades of horror cinema, easily spanning fears of communism from the turn of the century and in the 1950s and, well, fears of communism in the 1980s: that the people that you see every day, your neighbors, your friends, or the polite young man working the receptionist's desk, might secretly be your enemies.

Directors in Italy picked up where *Psycho* and *Peeping Tom* left off to form their own pulpy, stylish take on human violence with giallo. Named after the yellow covers of cheap crime novels (originally those published by Mondadori, starting in 1929, but eventually yellow became the go-to cover color for publishing houses publishing pulp), gialli delivered crime thrillers that used sensory motifs and violence as transgression to tensions in Italy around the time—similar in some ways to shifts that were occurring in America, but without the repression of a Production Code.

The Girl Who Knew Too Much (1963, dir. Mario Bava), with its undeniably pulpy mood and style, is usually identified as the first giallo film, but we often associate the aesthetics of the genre with later entries, like the vibrant color-saturated sets and sensational murder scenes of *Blood and Black Lace* (1964, dir. Mario Bava) and the black-gloved killers and gloppy red blood of *The Bird with the Crystal Plumage* (1970, dir. Dario Argento). A lot of the stylistic elements built up by gialli would be borrowed when American slashers would begin to hit their groove in the late 1970s and early '80s. In the meantime, the 1960s would still see social tensions rise and spill over onto the screen, just not in such a splash-tastic, Technicolor way.

VIOLENT ENDS (LATE 1960s–1970s)

What scared us? The Vietnam War, Cults, Serial Killers

In public, people were taking to the streets to protest racist policies and to march for civil rights for Black Americans; by the late 1960s, public spaces were also filled with bodies joining the anti-war movement, and still others were protesting for an end to institutional sexism. With society practically vibrating with civil unrest and pushing for change (and others in power pushing back against it), it's unsurprising that horror movies started to reflect fears of what that change might entail.

As social commentary from this era, I'd be remiss if I didn't mention *Night of the Living Dead* (1968, dir. George A. Romero). This is the movie that usually comes up in conversation first when people talk about cultural commentary in horror. Of course, Romero didn't necessarily intend his story of strangers trapped in a house while undead ghouls pressed in from every direction as a commentary on race and society. But the moment he cast a Black actor (Duane Jones) as the surviving hero Ben, who outlasts a night of relentless terrors only to die by the hands of a white police officer in broad daylight—a police officer who may or may not have recognized that Ben was not a ghoul at all before he pulled the trigger—it became very hard *not* to read the film as a social commentary.

Of course, racial tensions weren't the only issues making the people in power shift uncomfortably in their seats. Second-wave feminism, the introduction of the birth control pill in 1968, and the *Roe v. Wade* decision in 1973 all clearly influenced horror in this era. There were anxieties about what this so-called sexual revolution would do to the picture-perfect ideal of the nuclear family that was produced and promoted in the 1950s.

More tangibly, the discovery that the drug Thalidomide, prescribed in the mid-1950s worldwide for morning sickness, had teratogenic effects and could cause severe congenital abnormalities in growing embryos (if the affected embryos managed to survive) took frankly ableist fears that children may be born disabled and produced monstrous depictions of children. Together, these resulted in a lot of pregnancy horror, like *It's Alive* (1974, dir. Larry Cohen), *Rosemary's Baby* (1976, dir. Roman Polanski), demonic children like Damien in *The Omen* (1976, dir. Richard Donner) and Regan MacNeil in *The Exorcist* (1973, dir. William Friedkin), and a number of films that seemed to punish women for apparently destroying the nuclear family ideal, like *The Stepford Wives* (1975, dir. Bryan Forbes) and *The Brood* (1979, dir. David Cronenberg).

Cronenberg in particular rose to prominence for focusing on the body, especially the sexualized body, as a site for horror. Under his direction, human bodies developed pulsing parasitic nodules that ramped up their sex drives (*Shivers*, 1975), or developed bizarre genital-like formations where they didn't belong—like a phallic armpit stinger (*Rabid*, 1977) or a distinctly yonic new hole in an abdomen (*Videodrome*, 1982)—and generally saw perverse invasions and transformations. These films had a huge role in developing body horror into a horror subgenre unto itself.

By the end of the 1960s and into the 1970s, talk of cults

and serial killers became common. We can see echoes of fears stirred up by the Manson family cult and murders clearly in films like the X-rated *I Drink Your Blood* (1970, dir. David E. Durston) and more obliquely in folk horror films like *The Wicker Man* (1973, dir. Robin Hardy) and *The Blood on Satan's Claw* (1971, dir. Piers Haggard), where hippie communes are replaced with pagan groups with occult or satanic practices.

News of so many nicknamed serial killers at large in the United States around this time inspired new fears doubly represented as human threats that might be lurking in public spaces or their own backyards, and threats that might take the extra step to invade their homes and safe spaces. Everywhere you looked there were new threats becoming household names, from "the Dating Game Killer," to "the Golden State Killer," to "the Son of Sam," "the Hillside Stranglers," "the Vampire of Sacramento," "the Torso Killer," and more. These real murders paved the road for their cinematic counterparts: the human violence in *The Texas Chain Saw Massacre* (1974, dir. Tobe Hooper), *The Town That Dreaded Sundown* (1976, dir. Charles B. Pierce), and extremely violent home invasion films like *Straw Dogs* (1971, dir. Sam Peckinpah) and *The Last House on the Left* (1972, dir. Wes Craven).

SCARE SPOTLIGHT:
BLACK CHRISTMAS (1974, DIR. BOB CLARK)

Black Christmas is often cited as the first of the new slasher subgenre, building off the proto-slashers *Psycho* (1960, dir. Alfred Hitchcock) and *Peeping Tom* (1960, dir. Michael Powell), both released over a decade earlier. The film fits perfectly among other movies of this new era concerned with serial killers and sexuality: the plot follows an unnamed, unseen (except fleetingly as a pair of hands or a watching eye) killer who methodically stalks, taunts, and kills women in a sorority house at Christmas break. His cryptic telephone calls to the house recall the urban legend of the babysitter and the killer upstairs, but otherwise reveals nothing about the killer's motivations (although these would later be developed by Glen Morgan in his 2008 remake of the film, fully sanctioned by Clark).

It was scary because a home was being violently invaded for no real reason, and no real prevention was possible. With real families in this decade still reeling over news reports of serial killers and rapists breaking into complete strangers' homes to enact violence, this story hit close to home. Reportedly, *Black Christmas*'s television premiere years later in 1978 was met with controversy, since its appearance on TV screens across America coincided with sorority murders by a then-unknown killer (later to be identified as Ted Bundy) mere weeks earlier.

Black Christmas put us as the audience into the killer's shoes. The perspective was filmed with a head-mounted camera setup created by camera operator Bert Dunk specifically for the film; the Steadicam wouldn't be introduced until 1975. You can see the genetic connection between *Black Christmas* and the slashers that would follow. John Carpenter's *Halloween* (1978) opens similarly with a scene told from an unseen killer's perspective, although, unlike in *Black Christmas*, the killer is revealed to us in a literal and figurative unmasking.

In an interview with Icons of Fright, director Bob Clark jokes that he had once had a conversation with John Carpenter pre-*Halloween* as to whether he'd ever make a sequel to *Black Christmas*. He had no plans to dig deeper into the *Black Christmas* sandbox, and told Carpenter as much, but that if he ever did a sequel, "it would be the next year and the guy would have actually been caught, escape from a mental institution, go back to the house and they would start all over again. And I would call it *Halloween*." While this sounds suspiciously familiar, Clark goes on to say that *Halloween*, while definitely drawing inspiration from *Black Christmas*, is absolutely its own film and wholly an original creation belonging to Carpenter and Debra Hill.

In the same year that Sally Hardesty (Marilyn Burns) found herself laughing in fear in the back of a pickup truck, the final and only survivor of the Sawyer family's violence in *The Texas Chain Saw Massacre*, *Black Christmas* furthered the concept of the Final Girl with Jess (Olivia Hussey) as a woman who discovers horror and manages to resourcefully stay alive while her friends are picked off like scabs around her. That said, Jess is missing a lot of the Final Girl standards: she smokes and drinks, has sex, and is considering an abortion when she discovers she's pregnant. Altogether she's a portrait of a second-wave feminist and liberated woman, officially free to make choices about her own body since *Roe v. Wade* was passed the year before. For contemporary audiences she seems cool as hell, but in 1974 her depiction, along with those of her coeds, were considered hyper-sexualized (critic Gene Siskel, who hated most horror movies anyway, famously derided the characters as "junk roles" who talk dirty). The film doesn't *quite* treat Jess like a Final Girl either: after seeming to be rescued, she is ultimately left in the house with the killer, sedated and lying in bed, and her fate is left ambiguous.

To simplify Carol Clover's definition, a Final Girl was originally described as a woman who acts as an embodiment of terror, who is aware of the killer, either through the discovery of her loved ones' bodies or by watching the villain kill them right in front of her, but who manages to survive long enough to either be rescued or to kill the villain herself. Jess Bradford checks some of these boxes, but not enough to be more than a precursor to a definitive Final Girl. The trope wouldn't be solidified as we know it today and cemented in our hearts as a horror tradition until Laurie Strode would stride on-screen four years later in *Halloween*.

This new obsession with violent serial killers likely helped to pave the way for violence entering mainstream cinema in a big way. Violent exploitation films, previously relegated to low-budget grindhouse theatres, started to get booked on bigger screens.

When it comes to film, "exploitation" is more of an approach than a genre. As an approach we can loosely define the exploitation film as a work that keys into current trends and untapped audiences and—well—exploits them, often while couching content in lurid imagery and reinforced stereotypes. By this definition, exploitation films are defined by the audiences that they intend to exploit: blaxploitation films have been largely produced by and for Black audiences, Ozploitation deals specifically with Australian themes and settings while making the most of the dawn of the R rating in Australia in 1970, and so on. It was under this exploitation film umbrella that subgenres like the slasher and the splatter film could thrive. While exploitation cinema emerged as early as the late 1950s, we tend to associate the classification with the gorier, more violent horror films of the 1970s, mostly meant to target teenagers and young men. The Hays Production Code was officially over in 1968, giving way to the MPAA rating classifications in nearly the same form we use today. Filmmakers no longer had to worry about abiding by the code's thirty-six rules for propriety (not that they weren't already subverting the code any chance they got). Inevitably, horror films got a lot more violent. As you might expect, this is also when a lot of horror film traditions were born.

Vampire movies, while they never really left the scene, seemed to explode anew in the 1970s. But the Universal Classic Bela Lugosi type (*Dracula*, 1931) wouldn't cut it anymore. The dissolution of the Hays Code meant that religious themes, especially perversions of religious themes, could be explored anew, not to mention the sexual metaphors that often go hand in hand with vampire folklore. So it isn't really surprising at all that the era of the sexual revolution was a welcome space to revisit fanged fiends. Of note were films featuring Black vampires, riding the very specific wave of blaxploitation. These were works like the intricate art film *Ganja and Hess* (1973, dir. Bill Gunn) and the vampire film *Blacula* (1972, dir. William Crain), the latter of which would spawn a series. In different ways, these films used the classically othered vampire figure to explore issues of race and identity. Other, non-vampire blaxploitation films produced during this period include *Blackenstein* (1973, dir. William A. Levey), which, of course, was a Black Frankenstein film (set against the Vietnam War), and the zombie revenge flick *Sugar Hill* (1974, dir. Paul Maslansky).

Sensing an opportunity to cash in on this movement of low-budget high violence, studios started to get in on the exploitation action. In 1980, Paramount took a gamble and picked up the independently produced *Friday the 13th* (1980, dir. Sean S. Cunningham) and spun it into a franchise after its wide release turned out to be wildly successful. This would mark the start of the tidal wave of slasher franchises that would define the horror landscape for the next decade.

SLASHERS, SATANIC PANIC, AND VIDEO NASTIES (1980s)

What scared us? Teenagers, Threats to Family Values, Communism (...Again)

When you try to classify horror in the 1980s, a clear theme is hard to pin down. VHS videocassette tapes had become available for families to start renting and watching movies in their own homes instead of having to catch them on cable or in the cinemas. This was a bit of a boon for low-budget horror movies because they could be distributed direct-to-video, while they probably wouldn't have been released to many, if any, movie theatres. Some of the earliest direct-to-video movies—the ones that weren't video music albums—were horror movies, like *Blood Cult* (1985, dir. Christopher Lewis) and the blaxploitation B-movie *Black Devil Doll from Hell* (1984, dir. Chester Novell Turner).

Perhaps channeling the excesses of the decade, the genre seemed to veer toward fantastic elements. While the slasher genre was still going strong, the more human killers were yielding to supernatural weapon-wielding murderers like Freddy Krueger in *A Nightmare on Elm Street* (1984, dir. Wes

Craven). Existing slasher staples like Jason Voorhees and Michael Myers just seemed to become more explicitly supernatural as their series progressed through the decade.

Even contrast *The Slumber Party Massacre* (1981, dir. Amy Holden Jones) and its sequel *The Slumber Party Massacre II* (1987, dir. Deborah Brock). The first features Russ Thorn as a bizarre but definitely human serial killer who wields an industrial drill to attack anyone who crosses his path (especially if that person is a woman). Fast-forward to the sequel and our killer has been replaced by a singing, dancing driller killer with a drill-mounted electric guitar and a Freddy Krueger–esque ability to warp perceptions of reality. His own realness is also questionable. Both movies are in line with killer aesthetics at the time of their release—like a toilet paper roll, horror seems to be moving through aesthetic trends faster as we approach the present.

In 1984, PG-13 was added to the MPAA rating system, which ushered in a new era of horror marketed to a wider family audience—like Joe Dante's *Gremlins* (1984), which might have been a bit of a confusing experience for families who expected the puppet-driven film to be more of the *E.T.: The Extra-Terrestrial* (1982, dir. Steven Spielberg) variety. This addition to the ratings system might have also had a hand in chasing horror from a countercultural niche into a more mainstream light. Millennials can thank the new PG-13 for the fun-for-the-whole-family horrors that gave them childhood nightmares, like *The Gate* (1987, dir. Tibor Takács) and *Critters* (1986, dir. Stephen Herek).

Recoiling from the splatter and violence of the exploitation films of the 1970s, the U.K. experienced a wave of moral panic in the early 1980s that led to the ban of a lot of horror films labeled as "Video Nasties." What resulted was the Video

Recordings Act being instituted in 1984, and the eventual accumulation of seventy-two banned films. The criteria that were implemented for banning films seem inconsistent at best. Some of the usual suspects like *Cannibal Holocaust* (1980, dir. Ruggero Deodato) and *Blood Feast* (1963, dir. Herschell Gordon Lewis), and the film that likely launched the Video Nasties moral panic, *The Driller Killer* (1979, dir. Abel Ferrara), were among the earliest films to be banned (even if by '80s standards many of the depictions of gore and blood, especially in *Blood Feast*, were already verging on campy). On the other hand, not even critically acclaimed, award-winning horror was immune: *The Exorcist* was never officially prosecuted or banned—you won't find it on any Video Nasty lists—but the BBFC did manage to put up major obstacles to its release on home video in the U.K. *The Exorcist*, rated uncut and 18A, finally made it into homes and video stores in 1998. A number of the films banned under the Video Recordings Act, which began to lose steam around the late '90s and was officially replaced by a new Video Recordings Act in 2010, have been re-rated and released only relatively recently in the U.K.

The United Kingdom wasn't the only country reeling with moral panic; in the United States, the Reagan administration was pushing for a return to conservative family values. Reagan blamed poverty, which he described as "welfare culture," on the disintegration of traditional family ideals. In 1984, he called for a "rededication to bedrock values of faith, family, work, neighborhood, peace, and freedom." A year later, he dug his heels in deeper in his State of the Union message, stating that "as the family goes, so goes our civilization."

Satirical skewerings of Reagan-era family values in horror look a lot like parodies of midcentury *Leave It to Beaver* ideals. The real threats in films like *Parents* (1989, dir. Bob

Balaban) and *A Nightmare on Elm Street* (1984) were the parents who continued to perpetuate the beliefs and values that they were taught by bestowing them upon their children. The other side of the Reagan administration involved a neoliberal economic shift (including, unsurprisingly, major tax cuts afforded to the wealthy and benefits cuts to the poor) that was dubbed "Reaganomics." As a president, he was anti-communist and pro–mass surveillance. He celebrated consumerism and the rags-to-riches idea of the American Dream. Clear horrors that comment on these facets of Reagan-era society are *They Live* (1988, dir. John Carpenter) and *Society* (1989, dir. Brian Yuzna), both of which set up worlds filled with alien imposters—echoes of the *Invasion of the Body Snatchers* narratives of past anti-communist waves.

A HORROR ... SLUMP? (1990s)

What scared us? Serial Killers (Again), Social Turmoil (Again), the Apocalypse

When horror fans bring up the 1990s, there's a weird pattern of people describing the decade as a bit of a horror drought, if not the decade where horror died. I personally disagree with this take, but I am also biased because this is the era when I came of age as a young horror fan. I grew up through childhood nightmares soaked in scares from *Gremlins 2: The New Batch* (1990, dir. Joe Dante), *It* (1990, dir. Tommy Lee Wallace), *Candyman* (1992, dir. Bernard Rose), and *The Lawnmower Man* (1992, dir. Brett Leonard)—somehow absorbed into my consciousness without actually watching the movies. This absorption was thanks to movie posters and cardboard standees at the local video rental store and trailers that aired on TV when I should have been asleep. My true gateway to horror in the '90s, though, came in the form of thrillers like *Single White Female* (1992, dir. Barbet Schroeder), *The Hand That Rocks the Cradle* (1992, dir. Curtis Hanson), and *Kiss the Girls* (1997, dir. Gary Fleder). Like a lot of kids, I wasn't allowed to watch scary movies; unlike for a lot of kids, titles that the internet qualifies as "erotic thrillers" were fair game. According to my mom, this was because thrillers were "more realistic." Go figure.

Horror in the '90s pulled back dramatically from the flash and fabulism of the previous decade and turned the lens to more realistic, and sometimes procedural, portrayals of horror. A lot of the horrors from this decade tended to straddle the line between thriller and horror. In particular, the crime thriller, the psychological horror, and movies built around serial killers flourished. The capture of serial killer Jeffrey Dahmer in 1991, along with other infamous crime stories, like the capture of Canadian killers Paul Bernardo and Karla Homolka in 1993, and the murder of six-year-old JonBenét Ramsey in 1996, helped spur the popularity of the subgenre. The public had renewed interest in true crime, and in consuming narratives that claimed to tease apart the inner workings of a killer's mind. This interest gave us the twisty, sometimes cerebral violences of *The Silence of the Lambs* (1991, dir. Jonathan Demme) and *Se7en* (1996, dir. David Fincher).

As Alexandra West notes in *The 1990s Teen Horror Cycle: Final Girls and a New Hollywood Formula*, teen movies in the 1990s were born of an intersection where "male run studios were willing to recognize the powerful intersection between women, horror, youth, and films. The heyday of the 1980s slasher films had died at various stages with killers at the forefront, and now it was time to focus on the Final Girls."

Easily the most popular Final Girl to arrive with this shift was Sidney Prescott (played by Neve Campbell), the teen survivor of *Scream* (1996, dir. Wes Craven). While not an especially developed character in the first installment of the franchise, Sidney stands out among Final Girls for breaking the rules so painstakingly set up within the movie universe. She has sex with her boyfriend, she claims ownership of her situation in a way that almost seems to break the fourth wall ("Not in *my* movie," she says as she shoots one of her would-be killers), and yet she still comes out on top (although, understandably, not without trauma that is explored in the sequels). Here was a Final Girl we could celebrate for transcending the frankly suffocating social rules meant for women relegated to the Final Girl role.

In many ways, the 1990s Teen Horror Cycle felt like the response to the John Hughes Brat Pack movies of the 1980s, but rather than subverting those usually feel-good comedies, a surprising number of teen horrors reinforced the tropes, character archetypes, and messaging that we have come to expect from teen movies. Also, despite putting the Final Girl figure front and center, and often sporting narratives that, at first glance, appear to be eschewing ideas of conformity, upon a deeper look these films seem to punish teens for pushing boundaries and striving for independence, much as earlier psychological thrillers like *Fatal Attraction* (1987, dir. Adrian Lyne) punished independent or sexually aggressive women for daring to violate patriarchal structures. At the end of the day, horror movies for teens were still being made predominantly by adult white men.

The Craft (1996, dir. Andrew Fleming) feels like horror's countercultural answer to *Clueless* (1995, dir. Amy Heckerling). Taking the place of the polished, bubbly, and fashionably dressed rich girls of *Clueless* are the disillusioned lower- and lower-middle-class high-schoolers who dabble in magic to improve their individual lots in life and love. Each of the teen witches in *The Craft* is punished in turn for seeking to harness power that "shouldn't" belong to them. Similarly, *The Faculty* (1997, dir. Robert Rodriguez) gives us a group of teens fighting to hold on to their individuality against a parasitic alien race that assimilates its hosts into a hive mind. The teens, who at the beginning of the film represented *The Breakfast Club*-esque social archetypes, from the goth loner, to the drug dealer, to the football jock, find themselves at the conclusion of the film—aliens defeated thanks to their pluck—drifting further from their initial archetypes and closer than ever to the status quo, seemingly happier for having shed those hard-won identities without the help of an alien threat.

Meanwhile, Japanese horror embraced the end of a millennium with a slew of apocalyptic horror films—notably, *Suicide Circle*, released in the United States as *Suicide Club* (2001, dir. Sion Sono), *Uzumaki* (2000, dir. Higuchinsky), and *Pulse* (2001, dir. Kiyoshi Kurosawa)—which all looked at alienation, isolation, and the importance of human connection when all of our communication seems to be mediated by either technologies or consumer products and media. The closest American counterpart I can think of from this period with this theme is *The Matrix* (1999, dirs. Lilly Wachowski and Lana Wachowski), although *The Matrix* is of a distinctly sci-fi flavor and the Japanese films mentioned above are very effective horrors.

HORROR FOR A NEW
MILLENNIUM (2000s)

What scared us? Terrorism, Travel,
Technology, Torture

A strange whiplash occurred in North America as society tipped over into the year 2000. Movies were tiptoeing
around depictions of violence, especially violence involving
teens, after the Columbine High School shootings in 1999
left America feeling bruised. If movies featuring teen violence resonated, it was because death was dealt by strange
and supernatural means, set apart from real-world human
behaviors—by werewolf attacks in *Ginger Snaps* (2000, dir.
John Fawcett), and by Death itself in *Final Destination* (2000,
dir. James Wong). Teen screams featuring human killers, like
Scream 3 (2000, dir. Wes Craven), only served to poke at the
bruise.

Filmmakers in other parts of the world had no qualms
with centering horror upon schoolchildren—*Battle Royale*
(2000, dir. Kinji Fukasaku) depicts a class of fifteen-year-
olds being forced by adults to wield weapons and engage
in battle with each other, a narrative that reminded the director of the horrors of his youth, forced to work at a muni-
tions factory during World War II and consequently having
to see his classmates die when the factory came under fire.
Although considered a cult classic now, the first theatrical
release of *Battle Royale* wouldn't happen in the United States
until 2011, over a decade after its initial release in Japan.

But then on September 11, 2001, four airliners were hijacked in a coordinated terrorist attack. Two of the planes
crashed into the World Trade Center in New York City, killing thousands, the third was steered into the Pentagon in
Arlington, Virginia, and the final plane crashed into a field

on its way to Washington, DC. President George W. Bush responded to the attack by launching the War on Terror, which persists at the time of this writing, almost twenty years later, and which launched a sequence of events that changed public perceptions of violence forever.

Torture as a form of violence isn't new by any means, but for the most part, people in North America were able to go about their daily lives without thinking about torture happening in other parts of the world, let alone at the hands of their compatriots. In the aftermath of 9/11, at Abu Ghraib and the Guantanamo Bay prison, the realities of torture were being unavoidably thrust into the public eye. With this new discomfort, along with new xenophobia created in the wake of 9/11 and the Bush administration, a brand-new horror subgenre was born to articulate fears of violence at the hands of other people, specifically "othered" other people (read: not American).

The term "torture porn" is often used to describe the horrors of this new subgenre—although that term is met with criticism. The addition of "porn" to the term implies a voyeuristic appeal to watching extreme depictions of violence and, for the most part, people don't tend to describe the viewing of such entries as *Hostel* (2005, dir. Eli Roth) and *Turistas* (2006, dir. John Stockwell) as enjoyable so much as they create safe spaces to explore the horrors of senseless violence and have the potential to be cathartic. Both *Hostel* and *Turistas* deal with horrors that Americans might face if they leave their homeland; entries like *Saw* (2004, dir. James Wan) bring torture into American spaces as a reminder that Americans are just as capable of torture as the non-American "other" that we are told to fear.

If there's a signature element of torture horror, outside of ultraviolence, it's that there is nobody who swoops in to save the day at the end and almost everybody dies. If there is a survivor, a bespoke Final Girl, the genre differs in that torture horror never seems to conclude with society restored to any sort of order. And we, as an audience living through a decades-long war with no resolution in sight, don't exactly expect to see order restored.

New French Cinema (or French Extremity) is often associated with the torture horror movement, but, despite surface similarities, the two subgenres are distinct. French Extremity films, such as *Martyrs* (2008, dir. Pascal Laugier), *High Tension* (2003, dir. Alexandre Aja), and *Raw* (2016, dir. Julia Ducournau), are graphic and transgressive, and the violence depicted is meant to explore the limits of the human body (and will), but these films almost always involve a narrative and structural complexity not present in torture horror films. While some horror fans see French Extremity films as a challenge to how much grim imagery they're willing to stomach, there's a distinct national identity to the subgenre that seems to specifically criticize France and the French film industry for its real tolerances (or, at the very least, inaction) toward violences such as racism, rape, and pedophilia.

Perhaps surprisingly, given the United States' desire to double down on its own national identity during this era, we saw a spike in the popularity of adaptations of Japanese and Korean horror films being brought into North America from across the world. Usually these adaptations took the form of swapping out the original stories' protagonists for a usually blond, white American woman: Sarah Michelle Gellar for *The Grudge* (2004, dir. Takashi Shimizu), Naomi Watts for *The Ring* (2002, dir. Gore Verbinski), and, for a brunette exception, Jennifer Connelly in *Dark Water* (2005, dir. Walter Salles). These films are distinctly supernatural in nature, dealing primarily in vengeful spirits. In their original forms, these films speak to tensions between the ideals of "traditional Japanese" roles and sociocultural transformations that promise to move Japan further away from its past. In his analysis of contemporary Japanese horror, *Nightmare Japan*, Jay McRoy sees both *Ringu* (1998, dir. Hideo Nakata) and *Dark Water* (2002, dir. Hideo Nakata) as emblematic of "the various (re)constructions of the 'family,'" given that both films feature a single mother confronting ghosts.

The shift back toward violence made room in the early and mid-2000s for glossy remakes of horror classics reworked and recast with teen heartthrobs and influencers to specifically target teen audiences, a natural extension of the 1990s Teen Horror Cycle. This was the era that saw the Vincent Price vehicle *House of Wax* (1953, dir. André De Toth) remade with Paris Hilton (2005, dir. Jaume Collet-Serra), William Castle's classic *13 Ghosts* (1960) remade as *Thir13en Ghosts* (2001, dir. Steve Beck), and slasher originator *Black Christmas* (1974) remade as *Black Xmas* (2006, dir. Glen Morgan). Although often disparaged for "ruining" the original films, the teen horror remakes have lately been seeing a resurgence of appreciation from horror fans.

HORROR MOVIES TODAY AND LOOKING TOWARD THE FUTURE (2010s–?)

What will scare us next?

It can be hard to place trends in horror while you're in the middle of a cycle. I'm sure ten years from now, critics will be able to cherry-pick one or two major events to highlight in the same way I've treated every other decade in this chapter, but while history is actively unfolding around you, it's easy to see factors for every facet of life shaping horror without any one dominant trend pointing to what presently has the greatest influence.

Recent horrors have seen a return to familiar stomping grounds, like familial horror, with *Hereditary* (2018, dir. Ari Aster) and *The Witch* (2015, dir. Robert Eggers), which, like the familial horrors of the 1980s, explore intergenerational horror and the sins that parents visit upon their children. Where *A Nightmare on Elm Street*, for example, told this story with a bright, darkly comedic palette, these new horrors-at-home are much more bleak, both in coloring and in outcome.

Ongoing social movements formed to combat systemic inequities, such as the Black Lives Matter movement, paired with calls for better representation in the film industry, have allowed for a slow but ever-growing presence of American horror films from historically marginalized perspectives. *Get Out* (2017, dir. Jordan Peele) managed to garner a lot of attention for its quietly terrifying look at the myth of a "post-racist" society. *Candyman* (2021, dir. Nia DaCosta) revisits the '90s horror franchise through a contemporary lens. Other films, like the Spanish film *The Platform* (2020, dir. Galder Gaztelu-Urrutia) and the South Korean film *Parasite* (2019, dir. Bong Joon-ho), directly take on class disparity and poverty.

As this book was being drafted in 2020, the world went on lockdown as a novel coronavirus, SARS-CoV-2, known colloquially as COVID-19, spread in a global pandemic. In a fascinating turn, as the public was waiting to learn more about the virus that was quickly taking hold across the globe, a nearly decade-old movie, *Contagion* (2011, dir. Steven Soderbergh), jumped to the top of the rentals list on Apple iTunes, not to mention top ten popular streaming lists where it was available. There was comfort and catharsis in watching a terrifyingly virulent infection paralyze the planet, and a vaccine successfully manufactured within a fictional space on-screen (yes, I was one of those people who watched *Contagion* while in lockdown)—it defined a sort of arc of events that we could expect to more or less follow in the real world where there was only uncertainty.

The COVID-19 pandemic also brought us *Host* (2020, dir. Rob Savage), which unspooled its narrative over the length of a single forty-minute Zoom call. *Host* reflected the stresses of trying to connect with loved ones over unreliable technology during quarantine, while adding in a supernatural twist.

Horror has been right next to us, exploring cultural shifts as we go through them. One of my favorite aspects of returning to older horrors, especially horrors that predate my lifetime, isn't so much that I get a peek into what was making the films' original audiences collectively anxious at the time. It's more that I get a snapshot of context telling me *why* they were afraid and how they engaged with their fears. In the one hundred–ish years that we skimmed through during this chapter, we saw a lot of social fears that repeated themselves. Even so, when horror movies revisited fears, visual representations and filmic approaches to those familiar fears were often, if not always, transformed.

Speaking of representations, it's time to move on to one of the most important genre mainstays, the one responsible for giving recognizable physical forms to even our most nebulous fears: the monster.

IN CONVERSATION WITH ALEXANDRA WEST

Alexandra West is the author of Films of the New French Extremity: Visceral Horror and National Identity *and* The 1990s Teen Horror Cycle: Final Girls and a New Hollywood Formula. *She is the co-host for the* Faculty of Horror *podcast, which tackles "all things horror with a slash of analysis and research."*

People, horror fans included, often cite the '90s and early '00s as a period that experienced a relative dearth of horror movies. Can you comment on this perception versus the reality of horror in this era?

Horror in the early '90s was just coming out of a heavily codified era in the 1980s with the rise of the slashers and all their sequels. Before that prestige horror like *Rosemary's Baby, The Omen, The Stepford Wives,* and *The Exorcist* in the late '60s and into the '70s proved that horror could have huge cultural moments alongside then indie films like *The Texas Chain Saw Massacre* and *I Spit on Your Grave.* The early '90s still had a great horror films like *Candyman, Silence of the Lambs, Army of Darkness, Jacob's Ladder, Wes Craven's New Nightmare,* and *Misery,* among others, but they were all quite different. They weren't easily labeled, so it's harder to qualify them, which is what we like to do as fans and/or culture writers. By the mid-'90s, with films like *The Craft* and *Scream,* a clear trend emerged through box office receipts—teen horror, which borrowed heavily from films aimed at teens of the '70s and '80s.

In what ways, if any, are these '90s horror films reflections of their era?

My perception is that '90s horror films (particularly the teen ones) were heavily influenced by the rise of third-wave feminism, and wider access to media and the twenty-four-hour news cycle. Nineties teen horror has a strong emphasis on the darkness of being a teenage girl, particularly with many narratives centered around bullying and sexual assault (I think *The Craft* and *The Rage: Carrie 2* are good examples of this), while films like *Scream* incorporate those elements as well as the influence of a gratuitous news cycle that seeks to turn personal tragedy into national tragedy.

You mention that '90s teen horror borrows from the '70s and '80s. In what ways was teen horror in the '90s a response to the past and a template for teen horrors that we see today?

Nineties teen horror centers a female experience while grappling with trauma, the characters are less disposable, and the backgrounds of the protagonists are darker. *Final Destination* is an important turning point: it was just far enough away from the Columbine shooting (which affected the release of the other Devon Sawa–led horror film, *Idle Hands*) that audiences could handle teens getting readily and easily disposed of by the literal specter of death and the elaborate traps. The setups and wince-inducing deaths were an early indicator that audiences would respond positively to films like *Saw* and *Hostel*, which led the Torture Porn cycle.

Do you have any personal favorites?

The Craft and *Scream* were two films I grew up on, so they'll always be favorites. I think *The Rage: Carrie 2* is a much more powerful and heartbreaking film than people recognize, and *I Know What You Did Last Summer* is a very effective and entertaining slasher.

You've also done a deep dive into horrors of the New French Extremity and violent films that speak to French society. Setting aside how people often confuse these films with "torture porn," what are the social or historical elements that birthed this form?

I consider the rise of New French Extremity to be linked with the rise of authoritarian right-wing politics in Europe. After the bloodshed that happened throughout Europe during

WWII, Europeans are naturally more inclined to fear the rise of the right. In France in particular, the LePen family (Jean-Marie and Marine specifically), who both led the anti-immigration far-right National Front party, as well as mainstream politicians like Nicolas Sarkozy, spread fear and hatred. France has always seen cinema as an important art form, so it became a natural place for artists to react and showcase the horrors that were beginning to infiltrate their society.

What's the distinction between "violent films" and "films about violence"? Do these films have different goals for their audiences?

Films about violence depict characters before, during, and after violence enters their lives. It becomes important for audiences to know these characters and understand the impact of violence in their lives, how it changes them. Violent films tend to focus less on the characters and more on their deaths, which serve to titillate the audience to either cheer as two-dimensional characters meet their deaths or wince and look away due to the gore on-screen.

In terms of horror and national identity, are there other similar national horror cycles (not French Extremity or American horrors) that speak as strongly to a nation's social fears that you feel are overlooked or bear discussion?

I think Canadian horror has taken some interesting twists and turns in the last decade, with films like *Pyewacket, Possessor, Violation, The Void,* and *Come True,* among many others.

U.K. horror is having an interesting moment with contemporary anxieties, with films like *Host, Censor, Caveat, His House, Dashcam,* and *You Are Not My Mother.*

Latinx horror has produced some incredible films, like *La Llorona, Tigers Are Not Afraid,* and *Terrified.*

As a Canadian, I often think about body horror as specific to Canadian horror.

I personally think Canadian horror has more to do with identity, and body horror is a vessel for that. I also think the space and land that characters occupy is incredibly important to Canadian horror. It's not often touched upon but it's pretty central in many ways (see the French-English divide in *Pontypool,* the camping trip of *Backcountry,* the remote location of *Pyewacket,* and everything about *Blood Quantum* and *Night Raiders*).

Are you currently digging into a different era of horror?

I recently did a deep dive into the adult/erotic thrillers of the late '80s through the '90s, films like *Fatal Attraction, Single White Female, Basic Instinct, Sleeping with the Enemy, Dead Calm, The Hand That Rocks the Cradle, A Perfect Murder, Unlawful Entry, Jennifer 8,* and many, many, many more. Overall, they're all pretty reactionary to third-wave feminism to various degrees and culminate in some form of misogyny. There are also incredibly problematic depictions of mental health, the treatment of the few characters from marginalized communities is really awful, and there is an overall homophobic vibe in many of them. These were mainstream films that came out not too long ago (certainly in my lifetime anyway) whose politics are so contrary in many ways to our discourse now that it's incredible to see how far we've come and what we used to think was acceptable.

CHAPTER 3

HOW TO MAKE
A MONSTER

A horror movie isn't really a horror movie without a monster.

The monster, whether it takes the shape of an attacking alien, a boogeyman, or a masked killer, is what distinguishes horror from adjacent genres, like war movies or detective thrillers (although these genres do sometimes overlap). A monster, once it's revealed, must obviously be a monster, whether it's based on a historically or culturally familiar threat, like a vampire, a giant spider, or a man with a knife, or if it's something the audience has never seen before, like the graboids from *Tremors* (1990, dir. Ron Underwood), the alien organism from *The Thing* (1982, dir. John Carpenter), or the Behemoth from *The Mist* (2007, dir. Frank Darabont).

The monster in horror is a complex figure—we discussed in the last chapter just how its shape and approach can change to reflect the collective fears of the moment. That said, the monster always represents a threat of some form, whether it's a literal threat to the personal body or a figurative threat to social norms. But how do we give abstract threats physical shape? What are the traits that inspire special effects artists to mold foam and rubber into the jaws and claws of monsters? What moves digital artists to draw imposing creatures that feel like they've been yanked fully formed from our nightmares? For the visuals of a monster, we turn to recognizable, real-life threats with familiar traits, even if the monster itself appears to be completely novel. After all, while monsters are unnatural, their creators are always human.

While a completely novel monster sounds cool in theory, it would be hard to depict. Take, for instance, the monsters from *Bird Box* (2018, dir. Susanne Bier). The creatures are said to be incomprehensible, and the act of looking at them and trying to interpret their appearance drives those who see them to violent madness. How would you visualize such a creature on-screen? You couldn't. Those involved in the design of these creatures are humans who only have human knowledge to work with, so any creature they'd design would inevitably feature something recognizable. Even the most creative monsters in movie history remind us of something else.

It's easy enough to draw straight lines from traits that we see in most monsters, even the funky-looking ones, to something recognizable. Some are pretty obvious as familiar fears: *Eight-Legged Freaks* (2002, dir. Ellory Elkayem) features spiders of ginormous proportions. *Lake Placid* (1999, dir. Steve Miner) gives us a bloodthirsty giant crocodile. The Reaper breed of vampires in *Blade II* (2002, dir. Guillermo del Toro) are humanoids that have split, fanged lower jaws and probosci, traits that we associate with insect or arthropod mandibles. The grotesque and ancient Moder from *The Ritual* (2017, dir. David Bruckner) appears as an unlikely fusion of elk and floppy human corpse—two identifiable components. These hybrid creatures make us uncomfortable because they are hard to categorize as a whole, even though we can pretty easily categorize them according to their disassembled parts.

Keeping track of potential threats, obvious or not, is stressful. Constantly practicing hypervigilance, besides being super stressful, takes away your capacity to focus on other tasks, and humans aren't built to spend their energy only running or hiding. The key to conserving this precious energy is to recognize the threat before it becomes threatening. A lot of prey organisms do not possess innate recognition of potential predators and so must learn by association (or via social learning). Most prey animals look for visual information cues known as *key feature stimuli* to recognize threats. This involves noticing not only potentially threatening movement, but the shape, form, speed, and direction of that movement.

But how do you learn to recognize a predator when, as a human, you don't have any actual experience with predation?

The good news is, we're *really good* at picking up on potential threats. In chapter 1, we saw that threatening images—such as images of snakes, spiders, and guns—can trigger a threat response even when the images are flashed so quickly that the viewer might not be consciously aware that they saw the threat at all.

Which is great if you suspect that you're being hunted by a monster that's shaped like a snake, spider, or gun.

Beyond sight, humans also have pretty good hearing ability given their head size (a weird compliment, I know). While our hearing isn't spectacular by any stretch, we do have a solid ability to zero in on relevant sounds and block out irrelevant noises as static. This explains what's often referred to as the "cocktail party effect," a selective attention phenomenon where most people will hear their name when it's spoken from across the room at a party (relevant information! Someone is talking about you!), despite a number of other conversations (irrelevant!) creating competing noise. This skill has obvious benefits when you're avoiding monsters—it will help you notice monster sounds that indicate that the threat is nearby and in pursuit.

Since humans don't have a lot of practice identifying predators that aren't other humans, spiders, or snakes, I've built this handy-dandy guide to dealing with your horror movie predator:

Ask yourself, in order, the following questions:

1. Is it trying to kill you?

Seriously. This should be your first and most obvious clue. If yes, proceed to question two.

2. Does it have the physical tools to kill you?

These tools can be built-in, like sharp pointy teeth, slashing claws, and jaws that can open wide enough to give you a nasty bite (in academic terms, this aptitude for biting is known as gape size). If it doesn't have these traits naturally, does it have a weapon (or can it acquire one easily)?

Those first two questions will cover most monsters that clearly look like predators. But because horror monsters are a special form of predator, we need to ask a third question:

3. Whether or not you answered *yes* or *no* to question two: How could it kill you?

It's important to recognize that horror movie monsters have different ways to harm us, and their differing methods shine spotlights on different types of human fears.

The most obvious type of harm is, of course, physical harm from being bitten, beaten, and/or slashed by a monster's physical body. This type of harm accounts for most horror movie monsters, since physical attacks are visually interesting to watch. Physical harm can come as a result of the destructive power of a monster's sheer size or brute strength, as is the case with giant monsters like Clover from *Cloverfield* (2008, dir. Matt Reeves), or the supernaturally muscular, swamp-inhabiting Victor Crowley (Kane Hodder) from *Hatchet* (2006, dir. Adam Green), who can tear human bodies apart with his bare hands. Harm can also come thanks to natural fangs and claws, or with man-made weaponry, like Freddy Krueger and his knife-glove.

Another type of monstrous harm is from monsters who act as vectors for infection and disease. Zombies whose victims become infected to become zombies in turn fall under this category. Werewolves and vampires similarly can act as vectors for monstrous transformations, if their attacks play out in a way that leaves their victims alive and infected (in some vampiric cases, ritually). And then there are parasitic infections, like *Night of the Creeps* (1986, dir. Fred Dekker) and *Slither* (2006, dir. James Gunn), which see the body invaded by tiny monstrous organisms. Besides usually serving as some sort of metaphor for xenophobia, the surface presentation of these types of monsters first and foremost preys upon our fears of disease and infection. As we learned in chapter 1, blood, pus, and vomit are quick disgust cues that tell us to avoid something that might be infectious. For good reason, infectious monsters are rarely seen without biological goo to reinforce the threat.

Finally, there are monsters that cause psychological or emotional harm. These are the ghosts and the gaslighters. These are the monsters that trick you and make you paranoid, like the aliens of *Invasion of the Body Snatchers* (1978, dir. Philip Kaufman) or the haunting forces in *The Amityville Horror* (1979, dir. Stuart Rosenberg). They are the entities that convince children that they are a friend or playmate, like "Captain Howdy" (actually the demon Pazuzu), who makes contact with young Regan MacNeil (Linda Blair) in *The Exorcist* (1973, dir. William Friedkin), or the evil spirit Marcus (portrayed in ghoul form by legendary creature actor Doug Jones) in *Ouija: Origin of Evil* (2016, dir. Mike Flanagan). They are also the so-called friends and family members who make you doubt your reality, like Guy (John Cassavetes) in *Rosemary's Baby* (1967, dir. Roman Polanski) and toxic ex-boyfriend Adrian Griffin (Oliver Jackson-Cohen) in *The Invisible Man* (2020, dir. Leigh Whannell). In some cases, there's a complete lack of overt physical attack with these types of monsters, which can make them harder, or at the very least more confusing, to fight.

Monsters don't necessarily have to stick to just one of the above categories (and most of them won't). Ghosts might take over and harm your physical body through possession. A werewolf might rip your arm off at the same time that it's delivering a lycanthropic infection into your bloodstream with a bite. Some monsters may even have the tools to harm in all three categories.

SCARE SPOTLIGHT:
THE THING (1982, DIR. JOHN CARPENTER)

If there were ever a horror movie monster that managed all three categories of harm, it would be the titular Thing from *The Thing*. Not only can it physically harm you, it can engender dangerous levels of paranoia, and it can infect you like a parasite.

When it came to the creature design for the Thing, Carpenter was adamant that "what I didn't want to end up with in this movie was a guy in a suit." The design was created by Rob Bottin, whose many credits include *The Howling* (1981, dir. Joe Dante) and *Total Recall* (1990, dir. Paul Verhoeven), and supported (uncredited) by Stan Winston, whose likewise many special effects credits include *The Terminator* (1984, dir. James Cameron), *Aliens* (1986, dir. James Cameron), and *Lake Placid* (1999, dir. Steve Miner).

In the movie, you never really get to understand its true form, which, presumably, is the microbe-scaled entities that we see taking over and assimilating prey one cell at a time. We see this action unspool in low-resolution on an early-'80s computer screen, and it's hard to piece that clinical interpretation of the monster together with the result of its intrusion, which is a shape-shifting, tendriled beast made of uncountable alien units working together—kind of like how coral is actually made up of many tiny individual animals forming a larger body.

The Thing, when it's taking on the appearance of a multicellular organism, is an ambush predator. It waits until its newest prey is isolated before it attacks, in part to remain undetected and so prevent any risk of harm to itself. When it is threatened, though, it's capable of immediately changing form, drawing on traits that likely come from creatures that it's assimilated before. It's unclear why it behaves the way it does, and doesn't seem to have any reason to attack once it's safely hidden as an assimilated organism, except maybe that its survival relies on it aggressively spreading and assimilating as many living organisms as possible.

This isn't unlike the lengths that some real parasites will go through to travel from one host to another—the *Leucochloridium paradoxum,* or the green-banded broodsac, is a parasitic flatworm that, as larvae, will infect snails. As they mature, they hijack their host snail's eye stalks, turning them into swollen, pulsating appendages that wiggle like worms in the presence of light. The hijacking isn't just physical, either—where uninfected snails will prefer to hang out in dark spaces to avoid being seen by predators, like birds, infected snails will actively seek light and put themselves in danger. The goal? For a bird to come along and snap up the snail so that the flatworm can continue its life cycle in the bird's digestive tract. This is a form of what is known as *aggressive mimicry*, although it's a different scale of aggression when compared with the Thing's aggressive mimicry and assimilation.

Another parasite worth mentioning, more for the aesthetic than anything, is the horsehair worm. They prefer to infect insects like grasshoppers, crickets, and cockroaches, and will really make themselves known only if the insect ends up in a body of water (where the worm will escape) or if the insect gets crushed. If you've never accidentally stepped on a cricket infected with a parasitic horsehair worm, let me tell you: the visual of a surprise worm whipping its way out of a crushed insect carcass is distinctly Thing-like.

There's no single, unifying trait that makes a monster in a horror movie a monster except that it must be a threat. Something about it has to ping a warning in the back of our brains when we see it. It's easy enough to visually indicate a threat with sharp teeth or claws or a lethal weapon, but it takes a little bit more work to create a convincing monster that will give chase to a human.

While it definitely helps if the monster clearly looks like an obvious threat, this isn't a hard and fast rule. *The Blob* (1958, dirs. Irvin S. Yeaworth, Jr., and Russell S. Doughten, Jr., uncredited) and *The Stuff* (1985, dir. Larry Cohen) both built monsters out of amorphous goo. They each look about as threatening as Jell-O and Marshmallow Fluff, but once the movies establish their monstrosity—they can, and will, consume you—we accept them as scary for their bizarre predatory behaviors.

Most animals on Earth are engaged in some form of a predator–prey relationship: they are consuming prey or falling victim to predators or both. Humans like to consider themselves an ultimate predator, an *apex* predator. Nothing naturally preys on us and hasn't for a very long time. So, when a monster comes along and flips this current natural order, it's terrifying.

At first glance, it's kind of surprising that humans managed to survive and evolve into the creatures that we are today. Mammals first emerged in the Mesozoic era as small rodent-like prey. Over time, they split off into evolutionary branches, forming distinct orders, families, genera, and species according to the traits that they evolved to differentiate and survive. Humans today aren't especially fast compared to other animals; our bodies are squishy and easy to cut open, and our vision and hearing are good, but definitely not exceptional, especially once the sun goes down. We don't have any neat surprise defense mechanisms like fancy skin patterns that help us blend into the environment, or the ability to squirt jets of blood from our eye sockets like certain species of horned lizards. The most successful survival strategies that have presumably evolved since the first multicellular organisms appeared after the Cambrian explosion some 520 to 540 million years ago include camouflage, disguising yourself as something inedible, being poisonous or bad tasting, or possessing a thick armor—and humans evolved *none* of them.

This isn't to say that we haven't evolved survival strategies. If you take a standard human and squint at them, you can't exactly see the adaptations they've acquired to deal with predators. They're still there, but they're more behavioral than physical (and the physical ones, like myelinated nerve cells to transmit faster signals, aren't exactly visible to the naked eye).

Behaviorally, there are two major adaptive activities that humans evolved to survive: creating communities and inventing tools. Living and moving in groups is a common anti-predator strategy used by a number of organisms. When you're part of a community, everyone can take on a little bit of the work to protect the entire group. Humans' earliest hunting tools probably involved sharpened weapons to collect and consume animals living in tide pools. It wasn't long before early humans set their sights on larger prey, though, like elephants and bison. With a sort of confidence and determination unique to humans, neither the size of these creatures, nor protective adaptations like tusks and horns, seemed to deter early humans as hunters. If anything, it encouraged them. These hunting tools don't exactly equip us to take on other predators, though, so we've also gained adaptations to help us evade things that might be hunting us. We're also notably good endurance runners, in part thanks to evolved skeletal adaptations to help us run, and in part thanks to our sweaty and relatively hairless bodies, which help us dissipate heat more effectively. So, if we're not being chased by something that can out-sprint us and take us down quickly (or if we can evade it during its sprint) we might have a decent chance of surviving against a nonhuman monster if it's not built to be as good at long-distance running as we are.

These major adaptations translate directly to basic horror movie survival rules: don't split up the group, don't go anywhere alone, and use whatever you can grab to fight back. What we lack in tooth, claw, and natural armor, we make up for by finding tools that serve those purposes. And despite what horror movie character archetypes would have you believe, humans are actually pretty good at communication and collaboration.

Since human strategies to hunt prey and to defend against would-be predators both require the effort to find and use tools, it takes a lot of time and energy to avoid threats. The costs associated with self-protection, though, are balanced out by the hypothetical costs of getting caught. This can be referred to as the "life-dinner principle": less effort is required by the predator in a chase because, should they lose, they risk missing out on a meal, but they'll probably go on to live another day and capture another meal somewhere else. For the prey, should they lose the chase, they lose their life. Generally speaking, humans are used to running for dinner (and even that's being very generous, given that, for many of us, food gathering strategies amount to going to a grocery store or restaurant to procure food). But we definitely aren't used to running to avoid *being* something else's dinner.

THE MONSTER AS A PREDATOR

When it comes to the horror movie, monsters come in all kinds of flavors. In its most basic categorization, we can say that there are two main types of monster: the human and the nonhuman. We know what the former can be capable of; the latter telegraphs it to us with certain predatory traits.

A bunny rabbit and a mountain lion can both be described as fur-covered animals, but it wouldn't take you more than a quick glance to know that a bunny is prey, and likely not a threat, while a mountain lion is a predator and dangerous to approach.

A predator is defined by physical traits and behaviors

that help it subdue and consume its target prey. The traits are pretty easy to spot: predators, especially mammalian predators, usually have front-facing eyes for binocular vision that helps with hunting ("Eyes to the front—this animal hunts; eyes to the sides—this animal hides"), and jaws, teeth, and claws built for dealing with flesh. Those are the hard-and-fast rules and, while not universal, they seem to be the ones adopted most often when new horror monsters are created.

In terms of behaviors, knowing what kind of predator we're dealing with can give us major clues as to what kind of horror scenario we're dealing with and what we can best do to survive it.

Pursuit predators—predators that chase their prey—rely on the ability to suddenly burst into a sprint. Their speed is usually coupled with the ability to anticipate when their prey is going to make an evasive move and quickly change course to overtake them. In real life, animals like cheetahs and dragonflies fall under this particular type of pursuit predator. In horror, pursuit predation, especially in the form of monster chases, is pretty common, probably because the pursuit action gives us stressful, adrenaline-fueled sequences to watch. Examples include the fast zombies in *28 Weeks Later* (2007, dir. Juan Carlos Fresnadillo), the aliens from *Attack the Block* (2011, dir. Joe Cornish), and the Gwoemul from *The Host* (2006, dir. Bong Joon-ho). If you're being chased by this type of predator, you probably can't beat it by outrunning it (it's built to be faster than you). If you're lucky, maybe you can stay ahead of it until it runs out of stamina. But these predators don't usually behave by the same biological rules of, say, a cheetah, which can maintain its top speed for only twenty or thirty seconds before lactic acid buildup cramps their muscles and forces them to reduce their speed. Horror movie monsters of this variety are usually described as "relentless," so you're better off either trying to find a way to put a barrier between you and the monster making chase—always close the door behind you!—or practice literal herd immunity and put yourself among a crowd (and hope that someone else is picked off instead of you).

A subset strategy of pursuit predation is persistence hunting, also known as endurance hunting. These are the stalking predators that aren't necessarily able to outpace their prey. Instead, they intend to follow their prey until it's exhausted and gives up. These are the monsters behind every scene in a horror movie where the human being pursued is stumbling and panting, desperately trying to stay ahead of the threat but running out of steam fast. Most humans and slasher villains fall under this category. The T-1000 from *Terminator 2: Judgment Day* (1991, dir. James Cameron), the untethered from *Us* (2019, dir. Jordan Peele), and the creature from *It Follows* (2014, dir. David Robert Mitchell) could all be described as persistence hunters. Some of them, like the T-1000, can transition into a chase mode, but their strategy is defined by their never-ending pursuit, rather than by bursts of attack. Unlike their speedier counterparts, the key to evading persistence hunters is to get ahead of them and stay ahead for as long as you can without depleting your own energy stores. Because as soon as you stop to rest up, you're giving your dauntless predators the opportunity to catch up and catch you. Most horror movie monsters are some form of pursuit predator and, luckily for us, they're usually solitary.

On the other side of the coin are ambush predators. These creatures lie in wait for actively moving prey to cross their path. This requires stealth and is aided by an ability to blend into their environment, either with special adaptations such as camouflage, by hiding behind or under physical objects, or by burrowing. An ambush is effective only if the prey is too surprised by the attack to react. Trapdoor spiders and chameleons are both adept ambush predators. The former carves out a shallow burrow in the dirt and hides within, covering the entrance to their burrow with a "trapdoor" built from spider silk and camouflaging materials, like twigs, dirt, and pebbles. Tiny silk tripwires radiate from the burrow, and when unsuspecting prey walks by and vibrates the silk strings, the spider pops out of its hiding spot to nab its prey. Chameleons, on the other hand, hide in plain sight with color-changing camouflage, moving slowly toward their prey, only to close the final distance by unleashing a sticky tongue-strike. Horror movie monsters that behave like ambush predators are the alligators in *Crawl* (2019, dir. Alexandre Aja), the adult xenomorphs from *Alien* (1979, dir. Ridley Scott), or the Judas breed insects from *Mimic* (1997, dir. Guillermo del Toro). Ambush predators rely on the element of surprise, so the best way to survive an attack is to stay on the alert for threats and try to anticipate where they might be lurking in wait before they can get the jump on you.

SCARE SPOTLIGHT:
ALIEN (1979, DIR. RIDLEY SCOTT)

Alien is possibly one of the most thoroughly documented sci-fi or horror film productions out there. I'm not the first person to shine a spotlight onto the franchise, and I definitely will not be the last. One of the main reasons *Alien* has left such a deep cultural impression is because its monster is nothing short of groundbreaking for horror.

Alien writer and visual design consultant Dan O'Bannon was driven to have a memorable creature design. O'Bannon's first attempt at an alien threat, in *Dark Star* (1974, dir. John Carpenter), was much less successful. It looked like a beach ball with feet. According to O'Bannon in an interview for *The Beast Within: The Making of Alien* (2003, dir. Charles de Lauzirika), a lackluster rubber alien could be a powerful motivator: "It was our second try on that alien. I went away from *Dark Star* really wanting to do an alien that looked *real*."

The fully grown xenomorph in *Alien* was groundbreaking for a few reasons. For one, it showed us how we could depict an alien that didn't just look like a man in a rubber suit—although, admittedly, the adult xenomorph was still a man in a rubber suit, just a very elaborate one. For another, it generally proved that horror monsters can be shown fully on-screen without spoiling their scariness. We get to see the alien, and it feels not only realistic, but possible.

The factors that come together to make the xenomorph come alive in its various life stages go beyond H. R. Giger's famously strange and beautiful designs.

For one, the alien is clearly identifiable as a monster, and a threatening monster in its adult form with claws and teeth (in a snarling double-jawed mouth), and blood so corrosive that it chews through the metal components of a ship in seconds. But as a threat, it is wholly unfamiliar, synthesized from many mythological entities and cosmic imaginings, and neither the crew of the *Nostromo* nor the audience has any frame of reference for how to defend against this threat or, furthermore, how to destroy it. In the film itself, android Ash (Ian Holm) describes the creature as "[t]he perfect organism. Its structural perfection is matched only by its hostility.... A survivor, unclouded by conscience, remorse, or delusions of morality."

Its modus operandi as an adult is similar to that of many contemporary predators. The xenomorph is an ambush predator, almost always attacking from shadowy alcoves and hidden spaces on the ship. It's definitely strong enough and fast enough to stalk and chase down its prey (I have no stats on xenomorph stamina, but have you ever seen one get tired?), but it opts for stealth, waiting to pounce on an unsuspecting crew member as they walk down a corridor.

What's great about the xenomorph being an ambush predator is that this behavior ramps up tension in the already claustrophobic quarters of the ship. This effect made *Alien* ripe for memorable jump scares. In a key jump scare, ship captain Dallas (Tom Skerritt) is crawling through vents lit only by the light of a faltering flashlight and intermittent blasts from his flamethrower. Lambert (Veronica Cartwright) warns him over his headset that the alien is moving right toward him, but he can see no sign except darkness. He climbs down a ladder into another vent, turns his flashlight toward the camera and then away. There's an almost invisible cut that reveals a close-up of the alien, screaming, with its teeth bared and arms outstretched. The jump scare is effective: an attack is implied, even though we don't actually get to see the alien make contact with Dallas. Without the context of the scene, the alien looks like it's just jumping out and yelling, "Boo!" instead of preparing to kill Dallas off-screen.

In its face-hugger form, the xenomorph evokes fears and disgust tied to penetration, infection, and parasitism. O'Bannon cited parasitic wasps as an inspiration for this life stage, real insects that will infect caterpillars with eggs that will hatch into larvae that will then feast on their host from within. One species of parasitic wasp, *Epirhyssa johanna,* has a spindly, bowed shape that seems to be echoed somewhat in the adult xenomorph's skeletal, sinewy form.

The chest-burster is the life stage that gets the briefest amount of screen time, but it makes up for it by having the most iconic scene of the film. The phallic worm-shaped creature with teeth was inspired by unsettling art by painter Francis Bacon, designed by H. R. Giger, and brought to life by special effects artist Roger Dicken. What's most impressive about the chest-burster scene is that it's carried out in a brightly lit space, and when the monster is revealed, the camera lingers on it, letting the audience fully take it in before it screams and scurries away to grow into its adult form.

Every form of the xenomorph reveals its power to invade and destroy the human body, but it betrays no obvious weakness. I think this, combined with its believable and obviously threatening design, is what makes it so scary.

As Axelle Carolyn, a filmmaker whose credits include *Tales of Halloween* (2015) and *The Haunting of Bly Manor* (2020), once said: "At no point in the Alien movies, and definitely not in the first one, do you feel like what makes us human is the thing that allows us to beat this creature."

Another major factor in predation strategy is a social one. Is your monster a solo artist, or does he work well with others? While I said before that most horror monsters are solitary, the genre is not without its monsters who prefer group tactics. Needless to say, your chances are better if you are being pitted against one monster rather than a pack of them, who can use strategies such as flanking or coordinated movement that can steer you into a corner, like the raptors from *Jurassic Park* (1993, dir. Steven Spielberg) or the werewolves in *Dog Soldiers* (2002, dir. Neil Marshall). Cooperative hunting can also grant small, unassuming-looking threats, like the gremlins from *Gremlins* (1984, dir. Joe Dante), the vesps from *The Silence* (2019, dir. John R. Leonetti), or the brood children from *The Brood* (1979, dir. David Cronenberg), an unexpected advantage against larger prey.

THE HUMAN (OR HUMAN-ISH) MONSTER

Now that we have covered monsters who remind us of animal predators, it's time to turn toward the types of monsters who look just like us.

In 1970, an obscure Japanese journal called *Energy* published an essay called "Bukimi No Tani," by Masahiro Mori, a robotics professor at the Tokyo Institute of Technology. At the time, the essay didn't exactly make any ripples, let alone the splash that it would make decades later when it entered pop-cultural consciousness. The essay proposed that people will respond favorably, even empathetically, to humanlike robots, but only up to a point. As Mori mapped out his concept, he demonstrated a theoretical point at which humanoid robots would be received with fear and revulsion as they approached but didn't *quite* capture humanlike traits.

That dip in comfort is what is widely known today as the "uncanny valley." The feeling of "uncanniness" was once described by Freud as a sense of fear associated with novelty or unfamiliarity, while German psychologist Ernst Jentsch framed uncanniness in terms of uncertainty. There has been little research to drill deeper into what exactly makes up the specific feeling of uncanniness, but in 2008, researchers Chin-Chang Ho, Karl MacDorman, and Zacharias Pramono did conduct a small study that surveyed 143 Indonesian adults with little exposure to robots and asked them to rate their emotional reactions to randomized videos of humans or robots. Ho's team suggested that the feeling of uncanniness might be more related to a sense of eeriness, or a cocktail mix of fear, disgust, nervousness, dislike, and shock, rather than strictly a sense of "strangeness." This doesn't exactly do too much to define the feeling, except maybe to articulate that it's hard to capture the feeling of "uncanniness" strictly using words. You sort of have to experience it yourself to understand.

On a typical uncanny valley graph, the first peak shows subjects that have low human likeness, but high likeability, like stuffed animals or toy robots. As the subjects become more human, we see likeability increase before sharply dropping off (with a human corpse sitting at the bottom of the valley). Likeability starts to increase again as the subject gets closer to our ideal: a living, healthy person.

Cultural factors definitely affect what sits on a peak or in the valley. In Mori's original graph, the *okina* mask (a Japanese Nō theatre mask that represents a pleasant old

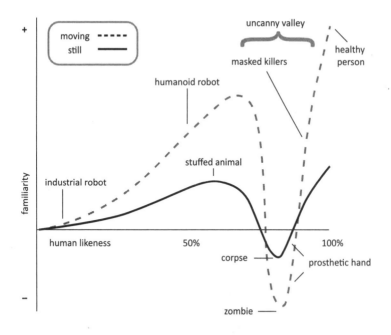

Drawing based on "Mori Uncanny Valley" by Smurraryinchester, which is based on an image by Masahiro Mori and Karl MacDorman, used under Creative Commons Attribution-ShareAlike 3.0 Unported (CC BY-SA 3.0).

man) and *bunraku* puppets are both situated as having both high human likeness and high likeability. If you're not, for example, familiar with traditional *bunraku* theatre, you might find the puppetry and their complex movements and mechanical facial expressions uncanny, strange, or unsettling.

When it comes to robot design, engineers are aiming to design models that appeal to us and so don't fall into the uncanny valley. Horror filmmakers, on the other hand, absolutely exploit monster designs that will land us squarely in our discomfort zone.

If we tweak Mori's representation of the uncanny valley to encompass horror monsters, it might look something like this:

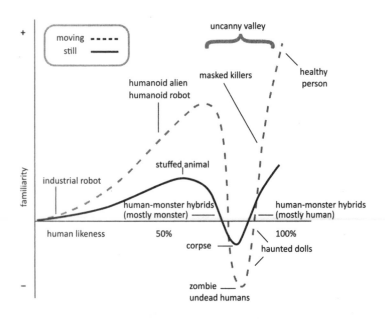

Drawing based on "Mori Uncanny Valley" by Smurraryinchester, which is based on an image by Masahiro Mori and Karl MacDorman, used under Creative Commons Attribution-ShareAlike 3.0 Unported (CC BY-SA 3.0).

While the phenomenon of the uncanny valley is widely accepted as plausible, we haven't been able to pinpoint exactly *why* we find ourselves falling headfirst into the valley when we come across a creepy doll, a masked killer, or a strangely humanoid monster. A few hypotheses do exist, though, and they fall into two major categories of explanation: that that uncanny feeling is an automatic, perhaps even evolved, reflex of perception that serves to protect humans from threat; or that the bad vibes are the result of cognitive processing that reveals a mismatch between what we are seeing and what we would expect to see.

When Mori first described the phenomenon in 1970, he posited that the uncanny feeling might be connected to the former category, as a mechanism for human self-preservation. Researchers have taken this idea and tried linking the uncanny valley to feelings of disgust and pathogen avoidance, arguing that the "off-ness" of imperfect human replicas could be interpreted as potential signs of disease that we want to avoid catching. It's possible, too, that the aesthetic of an uncanny human replica is alarming because it's a swing-and-a-miss at attractive physical traits that we tend to seek out in humans. It's not like we necessarily look at androids or monstrous humanoids with hopes to procreate—not to drag the vocal crowds on the internet who wanted to get physical with the fish-man after seeing *The Shape of Water* (2017, dir. Guillermo del Toro)—but researchers such as David Hanson (2005) have suggested that maybe we're creeped out by uncanny replicas not because they're unrealistic-looking, but because they just don't have those attractive traits we tend to subconsciously seek out in other humans. Others have suggested that our desire to avoid uncanny objects is as simple as that a shambling zombie or a pale-faced puppet reminds us of our own mortality or of a fear of the loss of control over our own body, because uncanny creatures don't quite look real or alive. They just look like a facsimile of life.

On the cognitive end of our hypothesis scale, we have theories that suggest that the uncanny valley experience is thanks to our knowledge and past experiences telling us to expect one thing (like, a living, breathing human) and our senses telling us that something doesn't quite match up with that expectation. This mismatch can be something as simple as an apparent child speaking with a demonic voice, like fully possessed Regan in *The Exorcist*, or completely black eyes, something we attribute to evil or demonic characters in contemporary horror. Even someone like Michael Myers (Nick Castle), whose eyes are usually hard to make out behind his pale mask, is described as uncanny by Dr. Loomis, who says that he has "the blackest eyes, the devil's eyes" in *Halloween* (1978, dir. John Carpenter).

Finally, there is the theory that uncanniness is born of what's known as *categorical uncertainty*. Humans tend to project human traits onto nonhuman animals and objects—we like to understand nonhuman entities, from pets to houseplants and beyond, in human terms.

When we can't understand a creature's actions in human terms, it makes us uncomfortable. In horror movies, this translates to trying to justify nonhuman monsters' behaviors by projecting human emotions onto them. One of the scariest things about these predators is that we don't understand how they think. They don't necessarily have humanlike rationales or motivations for doing what they do. Despite being humanoid (and likely mutant humans), do the cave-dwelling crawlers from *The Descent* (2005, dir. Neil Marshall) have any specific agenda against humans when they're stalking Sarah (Shauna Macdonald) and her friends on their Appalachian caving misadventure? Probably not. They might not even have any deep understanding that their human prey are any different from the dead deer that we find in the forest at the beginning of the movie. The crawlers are just being monsters. Monsters don't tend to live by human value systems, if they're even aware of human values at all.

In their review of theories to explain the uncanny valley, Shensheng Wang, Scott Lilienfeld, and Philippe Rochat (2015) proposed another theory: that dehumanization is at work. Similar to the phenomena at work for the categorical uncertainty theory, humans are particularly sensitive to noticing faces and to attributing personality to things with faces. We can thank the inferior occipital gyrus in the brain for its quick visual detection of face-like shapes, as well as for its direct line to the amygdala. The amygdala, then, can also be implicated in how much we trust uncanny faces—studies have suggested its involvement not only in face processing, but also in trust evaluation, anthropomorphizing, and general formation of social impressions. This all has obvious ties to the threat evaluation and response role that we discussed for the amygdala in chapter 1, and so would of course be implicated when it comes to the possible threat of uncanny figures.

The basis of the dehumanization theory is this: if the Thing with a Face does not meet those expectations of what we've projected onto them, the mismatch sets off alarm bells. The advantage to being able to apply faces to objects during early visual detection could mean life or death with a threat suddenly entering into view. Sure, it might be a false alarm and that possible monster might actually just be a faceless coat hanging from a hook on the back of your bedroom door, but remember: those embarrassing false alarms caused by misidentification are greatly outweighed by the advantages of correctly identifying a real threat even once.

When it comes to horror films, it's usually important to the audience that they be able to separate the monsters from the good guys. To help us out when they would otherwise just look like regular humans, monsters often come with masks.

Masks And Faces

Masks are the easiest way to visually divide a human monster from their humanity, which is why they serve as such handy shorthand for monstrosity in horror, especially the slasher subgenre. According to Thomas M. Sipos, author of *Horror Film Aesthetics: Creating the Visual Language of Fear* (2010), masks serve to empower slashers and heighten their horror, not only by replacing their human features with a disturbing visage, but by rendering the weapon-wielding killer anonymous and inhuman. The masked killer fits squarely into the uncanny valley conversation. Whether evil, undead, or granted a supernatural ability boost, masked killers are decidedly human under their disguises.

Beyond hiding features, masks also hide emotions. This puts us at an immediate disadvantage because we can no longer read the usual social cues that we're hardwired to pick up from facial expressions. There's no way to read what this masked figure might be thinking, feeling, or intending. Coupled with shadowed eyes and neutral stances (think Michael Myers standing next to the hedge), masked killers become even more inscrutable and unpredictable from a potential victim's point of view.

But it is completely possible to make a human face, sans mask, feel unfamiliar. The original poster for the movie *Orphan* (2009, dir. Jaume Collet-Serra) serves as a great test case for taking a child's face and making it creepy without the usual horror shorthand like blacked-out demonic eyes or blood or even a sinister smile. The poster's tagline declares THERE'S SOMETHING WRONG WITH ESTHER, as if this weren't immediately clear from the image of Esther herself. The image is simple, just actress Isabelle Fuhrman's face, her gaze straight into the camera. In fact, her expression, other than some slight shadowing around the eyes, is neutral. It isn't obvious at first, but the image is unsettling without any blood or obvious horror because it's *too* symmetrical. Esther's face on the poster is an image of half her face, mirrored.

The irony is that humans have historically valued symmetry as a sign of health and attractiveness. Biologically speaking, humans present what's known as *bilateral symmetry*: if you sliced a person in half along their mid-sagittal plane, so a line running down the middle of the forehead, straight down the center of the sternum, through the belly button, and beyond, and split those two halves apart, the two sides should be relatively equal. That's the intent of the human body's basic design, but obviously it's not 100 percent what we get with execution. Between factors affecting embryonic development, and internal and external effects on our bodies through growth, development, and aging, we see effects that make us appear less symmetrical. The Evolutionary Advantage theory posits that people who are more symmetrical must therefore be healthier because they've experienced fewer illnesses or adverse health conditions. The theory then follows that people find symmetrical features more attractive because their good health indicators mean a better chance for reproductive success.

It's a little cringeworthy, but the Evolutionary Advantage theory has had its bursts of popularity. Early twentieth-century state fairs in the United States and Canada would often feature "Better Baby," "Most Scientific Baby," and "Fitter Family" contests. These are exactly what they sound like, which is to say, the human equivalent of entering your prized pumpkin or pig into a contest for a chance at a ribbon or medal. Families could sign up to have their infants and families measured, tested, and generally prodded at by researcher judges who decided which entrants had the most ideal traits. The goal of these contests, of course, was to quietly popularize eugenics ideologies.

We still see echoes of this history today. Every once in a while, magazine headlines will circulate to announce which celebrities are the most attractive "according to science." The metric used to evaluate attractiveness for these pieces is almost always facial symmetry, or how evenly matched both sides of a face would appear if we were to draw a line down the middle and compare. Apparently "scientists" agree that more symmetry equals a higher attractiveness score. And yet too much symmetry, as we see in the *Orphan* movie poster, is uncanny and makes us uncomfortable.

Another crappy side effect of this practice of equating symmetry with attractiveness is that it equates a lack of symmetry with unattractiveness, unfitness, and a culture of disgust toward people with facial differences or physical disabilities.

It's a culture that's found a foothold in horror history, with facial differences especially being used as visual shorthand for monstrosity. We've seen this as early as the silent film *The Phantom of the Opera* (1925, dir. Rupert Julian), with false teeth and hidden wires that yanked the Phantom's (Lon Chaney) nose upward, and the tradition has continued with killers such as the murderous son of Frau Brückner (played by Davide Marotta) in *Phenomena* (1985, dir. Dario Argento), and Francis Dolarhyde in *Red Dragon* (2002, dir. Brett Ratner), played by Ralph Fiennes, who also notably portrayed an even more well-known villain with facial differences—Lord Voldemort in the *Harry Potter* franchise.

When we discuss the uncanny valley, the conversation is usually centered on still images of faces and figures that deviate from so-called standard human faces and figures. Uncanniness can go so much deeper, though, especially once movement is introduced.

Moving Makes It Worse

In his original essay about the uncanny valley, Mori notes that movement intensifies the sense of eeriness we can feel, effectively digging the valley even deeper.

It's an effect we see all the time in horror; humans displaying jerky and erratic movements on-screen telegraph that something is wrong, like *supernaturally* wrong, and definitely threatening. Possession movies and pretty much every zombie movie fall under this category.

To take a possession movie example, in *Annabelle: Creation* (2017, dir. David F. Sandberg), we see a young girl called Bee (Samara Lee) from behind as she hums and sets up a tea party for her dolls, including the titular Annabelle. Suddenly, with bone-crunching sounds, her neck and elbows crank to unnatural angles. When she turns and walks toward Esther (Miranda Otto), her feet are turned so fiercely inward that she is practically walking on the outside edges of her feet and ankles. Her movement looks uncomfortable, jerky, and decidedly inhuman. These movements are often achieved with undercranking, or other techniques to make the actors' movements appear unnatural, such as recording actors moving backward and then reversing the footage so that they appear to be moving forward, but with unusual gaits. This is part of what makes the nurses' movements in the live-action *Silent Hill* (2006, dir. Christophe Gans) adaptation so effective, not to mention the ethereal stairway ghost from *Poltergeist* (1982, dir. Tobe Hooper), who was similarly shot moving slowly backward up the stairs, only to have the footage later reversed to make it appear as if the spectral figure were floating down into the Freelings' living room.

Erratic movement is scary because it's unpredictable. We can't anticipate how an erratically moving monster is going to move next—or in what direction—and so we can't plan how to fight or escape. It might not be surprising to realize that the crown for most disturbing movements doesn't belong to the shambling zombie or to the contortionist moves of a possessed human. That prize belongs to none other than the humble spider.

Spiders are special. There's a large body of research spanning decades that shows that spiders freak people out more than they have any right to, and that fear responses to spiders are especially tenacious. It's been proposed that the reason it's such a common fear is because we've evolved to find spiders repulsive as a form of protection against potentially fatal spider bites, what Martin Seligman described in 1971 as "prepared fear learning." While it's true that all spiders are predators of some form, very few species of spiders are actually dangerous to humans—many spider mandibles are too small to even puncture skin, let alone cause any real damage with their venom. The idea of humans evolving a pretty common fear of them seems a little bizarre, especially since an outsized fear of spiders tends to outrank fears of other creepy-crawly arthropods, like wasps, whose defense mechanisms *are* actually designed to fend off larger threats.

To try to get to the root of what exactly creeps people out about spiders in particular, and to see if there was a common trait that binds those among us who fear spiders, a small study by Graham Davey (1991) polled 118 people and found that, although there was no clear consensus on what makes spiders so creepy, the most frightening features of spiders reported was their "legginess" and how they move suddenly. At the bottom of the list, interestingly, was their perceived harmfulness. The sample for the study is way too small to pull out any truly meaningful results, but it's still interesting to speculate as to why spiders' appearances and movements are freaky to us, but not the idea that they might cause harm. It's like we *know* that spiders aren't really all that threatening, but we can't help but be creeped out by them anyway.

Human aversion to spiders is so prevalent that it's an acknowledged issue slash fear tactic employed in video games. I would say that I have a pretty average discomfort with spiders, but video game spiders have always given me the heebie-jeebies. Whether it's the giant, venomous spider-baddies that can take you down in the *Dragon Age* franchise (2009) or decidedly cartoony spiders dropping from the ceiling in *Crash Team Racing* (1999), I'm liable to flinch when they appear. More recently the developers for the survival video game *Grounded* (2020) innovated an "Arachnophobia Safe Mode" among their accessibility options, to allow players to adjust the appearance of arachnid enemies to appear less spider-like. At Maximum Spider, the spider looks as it should, with a segmented body, eight legs, mandibles, and many eyes. By adjusting a slider toward zero, the spider first loses its legs, then its mandibles, before eventually appearing as floating textureless orbs with two red eyes—as far from a spider as possible.

As if tapping into this fear, some incredibly iconic horror moments have taken spider-like movements and gifted them to humans. In the cult found-footage horror *The Poughkeepsie Tapes* (2007, dir. John Erick Dowdle) there is a segment ("Poughkeepsie Tape #1826 Seg. 13j") that features a captive woman in the foreground with her mouth taped shut with packing tape, while in the background a man, the Water Street Butcher (played by Ben Messmer), approaches on all fours, wearing a black outfit and a neutral mask on the back of his head. The placement of the mask, combined with the grainy quality of the recording, gives us an illusion of inhuman anatomy and movement.

John Carpenter's *In the Mouth of Madness* (1995) features a crawling monster who *mostly* appears to be a woman, except that when she speaks to tell John Trent (Sam Neill) that "Cane has a job for you," her voice echoes demonically and, perhaps more horrifyingly, her head is twisted to face in the wrong direction. The grotesque torsion is visible on her neck, so that while she is crawling with her torso facing the ground, her chin is pointed straight up toward the sky (and vice versa before she flips her body around with joint-cracking ease).

And, of course, Regan MacNeil's spider walk (performed by stuntwoman and contortionist Ann Miles) headfirst down the stairs remains one of the most iconic images from *The Exorcist*, despite being cut from the original release of the film (it was cleaned up to remove visible wires and reinstated in the release of the director's cut of the film in 2000). Some fans quibble that the narrative suffers from its inclusion (after all, if Regan is able to leave her room after the demon Pazuzu fully takes her over, what prevents her from leaving at other points of the film?), but I think that minor plot transgression is worth the terrible sight of a young girl's contorted body traveling mindlessly down the staircase in an otherwise tidy family home, blood smeared across her face. Spider-walking Regan has become of a bit of a horror icon for her memorable movement, unlikely to be forgotten anytime soon.

MONSTERS THAT ARE HERE TO STAY

As horror fans, we like to talk about "classic" or "iconic" monsters—a gallery of creatures and beings that have earned the honor of a lasting image in horror's genre memory. New ghouls, ghosts, aliens, and cryptids, are entering the horror canon every day, but when you search online for best-of lists, the entries have been pretty much static over the past few decades, with only the rare new beastie managing to crack into the ranks.

Is there any common trait that binds fan-favorite monsters together? Not really. Nor does it seem that we have a psychological predisposition to certain types of monsters over others. In the last chapter, we established that monsters change over time to fit what we collectively need to see on-screen. George Romero's shambling undead in *Dawn of the Dead* (1978) share genetic material with Zack Snyder's fast zombies in his 2004 remake. Individual preferences might trend toward one type over another, but generally horror fans find room in their hearts for both.

In the early aughts, Stuart Fischoff was curious about the psychological appeal of favorite movie monsters. He and his team surveyed over one thousand participants to figure out which monsters stood out for moviegoers as clear favorites and why.

According to the study's participants, their major reasons for why a monster was their favorite had little to do with its capacity for murder, with superhuman strength coming in at number one, followed by intelligence, and then how the monster relates to depictions of "pure evil" or an otherwise lack of morality. The monster as a figure for moral exploration seemed more important to the participants than the monster as a strictly lean, mean killing machine. The study also included a measure for monsters that were favored for their overall sexiness. If you're curious, vampires were acknowledged as the sexiest of movie monsters, with, fascinatingly, Hannibal Lecter (as portrayed by Anthony Hopkins) coming in as a distant second.

Since this study was conducted back in 2003, not only have new generations of horror fans come of age, but we've seen the introductions of new iconic monsters, from Sam from *Trick 'r Treat* (2007, dir. Michael Dougherty), to the Pale Man from *Pan's Labyrinth* (2006, dir. Guillermo del Toro), to the Babadook from *The Babadook* (2014, dir. Jennifer Kent), to the updated Pennywise the Dancing Clown from *It* (2017, dir. Andrés Muschietti) and *It: Chapter Two* (2019, dir. Andrés Muschietti), to name a few. I'd be curious to see if and how tastes have changed. If user-generated lists on sites like Ranker.com can be trusted as representative, vampires might have lost their foothold at the top (which we *might* be able to attribute to the *Twilight* franchise causing both a jump and a slump in popular interest in vampires during the early and mid-2000s), while the xenomorphs from the *Alien* movies and the alien Thing of *The Thing* continue to hold strong in the top slots of a number of lists, decades after they first appeared on the horror scene. But if we consider that vampires as horror icons have predated horror films, they're not going to be gone for too long.

So far we've set the scene for a horror experience: we've discussed how to prime audience fear, we've grounded it in the context of horror history, and we've brought in monsters to embody threats. All we're missing is a little bit of atmosphere. It's time to get even more unsettled with sound.

CHAPTER 4

PUTTING FEAR IN YOUR EARS

Sound and music play an important part in horror film tradition. Audio is used across all cinematic genres to enhance the emotions of a scene and support a movie's storytelling. It's hard to imagine what *Jaws* (1975, dir. Steven Spielberg) would be like without John Williams's famous score, or *Halloween* (1978, dir. John Carpenter) without Carpenter's energetic 5/4 theme, or any of the many movies that feature children singing lullabies. It's funny; music isn't inherently scary, and children singing shouldn't creep us out as much as it does. One of the first instances of a child's song giving us the creeps in a horror movie is in *The Innocents* (1961, dir. Jack Clayton). Since then, it's been firmly established that if we hear children's voices, something spooky is bound to happen.

We take our cues from the sounds and scores of horror films. We know that sudden loud sounds are meant to make us jump and to enhance a startle. We know that when the score starts building and swelling with intensity, we should be preparing for some sort of tension or important moment. We know that when things get *too* quiet, something sudden and shocking is about to happen. And we are often introduced to musical motifs that help us identify heroes and villains. Think of the theme from *Psycho* (1960, dir. Alfred Hitchcock), composed by Bernard Herrmann: we hear the main melody when we are driving along with Marion Crane (Janet Leigh), and don't really hear it again until after she is murdered. This soaring melody can't belong to Norman Bates (Anthony Perkins) at all. The only thing we can ever associate with him is the *eee! eee! eee!* of screeching violins. Hearing the sounds and scores we expect in horror films allows us to play along as the audience.

Halloween further reinforces how important these horror music rules can become. John Carpenter once screened an early cut of *Halloween,* minus the sound effects and music, to an executive from 20th Century Fox. When she wasn't scared at all by the movie, he became determined to "save it with music." He worked with David Wyman to create the now-recognizable synth-based score and cut in all sorts of harsh-sounding stingers to coincide with the attacks of the Shape (Michael Meyer's credited character name in the first film of the franchise). Months later he ran into the executive again, and she said that she now loved the movie. According to Carpenter, the only thing he'd changed, the only thing that had made this difference, was adding sound.

Of course, that doesn't mean movies can't break their own rules.

28 Days Later (2002, dir. Danny Boyle) shows the power of sound and silence in equal measure. After a loud and chaotic prologue in which animal rights activists release violent RAGE virus–infected chimpanzees from a lab only to be attacked and infected themselves, the title card comes up in silence. Jim (played by Cillian Murphy) wakes up from a coma in a London hospital's intensive care unit. It is clearly abandoned. Horror movie rules dictate that with this much silence, a threat should be lurking just around the corner. There should be dead bodies on the ground. Instead, Jim wanders from abandoned space to abandoned space littered with trash in a way that signifies he has clearly awakened to some terrible aftermath. The only sounds are his own footsteps and his lone voice calling out "Hello."

As he wanders into Piccadilly Circus, the song "East Hastings" by Godspeed You! Black Emperor slowly simmers to life. (Fun fact: the song—the only song this scene could have been cut to, in Danny Boyle's mind—wasn't easy to get. Godspeed You! Black Emperor is a Canadian experimental music collective that's known for being very anticorporate in their politics; they don't tend to grant licenses to their music. Boyle may have managed to get an edited version of the song into his film, but he did not get permission to include it on the movie's soundtrack.) Despite the swell of music, Jim is alone in a strange London void of people. He opens a car door, and an alarm goes off, buried into the music. It startles him, breaking the dreamy state of the sequence. It's the first significant sound he's heard since waking up.

Boyle did experiment with playing the vacant London scene without any music—with unexpected results. It turned out that, without music, the silence in this scene was *too* scary, and the contrast between absolute silence and the sound of the car alarm was *too* jarring. "You couldn't do that in the cinema," he explained to Amy Raphael, author of *Danny Boyle: Authorised Edition*. "People would have heart attacks. Pacemakers would short circuit."

So, stripping sound from visuals clearly has an effect, but what about the reverse, taking visuals away? We do it when we think something scarier than we can handle might happen on-screen: we close our eyes, we cover our faces with our hands, or we hide behind our blankets or bags of popcorn to spare ourselves from seeing the worst parts of the movie. And does it work? Uh . . . no. Studies have concluded that closing your eyes against a scary scene is ineffective, because you can still hear what's going on—and whatever images your brain conjures up will probably be even scarier than the scene you're avoiding. Putting aside the fact that you're missing out on what might be great horror visuals, closing your eyes might actually be enhancing your experience of horror sounds.

One such study on this was done by Talma Hendler, a neuroscientist and psychiatrist at Tel Aviv University in Israel. She had volunteers listen to spooky, Hitchcockian music with their eyes open or closed, and did the same with comparatively neutral music. Brain scans revealed that the amygdala got fired up while participants were listening to the scary themes and unpleasant dissonance with their eyes closed. Other areas of the brain were co-activated with the amygdala, the locus ceruleus and the ventral prefrontal cortex (VPC). These areas are associated with both visceral and cognitive processing of emotional information. Interestingly, these results were not replicated when participants repeated the experiment in a dark room with their eyes open. It seems like having your eyes closed is an important factor.

Just like when you close your eyes to tune in better to your favorite song, closing your eyes helps you focus on sounds. Hendler and her team suggest that when we close our eyes, we're actually triggering a mechanism that helps the brain amplify certain information and better process and integrate the emotional experience attached to what you're hearing. Listening with your eyes closed, then, immerses you in the soundscape.

This immersion is part of why horror movies are often more effective when you watch them in a theatre with a good sound system (or if you happen to have a sweet surround sound setup at home). Humans typically have pretty good skills when it comes to sound localization, which includes our ability to sense the direction from which sounds are coming from and also pinpoint which sounds are more important than others. When you're watching horror in a space where you're surrounded by speakers, your immersion is higher because you're being engaged by auditory information that tells you more about your (movie) environment than what you're necessarily seeing on the screen. You might be seeing a close-up of a character but hearing a twig snap coming from behind you. The impression is then that you are the one with a killer behind you and at a greater risk than the character on-screen.

How music is applied to a movie goes a long way toward determining the overall mood of the narrative. Think of the iconic pub fight scene in *Shaun of the Dead* (2004, dir. Edgar Wright). Shaun (Simon Pegg) and his pals are trapped in the Winchester pub with zombies pressing in against the windows. The pub owner, an old man but also definitely a zombie, is trapped inside the pub with them. Shaun and others take turns pummeling the zombie with pool cues as Queen's "Don't Stop Me Now" plays on the jukebox, their whacks perfectly timed with the song's beat. In another room, David (Dylan Moran) frantically tries to find the right breaker to kill power to the jukebox, but ends up instead flashing lights on and off outside the pub, also in perfect synchronicity with the song. Imagine if "Don't Stop Me Now" were stripped away from this scene completely and replaced with a standard horror score. What's clearly a comedic scene automatically becomes something darker: a group of trapped people trying to fend off a zombie with useless tools like pool cues and throwing darts, while one of their own ineptly attracts more and more zombies to their location.

SCARE SPOTLIGHT:
A QUIET PLACE (2018, DIR. JOHN KRASINSKI)

The Abbott family has worked hard to build their homestead. They are as self-sufficient as possible, growing their own crops and mending their own clothing. Everything is hand-modified to meet their specific needs: they use large leaves instead of plates, their walkways are marked by a thick path of white sand, and they communicate almost exclusively in American Sign Language. Their quiet, rural life would seem idyllic if it weren't for the plague of monsters that kill anything they can hear.

In the world of *A Quiet Place,* as the name implies, silence is central to survival. This key component to the narrative posed a huge creative challenge for the film's sound design team, led by Erik Aadahl and Ethan Van der Ryn. In a reversal of the usual sound design process, Aadahl and Van der Ryn were required to strip all the sound away and add it back in bit by bit. As they built the soundscape back up, they had to establish rules early on for how they deployed sound so that they didn't introduce anything that would go against the logic of the film's world. According to Aadahl in an interview with *Vox,* the sound design team got into the habit of announcing, "Dead!" if someone noticed that something was just too loud. If the volume of an unmasked on-screen action was even a touch too loud and didn't attract any monsters, then the threat falls apart.

This meant that some sound developed in unusual ways. In most films, when nature sounds such as crickets or bird calls are part of the soundscape, lone cricket chirps and individual bird calls are layered in. There are cricket beds in *A Quiet Place,* but no single cricket stands out with louder chirps than the others. Because even for the crickets and birds, being louder than the base level of noise would automatically expose them to danger.

The few times the Abbott family have aural missteps, Aadahl and Van der Ryn made sure to push up the volume on the offending noise to enhance the contrast between the sound and the oppressive silence of the moments that precede and follow it. One of the few moments where music is played during the film, when Lee (John Krasinski) and Evelyn (Emily Blunt) take a moment for themselves to share a dance to a song played through Evelyn's earbuds, feels alarmingly loud, even though it's clear that the music is audible only to them.

There are actually three moments of complete silence, digital zero, in the film. These correspond with times when Regan's (Millicent Simmonds) cochlear implant is turned off (when we are seeing from Regan's perspective and her implant is turned on, we hear a low hum that we might not notice in a noisier film).

In return, the audience of *A Quiet Place* felt the tension of so much silence, and the unrelenting risk that someone, on-screen or off, might make a noise and attract death. Moviegoers anecdotally reported being super aware of the sounds they and the people around them were making while seeing this movie in theatres. Crunching popcorn and shifting noisily in your seat suddenly felt like a gross betrayal, as if the audience's sounds might affect the Abbott family's fate. Personally, this was one of my favorite in-theatre horror experiences ever. The power of silence, and the audience's collective motivation to participate in that silence, was palpable.

DISSONANCE

When it comes to scoring, the key in which music is composed has a similar influence on mood. We've historically attributed specific moods to different keys, but as a general rule major keys tend to be perceived as happier, while minor keys are sad. As far as research has shown, however, these perceptions are culturally informed, and don't have any scientific basis. Still, there are certain tricks to sound and music beyond stingers and scores that can get under our skin. This can be something as simple as which chords are played.

Dissonance involves unstable chords that demand to be resolved into more harmonious tones. They sound "wrong" and can actually feel uncomfortable to listen to, which can make them super-handy tools for building tension in a horror sequence. Believe it or not, there is actually a mathematical reason for this (and music is basically math, after all). The simplest way to put it is that if you play a chord of three tones, each of those tones has its own frequency. If you picture them in a linear fashion, each frequency looks like a wave with peaks and valleys. If you stack these three waves on top of one another, where they line up and where they don't can tell you a lot about their relationship to each other. Tones that have a relationship that's a whole number ratio tend to be consonant or harmonious and sound good together. The pattern they make will have a sort of symmetry. We can actually reproduce this symmetry as shapes known as Lissajous figures. For example, if two instruments are playing the exact same tone (same pitch, or a 1:1 ratio between the tones), the Lissajous figure produced would be a perfect circle. If two instruments are playing the same tone, but one is playing the tone one octave higher than the other (so a 2:1 ratio), then the resulting Lissajous figure would take the shape of a perfect figure eight. Tones that do not have relationships that are whole number ratios will tend to be dissonant or unharmonious and will sound *off*. Dissonance, with its use in tension building and release, does have its rightful place in music, though, especially rock. And despite its lack of harmony, people can still enjoy dissonance—I mean, heavy metal fans do exist.

One dissonant interval popular in heavy metal earned the nickname *Diabolus in Musica* or "the Devil in music," known in music theory terms as a *tritone* or an interval made up of three adjacent whole tones. Given its nickname, the story goes that the Church outright banned the use of the tritone, but there really isn't evidence to show that this was true. Tritones' dissonance doesn't exactly make them great candidates for church-friendly tunes, so composers were probably already avoiding them (and associating them with demons with a term like *Diabolus in Musica* probably didn't help either).

Can a music interval be so off-putting as to be truly diabolic? You can be the judge: the first three notes in the theme song for *The Simpsons* fit the bill for *Diabolus in Musica*, as does the interval between the tones in many fire truck and ambulance sirens.

Also, while you don't have to have perfect pitch to appreciate dissonance, you do have to be able to differentiate between tone sounds. Experiments done with amusic participants—people who are truly tone-deaf—demonstrated that they were immune to dissonance's effects.

Dissonance is far from the only sound that can make humans feel uneasy. There are other sounds that are almost universally considered to be unpleasant, like nails on a chalkboard. Still other sounds might make you feel uncomfortable without you even consciously hearing them.

SOUNDS ON THE FRINGES
OF HUMAN HEARING

The range of human hearing roughly spans 20 to 20,000 Hz. If your ears are young and the hair cells, a.k.a. the sound vibration sensors, aren't damaged, then you might hear frequencies that are higher or lower than this range in perfect lab settings. In general, high frequencies (although not necessarily super high) are designed to get our attention. We need to hear screams to respond to potential dangers, and baby cries to take care of our young. The sound of snapping branches or brush crunching underfoot might signal the presence of an approaching threat.

Younger ears tend to be able to pick up higher audible frequencies than adult ears, since these higher-limit frequencies start to drop off in most humans as we age. This was the inspiration behind the brief popularity of mosquito ringtones around 2008. These ringtones subverted an earlier use of high-frequency tones by shop owners who tried to deter loitering teens by playing unwelcoming sounds that only younger ears could hear. As ringtones, these sounds played at around 17,000 Hz and were marketed as a way for teens to discreetly hear their phones in class without their teachers noticing. The downside of this product is that the sound, while audible to teens, is also annoying. The teacher might not hear it, but classmates could and could complain about it. I feel really lucky that I finished high school right before this particular trend took off, even if that didn't stop me from playing around with mosquito tone generators online to see if my hearing was still "young enough" to hear them. My hair cells were still spry back then, but my most recent revisit to mosquito tones forced me to face the fact of my own aging and slowly diminishing hearing range.

At the other end of the frequency spectrum, sound that falls below the lower human limit of hearing is known as infrasound. Like all sound, infrasound travels in waves, but these waves are longer than those in audible sound and the peaks are farther apart. Even if we can't hear infrasound, we can still perceive the vibrations caused by it, especially if the sound pressure levels are high enough. Even when they don't realize they're hearing it, people exposed to infrasound might report a sense of uneasiness if they're sensitive to it.

In 2003, psychologist Richard Wiseman and acoustic scientist Richard Lord teamed up with composer and engineer Sarah Angliss to create a mass experiment to explore the spooky emotional effects tied to infrasound. They held two back-to-back concerts in the Purcell Room, a concert hall in South London. Some of the songs were laced with infrasound while others were infrasound-free. When later surveyed, the concert guests, without knowing which songs were infrasound-infused, reported more unusual sensations, awe, and fear during songs that had 17 Hz tones playing beneath the music.

You can listen to the infrasound-free version of a concert composition on Sarah Angliss's website. According to Angliss, if she had included any true infrasound tones in her piece, they wouldn't have survived the mp3 compression process. They relied on a hand-built infrasonic generator, an acoustic cannon made with a stiff sewer pipe and extra-long-stroke subwoofer, to create the low frequencies that they needed for their experiment.

It's been suggested that infrasound might make people feel odd if they're sensitive to it. Environmental infrasound has been blamed for what is ominously named the Hum. It was first reported as a mysterious droning, rumbling sound, similar to an idling truck engine, in Bristol, England, in the

1960s, and since then similar complaints have been lodged worldwide. Part of what's mysterious about the Hum is that it's hard to guess at where the sound might be coming from. Dr. Colin Novak at the University of Windsor in Ontario, Canada, decided to investigate what had come to be known as the Windsor Hum, to characterize it and to try to localize its source. He managed to record the Hum's presence on only a handful of days during his study, but he did get enough evidence to conclude that the Hum was real and registering around the 35 Hz mark (decidedly in the range of human hearing, but still qualifying as a low frequency). He suggested that the sound was originating from a blast furnace on Zug Island, south of the city and downriver of Detroit, Michigan. The island has historically been home to steel mills. Follow-up studies have concluded that Zug Island is probably not the source, but that hasn't stopped conspiracy theorists (the conspiracy goes that a U.S. Air Force program is behind the mysterious noise).

Like the Hum, most of the phenomena people have experienced thanks to infrasound have been easy enough to explain away as simple unpleasant sensations. But for some people, their experiences with low frequencies border on the paranormal.

One of the most fascinating pieces of research on the uncanny effects of infrasound was published by Vic Tandy and Tony Lawrence in 1998 in the *Journal of the Society for Psychical Research*. Tandy was inspired to investigate infrasound after a strange and unusual personal experience, what he dubs "The Case of the Ghost in the Machine." At the time of his experience, he was working as an engineering designer for a company that made medical equipment. His colleagues often gossiped about how their laboratory was haunted, and he recalls at least one instance when a cleaner left the building in distress because she thought she had seen some-

thing. As time went on, he began to note more weird oc-
currences: he kept feeling like someone was watching him,
and he'd turn to talk to a colleague that he swore was right
next to him, but there'd be nobody there. He started feeling discomfort. Sure, the laboratory could be spooky and
make strange noises, but this was something else. Finally
one night, when he was working alone, he noticed a ghostly
gray blur in his peripheral vision. When he turned to look at
it head-on, it faded and disappeared. He had no way to explain this apparition and it freaked him out . . . so he went
home.

The next day, despite his heebie-jeebies, Tandy went back
into the lab because he was entering a fencing competition
and wanted to use the lab equipment to work on his fencing
foil. He gripped the foil blade into a bench vise and left to
find some oil. When he got back to his foil, it was vibrating
frantically in the grip. Instead of deciding that the lab was
definitely haunted by some poltergeist, Tandy recognized
that the vibrations were coming from some sort of wave.
Then and there he developed an impromptu experiment using the fencing foil as a makeshift dowsing rod to pinpoint
the vibration's source.

Tandy and his coworkers weren't sharing the lab with a
ghost at all—they were sharing it with a standing wave. This
wave, caused by an extractor fan in the lab, was just the right
frequency to be reflected back completely by walls at either
end of the laboratory and create a sweet spot in the center
of the room, which was shaped like a long corridor. What's
more, this standing wave was vibrating at a frequency similar to the resonant frequency of the human eyeball. So, in
the right conditions, the wave was vibrating Tandy's eyeballs without him realizing and causing his strange visual
disturbances.

The effect of sound waves vibrating Tandy's eyeballs is

the same one that we see in action when a singer shatters a wineglass with their voice. Every material has a natural resonant frequency—a speed at which it will vibrate if it's disturbed by something, even if that something is a sound wave. When you flick a wineglass, you can hear the tone it makes when it vibrates. When a singer matches that tone frequency with their own voice, they are vibrating the air molecules around the glass with the same frequency as the glass's resonance (and, in turn, vibrating the glass). These vibrations put stress on it and cause it to deform. The louder the tone you make, and the longer you sustain it, the more the glass deforms, and the more prone it gets to weakening and shattering. Shattering wineglasses isn't a feat limited only to opera singers; it just takes a lot of effort. When the television series *MythBusters* captured singer and vocal coach Jaime Vendera shattering a wineglass with his voice (on his twelfth attempt), his voice registered over 100 decibels. For perspective, normal speaking voices usually register more in the 50-decibel range. It also helps if the glass that you're choosing to destroy is pre-weakened in some way, with small scratches or imperfections that can be aggravated by the vibrations.

Eyeballs are not wineglasses; they are squishier and (thankfully) more resilient to temporary deformations than rigid glass or crystal. The vibrations that Tandy experienced were *close* to the resonant frequency of his eyeballs, but his exposure was limited and it is unclear just how loudly that extractor fan was vibrating. Theoretically, at the right frequency and loudness, infrasound can have adverse effects on the body beyond some brief ghostly apparitions.

This brings us to one of the big infrasound legends: the Brown Note. Popularized in an episode of the television series *South Park*, the Brown Note is said to be an infrasonic tone that resonates on the human body in such a way that it has a laxative effect. Despite the massive number of videos online purporting to be recordings of the Brown Note, there isn't actually any evidence that these low-frequency tones are effective (unless you want to believe the online comments on these videos, claiming the tone's efficacy). It's also unlikely that a web video would have the sound quality needed to deliver an appropriate note. For the curious: yes, I did find a three-minute Brown Note video and listened to it. It even came with a warning not to proceed if I have bowel issues, which I shrugged off despite a chronic intestinal disorder. I'm almost disappointed that I didn't feel a single thing stirring in my guts.

Taking inspiration from Tandy's experiments, in 2008 a group of researchers attempted to create a "haunted" room by manipulating electromagnetic fields and infrasound. The room that they used was empty and featureless, white, dimly lit, and cold. Participants were given a copy of the room's floor plan and were asked to wander around the room alone for fifty minutes, recording any unusual experiences and where they occurred on the floor plan. They didn't know whether they were in a neutral room, or being exposed to infrasound, complex electromagnetic fields, or both. Most of the participants reported some eerie experience during their time in the room, whether it was feeling dizziness, tingling, a sense of something else's presence, or straight-up terror. Once the data was analyzed, however, this team found that these experiences were probably not being caused by either infrasound or electromagnetic fields (and they probably weren't being caused by a real haunting, either, although that would be a horror movie–worthy twist). The researchers suggested that the reported experiences were probably caused through the power of suggestibility. All of the participants were informed that they might experience unusual sensations and were asked to report on them as part of the experiment, so they were primed to be more receptive to any sensations that might be unusual.

With infrasound being implicated in so many spooky experiences—whether or not it's truly at the root of them—you can bet your butt that horror filmmakers have found a way to work infrasound, or at least near-infrasound, into their projects. Like in the haunted room experiment, viewers are already primed to be exposed to uncomfortable stimuli in a horror movie. Part of what makes infrasound so uncomfortable to experience when it's layered into a soundscape is that we can't pinpoint a source. If you can't identify what's causing these abstract feelings, your imagination might make up a reason primed by whatever you're watching on-screen. Director Gaspar Noé famously admitted to using near-infrasound (registering around 27 Hz) in the first act of his 2002 film *Irréversible,* as if a film with a ten-minute-long-take rape scene and extremely graphic scenes of violence wasn't already uncomfortable enough for viewers. *Paranormal Activity* (2007, dir. Oren Peli) is also said to have boosted its quiet, spooky moments with infrasound. In keeping with a found-footage style, this movie does not otherwise use a music soundtrack.

On a happier note, infrasound doesn't make all creatures great and small feel unease. As loud as a trumpeting elephant can sound, some elephant vocalizations are actually infrasound, in the range of 5 to 30 Hz. These vocalizations are known as "rumbles." The benefit of communicating in infrasound is that lower frequencies can travel farther without being absorbed or reflected by the environment, so elephant rumbles can actually let them communicate with each other when they are miles apart.

Mercifully, not all sound frequencies make you feel like garbage like infrasound can; otherwise we wouldn't enjoy music so much. For select people, some sounds even trigger a specific kind of pleasurable response. This is known as the autonomic sensory meridian response (ASMR)—and while it sounds like a clinical term coined in a medical journal, it's not. It was named back in 2010 by Jennifer Allen, an ASMR online community pioneer, who realized that the phenomenon would need a name before people would feel comfortable talking about it. The term describes a pleasant "brain tingle" that some people feel in response to sensory triggers. You might have heard of it before if you've spent enough time on the right social media channels. ASMR has become a sensation on sites like YouTube, where there are entire channels dedicated to whispering, gentle tapping, and other soft sounds that have the potential to trigger the response. ASMR even has a market beyond the internet, with paid immersive experiences such as Whisperlodge. Part theatre and part ASMR spa treatment, Whisperlodge is an intimate experience in which you find yourself in one-on-one scenes with the cast while they crinkle paper next to your head or stroke your face with soft makeup brushes.

As a newer phenomenon, there is little research to explain ASMR. The first peer-reviewed study was conducted in 2015 to try to classify the response. The researchers from this study suggested that there may be a link between people who experience ASMR and people who experience synesthesia, another phenomenon in which stimuli for one sense trigger sensations from another (like perceiving words as having a specific color, or sounds as having particular tastes). More recent studies have provided evidence for the relaxing effect that ASMR-sensitive people experience: their heart rate measures showed a marked decrease during ASMR videos, compared with people who do not experience ASMR and compared with their measures when watching neutral footage.

ASMR contrasts wildly with another type of sound sensitivity, termed *misophonia*, where affected people are prone to irrational anger or even violent responses when exposed to certain sounds. Often these sounds are ones that are commonly disliked, like the sound of another person chewing food, but the response is atypical and extreme.

When it comes to selecting sounds for horror, uncomfortable sounds like chewing and aggressive, decidedly anti-ASMR finger-tapping and clock-ticking are often favored because they ramp up disgust (in the case of chewing) and tension (in the cases of tapping and ticking). For someone who experiences misophonia, these sounds might risk causing a tension overload or just a hellish moviegoing experience. Outside of these misophonic outliers, though, when it comes to sounds on the fringes of human hearing, horror filmmakers should favor the ones that are meant to make us uncomfortable, like infrasound, over ones that might give you enjoyable brain tingles.

SCARE SPOTLIGHT:
THE BLAIR WITCH PROJECT (1999, DIRS. EDUARDO SÁNCHEZ AND DANIEL MYRICK)

In October of 1994, three student filmmakers disappeared in the woods near Burkittsville, Maryland, while shooting a documentary.

A year later their footage was found.

Heather, Josh, and Mike have been lost in the woods for days. They are armed with only their camera gear and some meager camping supplies. Tensions are running high as Heather remains bent on documenting every part of their trip, even when they come across strange cairns and hanging stick effigies, when they hear weird sounds outside their tent at night, when Josh disappears and something seems to be stalking them and leaving gifts of stones and human teeth. They do find Josh in the cellar of an abandoned house, standing motionless and facing a corner like in the myths they'd heard about the Blair Witch back in town, but they never do get footage to prove the existence of the witch—something unseen knocks Mike's and Heather's cameras, and presumably Mike and Heather, to the ground. Their footage was found, but their bodies were never recovered.

Sound in movies doesn't follow the same rules as sound in the real world. Some sound might be *diegetic*. This is sound with a source that exists in the world of the movie, actual sound that the characters on-screen experience just as clearly as you do. Other sounds might be *non-diegetic,* existing outside of the story's space. We hear the atmospheric music and sound effects added to enhance the mood of a scene, but these sounds aren't real or observable to the characters in the film. The balance between the use of diegetic and non-diegetic sound in movies can mean the difference between feeling like you're watching a recording of real events or being reminded that you're being absorbed into a fictional movie narrative. Playing with this balance can also blur the lines between spaces and create the ambiguity that is oh so appealing in horror, where the intention might be to have the viewers, consciously or subconsciously, ask themselves, *Is this really happening?*

Found-footage films hinge on this question, and standout found-footage films risk tricking their audiences into believing that they have documented real events. *The Blair Witch Project* is one of the go-to examples for found-footage films, and the absence of non-diegetic sound in the film plays a huge part in its effectiveness. The entire film is shot on the cameras being handled by the students, so we only ever see what they are seeing and are limited by where they choose to point their cameras and what they manage to actually get in focus. Likewise, we only hear what is picked up by their cameras' microphones. There is no obvious soundtrack to underscore the characters' emotional journeys, no foreboding crescendos or stingers to prepare us for scary imagery. The effect is that you feel like you're watching an amateur home video. What makes *The Blair Witch Project* scary is how real and unpolished it feels.

Despite holding *The Blair Witch Project* up as a masterpiece of diegetic-only sound, it wouldn't be right to say that the film has no score at all. *The Blair Witch Project* has a subtle and creepy score composed by Tony Cora, and you have to strain to hear it. It's probably most audible in the film's final moments, as Mike and Heather are running through the house searching for Josh.

In 2016, a sneaky sequel to *The Blair Witch Project* premiered at San Diego Comic-Con. Con-goers thought they were catching a premiere of a film called *The Woods,* only to find out that it was *Blair Witch* (dir. Adam Wingard) in disguise—the marketing campaign even went so far as to print and hang posters for *The Woods* and then change these out for *Blair Witch* posters while the movie was playing.

The Blair Witch Project is a tough act to follow, not just because of its impact on found-footage films, but because of its unprecedented viral marketing campaign. Both *Blair Witch* and an earlier sequel, *Book of Shadows: Blair Witch 2* (2000, dir. Joe Berlinger), failed to live up to the original. One of the most notable differences is this handling of diegetic versus non-diegetic sound and visuals. *Blair Witch* boasts a full score and obvious sound effects. This sequel also tries to pass itself off as a found-footage piece, but outfits the characters with earpiece cameras instead of the handheld and shoulder-mount cameras from the original film. This technology upgrade lets them gloss over some unlikely shots that would have been impossible for the original *The Blair Witch Project* team to capture with their two cameras. But some of those shots come from perspectives that don't match up with the sightlines we'd expect from a camera held at head level, and all of them are unexpectedly clean and in focus despite the fact that hair should be falling over the lenses. The newer film is also introduced with a title card, much like the one in the original film, that states that this footage was "assembled" rather than strictly "found," which means that the movie can handwave the fact that the footage acquired is polished and finely edited. This makes the finished product a far cry from the poorly framed and jittery shots in the original when the actors were in fact the camera people and, despite portraying film students, had minimal experience behind the camera.

THE SCREAM

We can't talk about sounds that scare without talking about the scream. And I'm not talking about Edvard Munch's famous painting, although it does give a great visual: the subject's eyes are wide and staring and his mouth is stretched open in an expression that can only be recognized as fear. If this painting had audio, you know exactly what sound that figure would be making.

No matter what language you speak, the sound of an adult screaming is universally understood as a vocalization of fear or alarm. Babies scream too, to express alarm like adults do, but also to alert their parents to needs like hunger or discomfort that they don't yet have words to describe. Screams are not only loud and shrill; they're also immediately recognizable as a distress signal.

Screams in horror movies tend to come in two flavors: the sudden and perfectly timed jump scare scream (an art perfected in YouTube screamer videos) that aims to startle the viewer, and the reactionary scream that aims to amplify feelings of fear by demonstrating a character's horror.

Despite the universality of the scream, the science of screams still isn't well understood.

In 2015, neuroscientist David Poeppel and his team launched an investigation to decipher what exactly is happening when we hear a human scream and what makes its sound so special. They created a catalogue of human screams both by downloading a collection of screams from movies and by bringing real people into the lab and recording their screams. These screams were added to a bank of sounds that also included spoken sentences, artificial sounds (like alarms and instrument sounds), and tones.

These sounds were then ranked by participants on the order of how scary they were on a scale from 1 (neutral) to 5 (alarming). Unsurprisingly, human screams stood out from the rest of the sound bank. The screams that freaked participants out the most were ones that fell into a range between 30 to 150 Hz. The scariest screams also showed the highest measures in a sound quality known as *roughness*. In sounds with high roughness, the amplitude or loudness is modulated very, very fast (between 30 and 150 times per second). Roughness makes scream sounds more detectable; it also makes scream sounds sound very unpleasant. This modulation places screams in the category of nonlinear sounds, sounds that distort when they are too loud and rough for the instrument projecting them—like a raw scream straining the limits of the human larynx.

Irregular, scratchy nonlinear sounds are often found in nature, usually in young animals whose cries need to attract their parents' attention. Similarly, humans respond more to baby cries that contain nonlinearities than ones that don't. Furthermore, studies focused on meerkats have shown that they don't easily habituate to nonlinear sounds—they are meant to be alarming, abrasive, and hard to ignore. It makes sense—these sounds indicate the presence of a potential predator. Survival requires us to not get used to the kind of sound that might point to something dangerous lurking nearby, whether that sound is a scream, a growl, a snapping twig, or a creaking floorboard. Although it's incredibly unlikely that sound designers are up to date on meerkat research, they have clearly been keyed into nonlinear sound's ability to evoke these feelings for a while now. A number of movies incorporate nonlinear sounds into their scores, notably *The Shining* (1980, dir. Stanley Kubrick), where violins swarm alarmingly as Jack Torrance (Jack Nicholson) chops through a bathroom door and delivers his most famous line from the film, "Here's Johnny!"

Poeppel's experiment also used fMRI to take scans of participants' brains as they listened to screams and neutral speech. Generally speaking, if you play any loud sound to a listener, that sound will activate the parts of the brain that process auditory information. In this experiment, he found that scream sounds also selectively activated the amygdala and fear circuit. This activation was sensitive to a scream's roughness. This sensitivity suggests not only an "acoustic niche" in the brain for processing human screams, but an ability to accordingly modulate a fear response to faked or less urgent-sounding screams and screams describing real fear.

Are any of these sound design techniques crucial to crafting the perfect scary atmosphere? After all, sound design in film only began to pick up real momentum with the advent of digital sound in the 1970s, and movies have existed for much longer than that. While you can build an evocative horror scene with tight visuals and narrative cues, sound (and the vibrations created by sound) can act as a special ingredient that takes a great horror sequence and escalates it to a scare that shakes you to your core.

IN CONVERSATION WITH RONEN LANDA

Ronen Landa is a film score composer. His horror film credits include The Pact *(2012, dir. Nicholas McCarthy),* At the Devil's Door *(2014, dir. Nicholas McCarthy), and* 1BR *(2019, dir. David Marmor).*

I feel like when I'm watching horror films I notice the things I expect to notice. I notice stings. I notice when that low hum comes in during tension-inducing scenes. When it comes to your process, how much of it is leaning on those familiar techniques?

So, it's interesting because you develop a tool kit. And some of those things I carry from film to film. There's a process for scoring horror films specifically that works for me, because there are some challenges that are specific to horror.

Horror is difficult because we're using all of these extended techniques and all sorts of interesting sound-making techniques; the idea is to be strange and to find weird noises that are *almost* traditional, but freak people out because they don't quite sound like they should. For instance, you can make a cello sound nasty and not pretty—people want that cello to sound pretty, so the unexpected sound is shocking and jarring. As much as I can, I try to use acoustic instruments and record them. I come up with those creative techniques myself and develop those ensemble sounds so that they're original. I don't want to use things that are only prefabricated and that I can just, like, plop in from a sample library.

But there's no way to show the director what it is that

you're going for in a mock-up unless you actually have the sounds. So I started to build a process where I have recording sessions before composing, and developing a lot of those sounds that I'll be using in these sessions. And from there I create an architecture for each cue, and color in with those sounds I developed. And so I use a lot of my personal sound library to build stings and other elements. But I try to create new sounds for each project. So, part of it is building that tool kit, which is a process tool kit, and also an actual sonic tool kit, and then part of it is understanding what's in front of you. And what's in front of you is the film.

How much do individual narrative elements of a film color your scoring? Do subgenres come with their own sound?

The way I would score one slasher film would be different from the way I would score another. If you listen to *Eloise* [2016, dir. Robert Legato], obviously there are horror elements, but there's camp to *Eloise* that's nowhere in *The Pact,* for example, or in *At the Devil's Door.* For the most part, the process involves looking at a specific film and the musical problems that the film presents. Not problems in a bad sense, but as in puzzles. My job is to solve those puzzles in a way that will move the audience and will help them connect to whatever the story is that we're telling them. I always think of music as the emotional glue in a film.

It's interesting because I'm always trying to tap into that emotion that I had when I first read the script or the first time I saw a cut of the film. What I'm trying to tap into is: *How did I feel when I first saw that?* Because it's always going to have that shock value the first time.

Usually, a film comes to me with some temporary music in it. So there's going to be music that I'm already responding to when I'm watching a scene for the first time. I'm trying to put myself in the audience's shoes, but I'm also trying to keep our thematic material and the sound of the film—each film, as I said, is different, and that's because I really put a lot of time into thinking, *What's the sonic universe for this film?* And I want that to be a thread that helps to create a more cohesive experience.

What's an example of a sonic puzzle that you've had to solve through your score?

In horror there's often that sense of *Is this film being done to me or is this film bringing me into something?* I think that those are the big questions. In *IBR* there's an interesting scene involving a cat. And that was a really hard scene to score. It was a complicated scene to solve musically because the filmmaker had set up a double scare, where you have the anticipated scare with the cat, and then a bigger unexpected scare immediately after. So there was this huge challenge there: How are we going to make both scares effective when they're so close together?

If we cranked both scares up to eleven it wouldn't work because it wouldn't feel earned. And I worked to build a sequence where the first scare would be unsettling and disturbing, more upsetting than scary. And then this scare comes when she's taken. And so there's a real progression there in the music. If you listen to the track without the visuals you can really hear the narrative cues of the scene as you're listening to it: the first smaller gut-punch scare and then the bigger *Omigod!* scare right afterward. That was tough! It was an example, on a micro-level, of how you have to earn your scares. Because if we had gone too big on that first scare, the second one would have fallen flat. It would have had a reduced impact. And really, in terms of story, the movie is about the second scare and not the first one.

Where does silence come into play?

Silence is a really important element in a horror film too. Usually the scariest scene in the whole movie is something quiet, without any music. But if you didn't have the music in other parts of the film, would that silent scene be as effective as it is? I don't know. It's like in music notation we have the idea of a rest—and understanding where to place that rest can so effectively enhance the drama. So, even knowing where *not* to score is essential when you're building an emotional sound-scape.

Is there anything that you feel that, as a horror composer, is often missing from the conversation about your work?

It's a good question. It's a generous question. I think that the thing that I'm constantly trying to stress when I'm having these kinds of conversations is the collaborative nature of the work. I'm an artist and I have a voice, and I really try to bring the most of myself to all of these projects. But all of them are reflective of a state of constant collaboration, working really closely with the filmmakers to achieve their vision. Different filmmakers have different relationships with music and expec-tations for how they're going to interface with their composer, but the best scores come from these really close-knit collab-orations of filmmakers and also with the musicians. I can't tell you how much, when I listen to Dan Tepfer, who played piano on *The Pact*. Or when I listen to Anna Bulbrook, who played violin on *The Pact*, or I listen to Karolina Rojahn, who played piano on *IBR*—when I listen to their performances, just to name a few, how much artistry they all bring to our recording sessions. All of the experimentation that we can do together, finding new sounds together. A lot of this stuff happens in a collaborative way. It's a rare kind of human connection. And it's very special. I'm really, very proud of that collaborative aspect.

CHAPTER 5

WHY SOME SCARES STICK WITH YOU

Sometimes horror movies stay with you after you leave the theatre. Even if the movie didn't seem scary when you were watching it, your brain might tell you to be on the alert, that the dark shadows in the corners of your room might be housing something insidious, that *maybe* you should sleep with the lights on.

The feeling might wear off after the sun comes up and you wake up whole and unharmed by the movie monsters, but sometimes the scares are deeper and stay with you for much, much longer.

You might have a movie that haunts you. If not, there's probably someone in your life who does, even if they aren't fully conscious of it. The movie that scares my wife more than any other isn't even a horror movie. It's *E.T.: The Extra-Terrestrial* (1982, dir. Steven Spielberg), a family movie about a peaceful alien that gets stranded on Earth and befriends children in an effort to contact his ship and make his way back home. *E.T.* scares her so much that, as an adult, she didn't have any memory of having seen it. When she told me that she'd never seen *E.T.*, I immediately pulled up a movie trailer. About fifteen seconds in, as soon as the lovable alien's face appears for the first time and tiny Gertie (Drew Barrymore) screams, my wife panicked.

"Turn it off!" she shouted. She was now *sure* that she must have seen it before, and been so scared that she'd suppressed the memory. Seeing a movie clip two decades later had unburied that fear.

Relatedly, my wife is also generally afraid of aliens, but this may be a sort of chicken-and-egg scenario: Did a fear of aliens make her automatically afraid of a pacifist extraterrestrial from a film made for children, or did childhood exposure to E.T. inform her fear of aliens?

Most evidence of long-term effects of scary movies is anecdotal: your uncle has been nervous about clowns ever since seeing *Poltergeist* (1982, dir. Tobe Hooper); your friend can't take a shower without thinking about *Psycho* (1960, dir. Alfred Hitchcock) or, for that matter, can't use one of those mirrored bathroom cabinets without thinking about so many other horror villains who might appear standing behind their reflection as soon as they close its door. (Honestly, how come bathrooms serve us so many scares? You'd rather not have to worry about monsters while you poop.)

My long-term scare is *Gremlins* (1984, dir. Joe Dante). My brain understands that it's a horror-comedy, and I think the actual movies are a good laugh, but that doesn't stop me from having an Annual Gremlins Nightmare or my general unease around plots that revolve around creatures that multiply in grotesque ways.

It's almost alarming how easy it can be to learn a new fear from a horror movie, especially if you are exposed to that horror when you are young. As part of a series of experiments exploring children's fright reactions to media, researchers Barbara Wilson and Joanne Cantor showed schoolchildren the snake pit scene from *Raiders of the Lost*

Ark (1981, dir. Steven Spielberg). They found that children exposed to that scene tended to avoid handling a live snake afterward.

Luckily for me, it's not especially likely that I'm ever going to come across a gremlin in real life, and my wife will probably never have to worry about meeting E.T. But some horror film residual scares might be tougher to avoid. Scary clowns do make appearances from time to time in real life, especially around Halloween. Most houses are equipped with showers, and personal hygiene demands that you should use them regularly. It's easy to see how these fears might spiral into something that affects how you go about your day-to-day living.

Long-term fears can be frustrating because as an adult you *know* that they are irrational and that they have a basis in a scary movie you saw years ago, but that knowledge doesn't stop you from feeling scared anyway.

This phenomenon can be explained in part by Joseph LeDoux's two-system model of fear memories. We know that emotional memories, including fear memories, are processed in the amygdala. This also includes physiological responses tied to those fear memories, such as tensed-up muscles, spiked blood pressure and heart rate, and release of adrenaline. We also know that these memories are highly resistant to change. Cognitive memories, on the other hand, are processed and stored in the hippocampus; these memories are squishier and easier to update.

LeDoux's idea is to consider the same event, such as seeing a clown in real life, as it is processed through these two areas. The amygdala is always geared to protect you from harm. It will react before you're necessarily aware of a potential threat, and it will certainly react faster than the hippocampus. While your amygdala is leaping to action, your hippocampus is more methodical and takes time to process the supposed threat. It appraises the clown in the context of the circus that you chose to attend, holds this clown up against scary clowns you've seen before, and relays the information to you that this clown is probably *not* a threat. This information can work as a tool to help you calm down and handle your situation. The amygdala's response is powerful, though, as its goal is to keep you alive. In cases where the amygdala and the hippocampus are at odds, the amygdala will often win.

The amygdala's knee-jerk response to fear memories is crucial in situations where a split second can mean the difference between death and survival, but it can be detrimental in cases where the fear that's been stored is a non-threat that's been mislabeled. Even in the moment, it's clear that the experience of seeing something unfold on-screen is different from experiencing that same event in the real world. But when something that scares you in a horror film becomes a lasting fear, it appears that the amygdala is storing the experience that you had watching the movie as if your survival depends on it. So even if your hippocampus has decided the circus clown is not a threat, if you're afraid of clowns, your amygdala might cause you to react inappropriately.

It's worth mentioning that not everyone is a fan of this two-system model: the major critique is that fear is best understood as an integration of autonomic, behavioral, and cognitive-emotional responses to danger (that we have evolved to protect ourselves) and that by reducing fear to two non-integrated systems, fear as an experience becomes subjective and unmeasurable. We'll circle back to LeDoux's model again in this chapter, but this is a humbling reminder that, despite so much effort and research going into understanding how the brain fires signals in response to fear, there's still so much about the actual mechanism of fear in the human body that even researchers still don't understand or agree upon.

In LeDoux's view, fear learnings established through the amygdala are indelibly burned into the brain and will possibly be with you for life, no matter how well you can reason that there's nothing to be afraid of. Thankfully, a growing body of research has suggested that these learnings can be erased.

The fear memories that the amygdala stores focus more on the emotional and sensory information of the memory than any nitty-gritty details. The term "flashbulb memory" was coined back in 1977 by researchers Roger Brown and James Kulik to describe an atypical sort of memory that is created for some people when they are faced with a surprising emotional event. Their research involved surveying participants in the wake of shocking events such as President Kennedy's assassination and asking them to provide detailed accounts of the moment in which they learned of the event. They would then be re-surveyed at a later date to recount the same event again. The idea of a flashbulb going off seems to suggest a moment captured forever, like a Polaroid that you can stick into an album and revisit and pore over. Brown and Kulik proposed that important traumatic events might be stored in vivid detail because in the moment we don't have time to analyze what's happening, but later we can review the details of the context and our emotional reactions to the event so that we can avoid similar trauma in the future.

The reality of flashbulb memories seems to suggest the opposite: in moments of intense, surprising emotion we are certainly forming emotional memory of what's going down, but that *emotion*, often with arbitrary accents of sensory information, is what gets sharpest focus. The flashbulb memory isn't the Polaroid at all; it's the flashbulb itself, which intensely focuses light onto a moment (and only for a moment) before popping out again. It's the *feelings* evoked in that moment, rather than the facts, that have staying power. In fact, other studies have found that you can easily introduce errors into the factual details of a person's memory, and that those errors tend to be recalled in future retellings of the memory. But unlike factual details, which get blurry over time, people tend to remember how they felt. One participant in Brown and Kulik's study recalled how stairs felt beneath his feet when he heard that Kennedy had been shot, even though the event had passed thirteen years prior; Kulik himself remembered that his teacher had been crying. These details seem trivial, and aren't necessarily helpful for facing a future threat, but they definitely resonate emotionally.

The same could be said about horror movie–inspired fears.

SCARE SPOTLIGHT:
JAWS (1975, DIR. STEVEN SPIELBERG)

It's dusk when Chrissie Watkins (Susan Backlinie) runs off from the beach bonfire, peeling off layers of clothes as a boy follows her down to the beach. She plunges into the ocean naked and swims out. Suddenly, something grabs her below the surface. Chrissie screams and thrashes as she's yanked violently through the water. She tries to cling to a buoy and call out for help before she's finally dragged under. The boy who followed her to the beach is passed out drunk on the shore. We don't see what got Chrissie.

Jaws is based on the 1974 novel by Peter Benchley, which in turn was partly inspired by shark attacks in resort towns on the New Jersey coastline in the summer of 1916. Four people were killed and one other was injured by the attacks between July 1 and July 12. Theories abounded as to what species was responsible and whether there were multiple sharks or just one rogue one—who became known in the media as the "Jersey man-eater." A summer heat wave drove people to these seaside resort towns, but people were afraid to swim. Some of the resorts dropped steel nets into the water to protect swimmers, but the damage was already done and a little steel mesh wasn't enough to dampen public fear. If those real events inspired panic, Jaws launched a fear of sharks into the stratosphere.

It's been suggested that Jaws is a huge factor behind prejudice against sharks, not only painting sharks as man-killing machines, but also warping public perception of shark attacks for the worst and boosting feelings that sharks should be killed. Conservationists have had their work cut out for them to try to educate the public about the true nature of sharks and a more accurate measure of shark attack risks. Even Shark Week, a Discovery Channel staple since 1988, was originally pitched as a way to celebrate sharks and to dispel misconceptions. That said, Shark Week has misfired more than a few times over the years because viewers appear to be more interested in seeing sensational programming than being educated.

As much as we can rationalize the actual risk of getting attacked by a Great White—statistically, you're more likely to be struck by lightning—it's a tough sell to your amygdala and fear circuits.

Jaws captured audiences' imaginations in the '70s, but how much lasting power can a movie have on public fear?

In the 1990s, Joanne Cantor asked undergraduate students to write about lasting frights that they experienced (or that they witnessed in others). Over three years (1997 to 2000), she collected over 530 essays. Overwhelmingly, these essays detailed the students' own fright experiences caused by fictional sources like horror movies. *Jaws* was one of leading causes. Of students who saw the film before they were thirteen years old, 43 percent reported that it made them uneasy about swimming in oceans or in swimming pools, even years later, writing such statements as "Sharks have become a terrifying creature to me to the point that I am not able to watch Discovery Channel documentaries or National Geographic presentations" and "This paranoia is still with me today. I know that sharks are not found in lakes and pools, yet, whenever I am in the deep end at a pool, I swim really fast to get to the edge (always looking behind me)." Remember, at the time of this study, *Jaws* would have been out for at least twenty years. It wasn't a brand-new film, and it probably wasn't a new film when first viewed by the students.

If you're curious, the other most-reported films that inspired lasting fear effects were *Poltergeist* (fear of clowns, trees, and television sets), *The Blair Witch Project* (fear of camping and forests), and *Scream* (1996, dir. Wes Craven) (fear of being home alone). My wife might feel validated that eleven participants also reported a fright reaction to *E.T.*, which for roughly one-third of them persisted into adulthood. For students who specifically reported persisting fear after a movie or show that they watched before they were thirteen, *Jaws* lost out only to the 1990 made-for-TV version of *It*. Between Tim Curry's turn as Pennywise the Dancing Clown and Bruce the mechanical shark, a generation of kiddos were scarred for life.

Scares that stick around seem to work with mechanisms similar to those we see in people with post-traumatic stress disorder (PTSD). The classic signs of PTSD include reexperiencing a traumatic event through vivid flashbacks, nightmares, or intrusive thoughts, being hypervigilant and being startled easily, having trouble sleeping, and avoidance. It's normal for people to experience some or all of these symptoms after a traumatic experience, but when they persist, become generalized, and disrupt your life, they become signs of disorder. As a diagnosis, PTSD has a long history under many guises, with its symptoms being described in old texts, like Shakespeare's *King Henry IV*, and in even older texts, like Homer's *The Iliad* and *The Odyssey*.

For the longest time, it was thought that PTSD only occurred as a result of the traumas of warfare, and that developing PTSD signaled a soldier's cowardice or weakness of character. Evidence for PTSD as a soldier's disease is shown through the many names it has had over centuries, such as "soldier's heart," "irritable heart," "combat stress," and "shell shock." It was only after the Vietnam War and around the start of the Women's Movement of the 1970s that other forms of trauma were recognized as causing similar long-term symptoms. In 1974, researchers Ann Burgess and Lynda Holmstrom conducted one of the first studies on rape and identified the flashbacks and nightmares experienced by rape victims as parallel to shell shock symptoms. They called this condition rape trauma syndrome. The term post-traumatic stress disorder appeared for the first time as its own diagnosis in the DSM-III in 1980.

Understanding PTSD helps us understand how fear can get out of control and disrupt a person's life, but it's hard to draw a true parallel between long-term fear caused by traumatic experiences such as war or abuse, and irrational but persistent fears and phobias from watching fictional narratives play out on a TV screen. Fear, whether mildly uncomfortable or life-affecting, is a natural outcome of emotional learning, but how does that learning kick in?

HOW DO YOU START FEARING?

Fear isn't spontaneously generated. It has a purpose: to help you avoid what can harm you. Sometimes fears are irrational and get amplified to the point that they are more harmful than helpful to healthy living, but fear has to *start* somewhere.

How we experience fear isn't a debate of nature versus nurture—as with most things, it's a combination of both. Scientists acknowledge that there might be genetic factors that can affect how predisposed we are to having big fear reactions and how well we can get over those fearful experiences (something that we'll look at more closely in a later chapter), and that some of the most common fears seemed to have evolved in humans as adaptations toward threats. But otherwise, social learning plays a big role in terms of how we grow into our fears.

It might help to understand how we learn fears by understanding how we learn, period. Learning fears often happens without you realizing that you are learning anything. The strong emotion attached to fear learning makes the memory that much more powerful and likely to stand the test of time.

One useful learning theory to consider is Piaget's theory of cognitive development, because it breaks learning into clear developmental stages based on how we build our understanding of the world around us and then learn how to apply reasoning and think about abstract and concrete concepts. Piaget's theory outlines four basic stages:

1. The sensorimotor stage encompasses infancy and language development, learning that you are separate and distinct from the world around you, and

that objects still exist when you can't see them (peek-a-boo is still a fun and exciting game in this stage).

2. In the pre-operational stage, which lasts until around age seven, you play pretend and look to the hows and whys of the world around you. You might have a hard time telling the difference between your point of view and someone else's. You can reason, but that reasoning is prone to phenomena like animism (like thinking that inanimate objects have feelings and motivations) or transductive reasoning (like creating a causal relationship between two specific but unrelated things: you heard a dog bark and then a door slam; therefore the door slammed because the dog barked).

3. The concrete operational stage, which begins at around age seven, is when you should be able to start solving problems, either through trial and error or by forming an opinion and putting it to the test. At this point, you should also be able to recognize that you aren't the center of the world and take other people's views and feelings into consideration.

4. In the formal operational stage, which begins at around age eleven, you should be handling more abstract concepts and tackling *what-if*-type problems that are more hypothetical than rooted in reality. You can predict outcomes and possible consequences to your actions (but you're also a preteen or teenager at this point, so you might not necessarily be practicing good judgment).

So does how old you were when you saw the Scary Thing affect how long that scare lingers? Not necessarily, but it might affect *what* scares you. When you're under seven years old or so (pre-operational), you are more likely to be scared by something that isn't necessarily a realistic threat; you're scared because something was loud or big or in your face. On the same tack, this age group might be afraid of something that isn't threatening at all, just because it *looks* scary. Eight- to twelve-year-olds (operational) are more likely be scared by more realistic threats like disease or death or war.

In a variation on their own experiment, the Indiana Jones snake avoidance study, Cantor and Wilson tested whether providing students with reassuring information about snakes, such as telling them that most snakes were not poisonous, affected their response to the snake pit scene. Older children tended to find this information reassuring, but kindergarteners tended to cling to the word "poisonous" and miss the "not" part of the statement completely. They ended up demonstrating *more* fear than if no statement had been provided at all. As you might imagine, telling preschoolers that what they're seeing on-screen is not real isn't a super-effective strategy either (and Cantor and Wilson have done other research that supports this!).

One famous—and famously unethical—experiment in fear conditioning in the 1920s involved a baby dubbed "Little Albert." Psychologist John B. Watson and his grad student Rosalie Rayner wanted to cook up a phobia in an infant. They knew that loud and unexpected noises, like a hammer striking a steel beam hanging behind your head, produce fear responses in babies, so they decided to pair that noise with something that shouldn't be automatically scary to a baby. Albert was allowed to play with a harmless white rat (that he wasn't afraid of) and they would bang the steel beam to scare him while he was playing. As we know from Pavlov's dog experiments, classical conditioning works: Little Albert started to show fear when his little rat friend was brought to him, even when there was no scary noise. Not only that, but he was afraid of other furry objects, like a rabbit or a dog, or a man in a Santa mask. This phenomenon, where a response can be triggered by a group of similar objects, instead of just being tied to one specific culprit, is known as stimulus generalization.

When it comes to inspiring fear, horror films use a combination of stimuli that give unconditioned fear responses (we naturally fear an attacking animal and its snapping jaws), and stimuli that we've come to associate with fear (like a white hockey mask). What's more, horror movies have a great skill for conditioning us to make new fear associations. If you manage to experience stimulus generalization, you might experience a less-intense version of the fear when you run into a real-life version of what the movie made scary, like if you watched *It* (1990, dir. Tommy Lee Wallace or 2017, dir. Andrés Muschietti) and suddenly felt nervous around all sewer grates and sink drains. Or if you watched *The Mangler* (1995, dir. Tobe Hooper) and developed an uneasiness around all sorts of laundry machines. The flip side of this model is that because the threats that we see in horror films are often *similar* enough to something threatening that we might encounter in real life, we will experience something approaching a fear response while we watch the film. Stimulus generalization doesn't have to apply to just fear responses, either; it can be used to elicit pretty much any sort of emotion, from disgust (useful for the horror film experience) to joy (probably less useful).

It's also possible to think of learned emotional responses as being "primed." Spreading activation theory dictates that we retrieve specific information through associated ideas. Like, if you were playing a word association game and were given the word "red," I probably couldn't predict what word you'd say in response. But if I'd primed you earlier in the game with a word like "fluid," you might be much more likely to respond with the word "blood."

In terms of predicting someone's response to a horror movie, we can look to how that person has been primed, either in the context immediately before watching the movie or in terms of their individual memories. Imagine that someone decides to watch *Friday the 13th* (1980, dir. Sean S. Cunningham), but they've never seen a scary movie before in their life, let alone a slasher or splatter film of any kind. *Friday the 13th* is full of blood and people being stabbed to death. Unless this person has never been introduced to the idea that knives are dangerous and can stab you, knives as a threat, and blood as something potentially upsetting, should already be represented in this person's memory. Seeing Jason Voorhees['s mom] stabbing a bunch of teens will not only activate those memories, but they will likely be reinforced with the new negative associations picked up while watching. In the same vein, they will pick up new cues and associations from the film (e.g., summer camps = creepy). So, the next time that person watches a movie with similar cues (assuming they don't decide that one horror film was enough for them), they might retrieve those negative memory associations anew.

It's easy to learn fears, to condition ourselves and make negative associations that we can carry forward into future experiences. Is it just as easy to unlearn fear? Is it even possible?

SCARE SPOTLIGHT:
THE LAST HOUSE ON THE LEFT (1972, DIR. WES CRAVEN)

Mari Collingwood (Sandra Peabody) and Phyllis Stone (Lucy Grantham) are teen BFFs driving into the city to see a concert. On their way they hear a report on the radio that criminals have escaped a nearby prison. They make a pit stop to buy pot and meet Junior, who just so happens to be one of these criminals. Mari and Phyllis follow him back to an apartment, where they are trapped by the rest of the fugitives and subjected to horrible tortures. There isn't a happy ending for anyone.

The Last House on the Left was Wes Craven's debut film. It was timely, released into the world in the aftermath of the Vietnam War and the Manson murders, and was an unrelenting tale of realistic violence. There were no supernatural monsters or ghosts or aliens or pod people. There was just violence inflicted on humans by other humans.

The story goes that *The Last House on the Left* couldn't score an R rating (being assigned instead an X rating), even after extensive edits. The movie had been revised to the point that it had lost its narrative and didn't make sense anymore. Frustrated, producer Sean S. Cunningham walked down the hall to someone who had just made an R-rated film and got their "This film is rated R" banner. They spliced the unearned banner onto the original version of the film and sent it out that way, MPAA none the wiser.

Upon its release, of course, the film's marketing leaned heavily into advertising its violence. It's most remembered for its tagline: "TO AVOID FAINTING, JUST KEEP REPEATING: IT'S ONLY A MOVIE...ONLY A MOVIE...ONLY A MOVIE." This marketing move was brilliant, and has been repeated in new forms time and again. The message itself also inspires a great question: Does telling yourself that it's only a movie actually help?

Telling yourself that what you're seeing on-screen is "only a movie," even if you already reasonably know that you're watching a movie, is a conscious act of distancing yourself from the threatening or upsetting information that you see. This lets you reappraise the information from a bird's-eye view and better shape your perception of its emotional significance. In turn, this might dampen your amygdala's response to the material. Not every person has the same capacity for distancing and reappraising, though. People with anxiety disorders, conditions that are already marked by a bias for interpreting information as high-risk or high-threat more often than in other individuals, tend to have a tougher time stepping back and reappraising information as nonthreatening after their brains have decided that a threat is there.

Allegedly, the tagline for *The Last House on the Left* came about when a marketing specialist was watching a cut of the film with his wife. She kept covering her eyes so she wouldn't have to see the on-screen violence against Mari and Phyllis, which prompted him to remind her that "it's only a movie."

I wonder if the strategy worked for her.

HOW DO YOU STOP FEARING?

Just because you like watching scary movies doesn't mean that you want to keep feeling scared after the credits finish rolling. So, how do you shake those heebie-jeebies? Here's what science has to say about your favorite anti-scare strategies.

Just Don't Think About It

You're lying in bed, trying to fall asleep, but you keep thinking about a particularly scary moment from a movie you watched that day. You weren't scared when you were actually watching the movie, but now that you're alone in the dark with nothing else to distract you, your thoughts are running away with it. The scary image keeps popping up uninvited. You'll just have to stop thinking about what's scary and think about something else to fall asleep.

Easier said than done, right?

Intrusive thoughts, or thoughts that you think without trying to, are a hallmark of the PTSD experience. They come without warning, they're hard to dispel, and they can be incredibly disruptive to people who experience them. While a lingering scare from a horror movie is in no way on the same scale as experiencing PTSD, understanding the mechanism of intrusive thoughts can give us clues as to what's happening in our brains when we get a case of the heebie-jeebies.

These intrusive thoughts have the potential to tip into another dangerous form of thinking called rumination, or the repetitive focus on something distressing—not to mention fixation on its causes or possible consequences. Rumination is the same mechanism that leads to negative thought spirals typical of depression. When you're in a deadlock of your own thoughts, you can't problem-solve, and so you end up amplifying whatever negative feelings you're granting focus. Like a cow chewing its cud (cows belong to a suborder of animals called ruminants), your brain keeps working over the same idea again and again instead of moving forward.

Rather than dwell on these thoughts, you can just *not* think about them. You can actively suppress them instead. To borrow a line from *Ginger Snaps* (2000, dir. John Fawcett), "If you don't like your ideas, stop having them." Suppression is a choice you make as part of an emotion regulation process. (This is distinct from *repression*, which is understood as a defense mechanism in which traumatic memories are detached from the events that created them and pushed into the subconscious, effectively causing a sort of amnesia around the trauma to protect the person who experienced it. It's one of the basic elements of psychoanalytic theory, but, to be honest, current psychological theory doesn't really support the repression model for dealing with trauma. If true repression happens, it's a rare occurrence, despite what movie narratives would like us to believe.)

To lift a situational example of suppression from *Ginger Snaps*, let's say you're Brigitte Fitzgerald (Emily Perkins) and you're dealing with the fact that your older sister Ginger (Katharine Isabelle) has been infected by a werewolf. The attack has torn a physiological and emotional rift between you both. It's one thing to deal with your sister turning into a literal monster, but it's another to deal with the distance forming between the two of you when you were, up until the attack, inseparable. You try your best to suppress your fear and stay close to your sister; you try to help her while mostly staying out of her way. You find out that your sister has killed a guidance counselor and could clearly be a danger to you, but you help her hide the body.

During emotion regulation for this situation, we see the brain's limbic system in action, with a few additional players:

- The superior temporal gyrus (STG), angular gyrus, and supplementary motor area (SMA) are areas important for processing information from the frontal cortex, the "thinking" part of your brain.
- The dorsolateral prefrontal cortex (DLPFC) is implicated in attentional processing.
- The ventrolateral prefrontal cortex (VLPFC)

is involved in sending signals of salience or providing an emotional gut-punch.
* And the anterior cingulate cortex (ACC) integrates and relays emotional information and generates your affect.

When Brigitte sees the guidance counselor's body on the floor, her VLPFC, SMA, angular gyrus, and STG receive emotional information from the amygdala. Appraisal of the situation then starts in the VLPFC, which examines whether or not there is a need for emotional regulation. And in this case, there *is* a need: Brigitte needs to suppress her fear to help Ginger hide the dead body and clean up the mess. The information from this decision is then projected to the DLPFC, where the actual regulation occurs. Finally, the DLPFC sends signals via the ACC back to the amygdala, SMA, angular gyrus, and STG, leading Brigitte's behavioral and physiological reactions to the situation.

It goes without saying that the trouble with suppression is that, while it may get you through a situation in the short term, it's really not a sustainable solution. Suppression might reduce your outward behavioral response, but it doesn't actually do anything to stop the emotional experience. It involves avoiding distressing thoughts or behaviors without actually dealing with what's causing them in the first place. Beyond that, suppression can impair your memory and actually *increase* your physiological responses to stressors. In Brigitte's case, she may have been able to suppress her fear well enough to help hide a body, but she's still undoubtedly scared of her werewolf sister.

Chase It With a Distraction

Maybe you like to immediately follow up your horror movie with a fluffy, familiar comedy, or maybe you prefer to curl up with a neutral book—anything that's lighter fare and a far cry from horror, so that you can forget the scary images you saw. There may be something to this method.

In 2009, researcher Emily Holmes and her team proposed playing Tetris as an early-intervention "cognitive vaccine" approach to preventing trauma flashbacks in people who had experienced traumatic events. Her idea was that memory consolidation—the process by which your brain converts short-term memories into long-term, stored memories—is particularly sensitive to being destabilized in the first few hours following an event. What's more, she suggested that the brain has only a limited capacity for memory consolidation at any given time, and that you can elbow the sensory memories of a traumatic event out of the running for consolidation if you can introduce other sensory information that can compete with it. She identified Tetris as a prime candidate because it requires mental rotations. It's so visuospatially disruptive that if you've ever stared at a Tetris game for too long, you might have noticed weird Tetris-like distortions when you finally turned your focus to something else. For example, if you tried to read a book, you might feel like the words were rotating on the page.

Participants in Holmes's study completed baseline assessments, including mood assessments, and then watched a twelve-minute video of graphic footage. The footage included stuff such as human surgeries, and real footage of accidents and drownings. The participants then reassessed their moods, did some filler activities for a half hour, and then were shown another film with neutral images that were recognizably from the traumatic film they had watched earlier. They were then randomly assigned to either play Tetris, or to sit quietly. The Tetris players reported fewer flashbacks both during initial testing and one week later; they also scored lower on the Impact of Events scale, a tool used to clinically diagnose symptoms of PTSD.

In the same vein as playing Tetris, putting on an episode of your favorite comedy show right after you watch a scary movie might help to prevent horror images from intruding on your thoughts when you're trying to fall asleep later. But unless the sensory information from the show is disruptive enough to compete with the scary stuff, it isn't surefire. Compare how busy your brain gets trying to rotate Tetris pieces to how busy it gets focusing on a comedy show. Your brain has to get distracted enough to essentially "forget" to encode the fear memory, so choose your distraction wisely.

Train It out of Your Brain

Humans are constantly bombarded with information. Some of it has emotional content, some of it has risk content, but by and large, most of what we see, smell, hear, taste, and touch every day is neutral and innocuous. You are less likely to remember something like what you had for breakfast last Tuesday, unless it was a special breakfast or you eat exactly the same things every day, because that information doesn't have the emotional glue to stick in your memory.

As for moments that pack an emotional or threatening punch, they can be neutralized too—if you are exposed to them often enough in a way that has neither a positive nor a negative association. This neutralization process is known as habituation.

Thinking back to the Little Albert experiment, if he had been deconditioned (like he ethically should have), he would have gone through a process that looked like his fear experiment in reverse. The researchers would have provided him a safe, neutral space to be exposed to fluffy white stimuli in small doses, crucially without any accompanying incident or noise, until he could engage with something fluffy and white, like a lab rat, without a fear response.

Once the trained response is gone, it's said to be extinct. Extinction and habituation are very similar concepts. Extinction deals specifically with the disappearance of *trained* responses, like Little Albert's fear, whereas habituation deals with the disappearance of *natural* responses—like when you jump at a single balloon being popped, but would have a smaller or no startle response if you were in a room where a lot of balloons were being popped over and over. The sound of popping balloons would stop being surprising and startling, and the effects on your reactions would quickly taper to no response at all. Extinction can take a long time. Fear at its root is meant to help protect us from harm—it can take a long time to unlearn it. But at least it isn't an impossible endeavor.

As a quick refresher: LeDoux's two-system model of perma-fear states that learned emotional memories that are stored in the amygdala are accessed almost reflexively and are resistant to change, while cognitive "information" memories that are stored in the hippocampus are easier to update. Newer research challenges that model and suggests that the brain is naturally equipped to revise or even erase specific learned behaviors, even if they are complex emotional learnings. The process for doing this is known as memory reconsolidation. You may have heard it said before that every time you recall a memory, you are not remembering the original event, but rather, you are remembering the last time you recalled the memory. This gets the gist of the process, but a more accurate way to describe memory reconsolidation would be to say that memory is an ongoing process. All of the facts, details, emotions, and sensations that were originally experienced get consolidated as a memory and stored until you retrieve them. Then they get reconsolidated, encoded, and stored again, like hitting "Save As" in your brain and deleting the original copy. In this way, a single memory goes through edits and revisions every time it's recalled and re-created. Sociologist and fear researcher Margee Kerr uses another awesome analogy for memory reconsolidation: it's like cooking your favorite meal. You use the same ingredients and follow the same recipe, but each time you make it, it tastes a little different.

This is good news if you have a memory that you'd like to forget, or at least dull. Every time you retrieve and reconsolidate a memory is an opportunity to revise the memory or interfere with the process in a way that stores the memory in a less emotionally triggering form. This can be done with a distraction method, such as playing Tetris per Holmes's research, by neutrally revisiting the memory until the emotional wallop (referred to in research circles as salience) has faded, or by a slew of other therapeutic tools, whatever works best for your individual needs.

There has also been research done into chemically interfering with reconsolidation. Studies have shown that beta-blockers, medications typically used to reduce blood pressure, might work to separate memories from the strong emotions associated with them. For folks with PTSD, this is done by taking a dose whenever they feel symptoms. The idea is that when you are experiencing a PTSD flashback, the memory you're recalling is returning to a squishy, alterable state; introducing a drug at this stage will interfere with how that memory gets filed away again. The link between recalling the memory and feeling fear should be broken. This effort has been super effective in animal studies, but has been hit or miss in human trials using veterans with PTSD.

Despite its potential as a treatment, not everyone thinks that interfering with memories in this way is ethical. These medications don't select specific memories and delete them—this isn't like the Lacuna procedure in *Eternal Sunshine of the Spotless Mind* (2004, dir. Michel Gondry), where you can selectively erase memories you don't want. Instead, the treatment dulls the emotions that you've attached to those memories. Some have argued that those emotions are an important part of memory and shouldn't be lost; rather, other therapies should be used to develop coping strategies that better manage those emotions. Others cite studies that show the use of drugs in this way not only interferes with emotional recall, but muddies details of the event in the memory. While this can help the memory to not be so intrusive, it can still spell out personal and legal consequences, such as if a treated person were asked to recall details of the event for a trial. Still others point out the potential for abuse of this treatment, such as military personnel administering it to soldiers to desensitize them to terrible acts.

We should all be grateful that our brains are capable of habituation and extinction because the world is a very scary place, and everything can technically be interpreted as a risk. Without habituation, we'd be on high alert 24/7.

Spoil It

Another way to avoid bad effects from a horror film is to take preventative measures. Prevention can take many shapes: you could watch with the lights on, during daytime, with a friend, or maybe read the synopsis in detail so you know exactly what's going to happen.

But does any of this help?

Measures like watching horror movies with the lights on come down to controlling your environment. If you're dealing with unknown, potentially threatening images on-screen, the least you can do is make sure that the environment around you is as unthreatening as possible. We've learned by association that if we watch a movie in the dark, we're more likely to experience a fright. If you're scared, the last thing you need is to be sitting in a dark room, or worse, in a dark house *at night*, where you cannot see if something is lurking in the shadows. If your room is bright, you can see that everything is safe when your brain is on high alert to search for a threat.

A good amount of research has been done on the impact of screen size on the movie-watching experience. Movies are generally designed for the big screen and are meant to have the best impact in the cinema. Where horror movies are involved, research has predicted that bigger screens might mean bigger fright responses, because you are confronted with a larger-than-life and more detailed visual experience, coupled with theatrical audio. So, if you're nervous about horrific imagery, consider watching the movie on a smaller screen, like a television, laptop, or phone screen, where the details are diminished and tiny, and, if you're sitting a distance away, can be a lot less immersive. A word of caution, though: be careful about wearing headphones while you're watching. With the sound being funneled directly into your ears, you might end up feeling like the film's soundscape is unfolding around you.

Having a friend nearby also ties into this theory in a very literal safety-in-numbers way. You're more protected against a threat if you're not facing it alone. Also, it's more fun to share a scary movie with someone else. This is another effect that can be helped or hurt by sitting in a cinema rather than at home. Exposure to the reactions of a crowd of people can heighten the scary moments, sure, but as many can attest, the shared experience of watching a horror movie in a packed theatre can also help to break up tension, as screams are often followed by laughter.

Spoilers are a measure for controlling against the actual scary content of the film. Although, to be honest, you don't need to hunt down an entire play-by-play of a film to be sufficiently spoiled. In most cases, you need to look no further than the movie's trailer.

These days, a good movie trailer is hard to find. As the main promotional tool for a movie, the trailer is an art form unto itself. And like many art forms, there is a level of mastery required to make trailers effective. Horror movie trailers are not the only culprits, but they are among the worst for lacking the necessary artful touch. More and more often, in their attempts to get butts in seats at cinemas, horror trailers will reveal the monsters or the biggest scares. It's frustrating, especially when you do sit down in the movie theatre and realize that the actual movie is just a drawn-out version of the trailer, and that you've already watched all the tentpole moments. How many times have you watched a movie trailer and thought to yourself, *Well, now I know exactly what's going to happen*?

The 2018 trailer for *Suspiria* (dir. Luca Guadagnino) opens with a student divulging her experiences at her dance academy to her psychotherapist. Over the course of two and a half minutes, we establish the premise and location, we meet the major players of the film, and we are told exactly who the villain is and that they are tied to something demonic. We are shown repeatedly that the dancers are at risk, through beautifully shot sequences and voice-overs, and that the instructors have secrets hidden in the dance academy's walls—we are even shown a secret passage. Compare this to the U.S. trailer for the original *Suspiria* (1977, dir. Dario Argento), which opens with a view of a woman having her hair brushed and decorated with a flower. When she turns, it's revealed that the woman is in fact a skull with a wig, which, incidentally, has zero ties to the film. The rest of the trailer is composed of context-free sequences of Suzy Bannion (Jessica Harper) running scared through some hallways, interposed with the film's title, while a voice-over warns about how scary the final twelve minutes of the film will be. Otherwise, there is no indication that this film is about a witches' coven fronting as a dance company.

Is one trailer inherently scarier than the other? Not necessarily, but one clearly gives away key elements of the film. It makes you wonder, does it actually matter if you know what's coming? What about reading spoilers, reviews, or plot synopses before you actually see the movie—does knowing make it less scary?

One study conducted by Kimberly Neuendorf and Glenn Sparks had groups of college students watch the classic horror films *The Texas Chain Saw Massacre* (1974, dir. Tobe Hooper) and *Night of the Living Dead* (1968, dir. George A. Romero). Groups would receive either a low, moderate, or high amount of forewarning about the film. For example, a "low" forewarning for *The Texas Chain Saw Massacre* stated: "The film you are about to see was rated R by the Motion Picture Association of America. Entitled *Texas Chain Saw Massacre*, it was produced in 1974 by Tobe Hooper."

A "moderate" forewarning added: "This contemporary horror film contains scenes of violence, including murder and dismemberment." And a "high" forewarning further added: "One key scene in the film shows a paraplegic being sawed in half by a chain saw–wielding masked maniac."

This study didn't find that any of their forewarnings affected their audience's reported feelings of fright or enjoyment while watching the movies. What did have an influence in their audience were prior fears, especially for *Night of the Living Dead,* where the prior fear was usually a fear of dead bodies. This influence existed even when viewers had seen the movies before. This supports the idea that when we've attached fear to a specific cue, we tend to experience that fear to a degree when we see it in film form. It also helps that these things we already fear are being presented in a *horror* film: it's being presented in a context that is frightening, and it's absolutely reasonable, if not downright expected, for us to be frightened by its presence in the film.

But before we can assume that spoilers have no effect, note that Joanne Cantor did a similar study using shorter clips (instead of the full movies), her forewarnings were auditory instead of written, and the forewarnings themselves were more different from each other than in the Neuendorf and Sparks study (even Neuendorf and Sparks acknowledge this in their own work). Maybe these differences in how the spoilers were delivered was crucial, because Cantor found that, in her study, forewarning actually *intensified* reported feelings of fright.

Despite mixed experimental results when it comes to the impacts of spoilers, we can say that scary movies aren't exempt from habituation. That's why many movie scares will make you jump the first time you watch, but not during repeated viewings, unless you are really, truly scared of what you are watching. Subsequent viewings of horror films can be (and often are) fun, but they usually aren't *scary*. In the same vein, seeing a scare play out in a movie trailer gives you that first exposure to the scare. You may still jump in your seat when you see the scare again in the actual movie, because other techniques in tension-building are at play, but the odds are that you'll recognize the moment and it will lack the novelty that your amygdala is so keyed to respond to.

There is a small risk for backfire, though. If you spoil yourself for the major scares, you might set yourself up to spend the movie trying to anticipate when they'll show up, unintentionally ramping up tension and priming yourself to be startled. And, of course, whatever fear memory baggage you're carrying with you into a movie will influence you more than spoilers will. If you've had a bad experience with a chain saw, *The Texas Chain Saw Massacre* will heck you up more than it will your buddy who has never seen a chain saw before, even if you know everything that's going to happen.

There is always a risk that scares will linger, and that they might linger for a long time, even if you *enjoy* watching horror films. Watching with the lights on and playing a round of Tetris afterward may go a long way to making sure the scares don't stick, but doesn't it seem like a lot of effort for the reward of sitting down for an hour or two to watch a horror narrative? Obviously, as horror fans, we love the genre and take enjoyment in having our pants scared off. But if you imagine the behaviors applied to another hobby—your friend tells you that they will only cross-stitch during the day, with a friend, so they won't get nightmares—it sounds ridiculous. What makes horror so appealing that we'll knowingly and willingly face the prospects of lost sleep to enjoy it?

IN CONVERSATION WITH
MARY BETH MCANDREWS AND TERRY MESNARD

Mary Beth is a horror journalist and editor in chief at Dread Central *with a focus on found footage, rape-revenge films, and gender representation in the genre; Terry is the creator and editor in chief of* Gayly Dreadful, *a horror site that takes on genre film and television from a queer perspective.*

Together, Mary Beth and Terry co-host a podcast called Scarred for Life, *which features creators from all facets of the horror film community to discuss the films that left major marks on them as children, from writers (I was invited to dissect my lifelong fear of Audrey II and* Little Shop of Horrors *[1986, dir. Frank Oz]) to film directors such as Brandon Cronenberg, who delved deep into* Poltergeist *(1982, dir. Tobe Hooper), and Natalie Erika James, whose choice was* A Tale of Two Sisters *(2003, dir. Kim Jee-woon). The podcast is also a space where these guests explore their passion for the genre and what served as their entry points. As Mary Beth described it to me, it's "an abridged version of someone's personal journey within the horror genre."*

Can you tell me a little bit about what inspired you to start this project?

Mary Beth: Well, funnily enough, Terry tweeted about it. He was like "Hey, this would be a really good podcast idea" and then I messaged him and said "I literally had an idea for this podcast years ago and never did it because I was by myself and didn't know how to do it." And he was like: "So, we should do the podcast, right?" and I said yes.

Terry: Yeah, it was—someone was talking about *Arachnophobia* [1990, dir. Frank Marshall] and I was, like "Oh. Yeah, this movie terrified me and legitimately has scarred me for life." When I tweeted that, a lot of people were like "Oh yeah, this movie and this movie . . ." and I was like "This would be a good podcast."

From my perspective, it all started because everyone started responding to this idea of movies that "scarred" them. Because I think that's what unifies us as horror fans is that scare as a kid that, like, a lot of people are either trying to re-create or trying to find over and over again because of the way that it made them feel at that age. I think it kind of gives everyone a sense of community because you can see what scared people as a kid. And I think that creates this shared idea of "Oh yeah, that movie really scared me" or "Oh . . . well, that movie didn't scare me but it made me start thinking about this movie," and I think that kind of shows that there is a connection between most horror fans.

It's interesting that you say "re-create." Can you elaborate on that a little bit?

Terry: Well it's like, you know, once you're thirty-nine years old and you've seen every horror movie that's pretty much come out, it seems like . . . you get kind of desensitized over time, and it's like, for me, I remember the very first time that I saw a movie that, like, challenged my thought process on, like, what was safe, because it was the first movie that I actually turned off. And it was at that point that I realized that things outside were dangerous.

There never seems to be a shortage of people who have baggage attached to some film or other. What sort of patterns have you noticed in your work so far?

Mary Beth: Well, I mean, I think something that has been surprising to me is how unified a lot of us are in things that scared us as kids. I think also—I think there's also a bit of a generational—well, not generational, but a bit of a gap between Terry and I because I'm younger and I grew up with a different set of movies. So sometimes our guests align more with what Terry saw when he was younger, and then what I saw when I was younger. *But* a lot of us—Ali Gonzalez talked about *The Ring* [2002, dir. Gore Verbinski] and I was terrified of *The Ring*. And then, just recently Dax Ebaben talked to us about *The Blair Witch Project* and I'm wearing a shirt that is printed with the introduction to *The Blair Witch Project*... it's interesting to see how many people had these related experiences because I felt very alone, I think, when I was younger, because I watched a lot of horror, but not a lot of people I knew watched horror. So, I was having these, you know, traumatic, I guess traumatic, scarring experiences, but didn't have anyone to share them with. And then this podcast has actually been really... vindicating is not really the right word, but it's been really validating, I think, in terms of what I found terrifying as a child a lot of other people found terrifying as children. And it's really validating as someone who felt very alone in her love of horror as a kid to find those people that, you know, experienced the same thing as you. It's just been really cool with Twitter, you know, and like this podcast bringing a lot of us together and unifying us even more than I expected. I think one more thing that has been really interesting that we talked about a lot recently on the podcast is the way that all of us have gravitated towards cover art in movie stores. Like that has been talked about so much and, again, I guess I never talked about it with my in-real-life friends or anything, but that experience so many of us had about gravitating towards this box art, and the visuals of that that terrify you and the narratives you built around those images? And so the other thing is, there's a movie I watched called *Carved* [2007, dir. Kōji Shiraishi] from a while ago. It's a Japanese movie and I was terrified of the cover forever. And then I watched it and it wasn't that scary. But it is really interesting, I think, how many of us loved box art and how that defined what was scary to us as kids even if we hadn't even watched the movie.

Terry: Yeah. What it reminded me of . . . I was thinking about that too because it's come up an awful lot recently. And I think it has to do a lot with the idea that—we just recently talked to B. J. Colangelo and she was talking about how her parents, when they would sit down and watch horror movies with her, and they would do what my parents did not do, and if it got scary, they would sit through it and talk with her because they knew that once whatever that person was going to create in their mind after the movie was over was going to be far, far worse than whatever was on-screen. And I think that that kind of ties into the box art, too, because I would see these pictures and it wouldn't have any context to it. And so, like, for me and *Deep Star Six* [1989, dir. Sean S. Cunningham], there was a man cut in half floating in the water. He was in an old-timey diving suit and it was just half of him. So, in my mind I had created this whole story about what happened to this guy and it terrified me. And I know that that seems to be a lot with people who see this art and have this visual image of it, and they might flip over and see a couple stills on the back. Like, I remember someone talking about the back of, like, Chucky—the *Child's Play* [1988, dir. Tom Holland] movie, with the knife and stuff. And they would see these images and they would create their own in their head and these stories without knowing the context and it would terrify them more. And so I kind of think that might be part of why there's that common thread.

Mary Beth: I agree with that 100 percent. It's like . . . the visuals that we're able to make ourselves. And as children, the imagination . . . as crazy as our imaginations go as kids. We make our own horror movies in our heads, basically, I think. Especially just looking at those pictures. Some people it terrifies, and some people, like us, are attracted to that. We're terrified but we want to know more and we want to dig into those images. That's where a lot of us are now.

Terry: It also just reminds me of the quote that Wes Craven used to say about how horror movies don't create fear, they release it. And it always seems to be that . . . I've always considered that it helps us contextualize what's going on in the world.

Which movies would you choose if you were guests on your own podcast?

Terry: I would say that it is a toss between *Alien* [1979, dir. Ridley Scott] and *Psycho*. I had grown up on, like, the 1950s horror and like the 1930s horror. So, like, Universal monsters and alien movies from the 1950s. My dad loved them. And the Vincent Price stuff. And, like, one day my dad was like, "Hey, you want to watch this movie called *Alien*? It has aliens in it." And I was like "Sure!" and I'm thinking like flying saucers and thinking, like, you know, fucking *The Day the Earth Stood Still* [1951, dir. Robert Wise] or that kind of thing. So I go into this and I . . . and the moment that it bursts out of his chest at dinner is the moment that stuck in my head for my life. My parents turned it off and I was like . . . they were staring at me with this excited look on their faces, so excited to terrify me. And I'm just, like, "Do you want us to turn it off?" And so we did, but at that moment it was like this realization that movies could be unsafe and that the world outside was unsafe. Because if an alien can burst outside of your stomach at any moment, then what the fuck?! *Psycho* scared me. And there's the same thing. I stopped halfway through because I couldn't handle it anymore. But, like, what I would end up doing, and I've talked about this in the podcast: I would end up going to seek out the sequel, because for some reason I could handle the sequel better. And then once I mastered this second movie, I could always go back to the first and I'd be fine. *Psycho 2* [1983, dir. Richard Franklin] and *Aliens* [1986, dir. James Cameron] weren't as scary, I guess? And then part of me knew what was coming. Whereas before it was this whole new experience for me. So, like, by the time the lady in *Aliens* is saying "Kill me" because there's an alien that's about to burst out of her stomach, it wasn't as terrifying as it was going into the first one.

Mary Beth: It would be *Jaws*. *Jaws* is the one I talked about on our first episode. *Jaws* was the one, it was the first movie I ever remember watching, and it's the first horror movie I ever saw. And it kept me from going into the ocean for years. That movie I think is one of them, and *Poltergeist*. So those two films shaped me, because *Jaws* was the first film I saw and then *Poltergeist*, I think just the imagery of *Poltergeist* stuck in my head, and I've always been really terrified of ghosts, and *Poltergeist* put images to my fears of haunted houses. And so that definitely got into my head. So those two are the ones that scarred me for life, I think.

CHAPTER 6

VIOLENCE AND MAYHEM

When I was young and Blockbuster Video stores still existed, I once had a debate with an employee because their store had consolidated horror movies and thrillers under the "action" section. It was the kind of debate that was thrilling for me as a know-it-all thirteen-year-old and probably not a debate at all—just a really annoying customer interaction—for the employee. If I'm being honest, my real reason for raising a stink is because I'd spent a good ten minutes looking for a horror film section that didn't exist anymore. But for my part, I thought I was really persuasive: horror movies deserved their own section (horror-adjacent thrillers were invited, too) because horror is a distinctly different viewing experience.

Both horror and action serve to excite the viewer, to quicken their pulses, but where horror movies are targeting fear as an emotional experience, action movies are trying to engage your attention with gunfights, Emmerichian explosions and cataclysms, and helicopters at sunset à la Michael Bay. Violence may be a feature in both action and horror, but it doesn't take a keen eye to notice that not only is violence a different tool when wielded by directors of different genres, but audiences also perceive action violence and horror violence differently. You seldom, if ever, hear about people linking action classics like *Mission: Impossible* (1996, dir. Brian De Palma), *Commando* (1985, dir. Mark L. Lester), or *Die Hard* (1988, dir. John McTiernan) to real crimes, but as soon as a movie's representations of violence tip over into the realm of horror, we're quick to point the finger.

That's why *The Exorcist III* (1990, dir. William Peter Blatty) was a focal point of serial killer Jeffrey Dahmer's trial—a VHS of the film was allegedly playing in his home during his arrest in 1991, although some accounts state that it was *Exorcist II: The Heretic* (1977, dir. John Boorman). It's why *Natural Born Killers* (1994, dir. Oliver Stone) was blamed for Columbine in 1999. It's why people clung to a spurious (and definitely racist) link between *Oldboy* (2003, dir. Park Chan-wook) and the Virginia Tech shooting in 2007—said "link" being that mass murderer Seung-Hui Cho brandished a hammer in a way that reminded someone of a scene in *Oldboy* . . . Yeah. It's why *Natural Born Killers* was blamed again, along with *American Psycho* (2000, dir. Mary Harron), for the Sandy Hook massacre in 2012. You might not consider some of these titles horror, but the rhetoric around these films at the time of blame wasn't quick to make the distinction. Infamously deflecting blame in a press conference, NRA executive vice president Wayne LaPierre referred to these movies as "blood-soaked *slasher films*" (emphasis mine).

We've spent a lot of time looking closely at how horror films build fear in their audiences by introducing potential threats of violence, but what about the follow-through? After all, most scares don't stop with a mere threat. We see the knife plunge into the flesh and the throat slashed by the killer. We see the monster consume its prey. We see the aftermath in all of its blood, gore, and body horror. Why is violence such a huge part of horror?

Huge amounts of research have been poured into studying aggression and media exposure to violence. Weirdly, a lot of the studies that are cited by the media as support for claims of a causal relationship between on-screen violence and violence in the real world don't demonstrate this effect at all. Neither does on-screen violence seem to make people less sensitive to depictions of violence in real life.

SCARE SPOTLIGHT:
CHILD'S PLAY 3 (1991, DIR. JACK BENDER)

On February 12, 1993, ten-year-olds Jon Venables and Robert "Bobby" Thompson walked not-quite-three-year-old James Bulger away from his mother at the New Strand shopping center in Bootle, England, just outside of Liverpool. They took the toddler on a two-mile walk into Walton Village, where they eventually brought him to a railroad embankment, beat and tortured him, and left his body on the tracks to be run over by a train (which he was).

Between surveillance footage from the shopping center, a number of witness accounts, and a series of interviews with both boys, we have a reasonably clear picture of what transpired after Jon and Bobby convinced the toddler to walk away from outside a butcher's shop. I'll spare you the gory details of the subsequent torture and murder, because the details are absolutely gory, and not in a fun and fictional horror movie way.

The manner in which James Bulger was killed was in itself horrifying, but the fact that the act was committed by children stirred both the media and public imagination into a frenzy.

A number of rumors were conjured as people tried to make sense of why children would commit such extreme violence toward a smaller child. One of these rumors was that at least one of the boys—Jon—had been desensitized by violent films. This particular rumor stemmed from the revelation that the last film that his father Neil had rented from the video store (on January 18, almost a full month before the crime) had been *Child's Play 3*.

It's a bizarre assumption that a connection could exist between the kidnapping, torture, and murder of a small child and possessed-doll Chucky's violent exploits. It's especially strange when you consider that this particular installment of the franchise sees Chucky mailing himself to a military school to harass teenaged Andy (aged up from six to sixteen and played by Justin Whalin), and while there is one young character that becomes Chucky's new target, the link between violent acts and small children is much weaker in this sequel than in the previous two films.

If you really stretch the imagination, you can find a few coincidental parallels between *Child's Play 3* and the James Bulger case, namely that their abuses included a small can of blue paint and, toward the end of the movie, Chucky has blue paint on his face from inserting himself in a military school paintball match; in addition, the climax of the film takes place in an amusement park ride that features carts on a track, and James's body was left on a railroad track. Like I said, these are big stretches.

Those involved in the case dismissed the idea of *Child's Play 3* as a source of inspiration for the boys, and it was never even submitted to the court as evidence. For one thing, Jon stated in his police interviews that he didn't like horror movies and that he hadn't seen the film (Bobby admitted to having seen a few minutes of *Child's Play 2* [1990, dir. John Lafia] when he'd walked in on his older sibling watching it, before he'd been kicked out of the room). His father also stated that he didn't show horror films to Jon—he rented movies like martial arts films and *The Goonies* for the ten-year-old. Perhaps he had sneakily found a way to watch it? But even then, a single video rental is hardly a motive. I can't stress it enough: *Child's Play 3* was not a point of discussion at the trial.

Which makes it all the more mind-boggling when the trial judge, Justice Morland, in his final address to the court, blamed the movie. "It is not for me to pass judgment on their upbringing, but I suspect that exposure to violent video films may in part be an explanation."

But this was on the tail of the Video Nasties era of the 1980s and it wasn't hard for this idea to take root in the public's mind. So, even though investigations into the matter had concluded that the boys hadn't watched *Child's Play 3* at all, and there seemed little chance that violent television was their inspiration to murder, the image of the Chucky doll had become inextricably tied to the case and splashed onto tabloid articles.

The incident may sound similar to a more recent violent event, which took place in Waukesha, Wisconsin, on May 31, 2014, in which two middle-school-aged girls, Anissa Weier and Morgan Geyser, lured their friend Payton Leutner into the woods, stabbed her nineteen times with a kitchen knife, and left her for dead, allegedly as a tribute to Slenderman. Payton survived.

Unlike Chucky, which exists only through the *Child's Play* film and television franchises and related merchandise, Slenderman is a multimedia figure with complex lore from a number of contributing sources from around the world. He might have been born from a handful of Photoshopped images in a forum thread, but now Slenderman lore encompasses found footage–style series, such as the YouTube series *Marble Hornets* (2009–2014, dirs. Joseph DeLage and Troy Wagner), alternate reality games (ARGs), video games, and a mainstream film, *Slender Man* (2018, dir. Sylvain White). While the narrative of the film *Slender Man,* which was shot and released after the stabbing, does not appear to act as a portrayal of the event, other films, like the Netflix-produced *Mercy Black* (2019, dir. Owen Egerton), not to mention episodes of the television series *Law and Order: SVU* and *Criminal Minds,* have more obviously based their plots around the event. As with *Child's Play 3* and the James Bulger case, the so-called Slenderman Stabbing stirred up old conversations about violent media and violent behavior.

This becomes a sensitive topic where mental health is involved. It's important to recognize, especially when unusual situations like this occur, that disorders like schizophrenia, while serious conditions, do not equate with murderous intent. Especially given that this chapter is discussing media depictions and how they can affect people, I really want to impress that there is more evidence that shows that stigma against people with schizophrenia, bipolar disorder, and other psychiatric conditions has been influenced way more by media depictions of these conditions than by actual media depictions of violence causing violence. Conditions like schizophrenia are not inherently dangerous to other people, and people with these conditions are not evil. The Slenderman Stabbing was an unfortunate situation in which a child with undiagnosed (and therefore untreated) schizophrenia happened to experience delusions and hallucinations tied to the violent media that she was consuming.

WON'T SOMEBODY PLEASE THINK OF THE CHILDREN?

Arguments linking on-screen violence to real-life violence have existed for as long as television sets have existed inside family homes (and, let's be honest, probably since the advent of cinema, but the discussion got a lasting toehold once television became popular). Television became available in the United States and Canada in the 1950s and people associate its adoption with increased violence, especially homicide, from the mid-1960s onward. Despite the huge body of research that's been dedicated to it, the evidence to support the notion that fictional violence breeds real violence is not as solid as you might expect. In fact, the results are maddeningly inconsistent.

Researchers trying to link the surge in crime to television screens have had to make pretty big reaches. Some have suggested that increased crimes committed by poor people were a result of them watching richer people live their fictional lives on TV. Committing crimes like theft was a way to reduce the discrepancy they saw between their poor lifestyles and those of the people on TV. The study that people tend to draw upon to "support" this conclusion—conducted by Karen Hennigan et al. in 1982—didn't actually find a link between crime rates in communities with television and communities without (a finding that has been confirmed again and again in larger, cross-national studies). But what I find interesting is that Hennigan's team specifically notes that it's unlikely that the rise in crime was due to people watching crime on TV and imitating it (the messaging we would receive decades later), because depictions of crime were uncommon on TV at the time. There was no graphic equivalent to *Law and Order: SVU*, and major broadcasting networks had similar production guidelines to follow. Even one of the first made-for-TV movies, the neo-noir *The Killers* (1964, dir. Don Siegel), was pulled before it hit the airwaves because it was considered too violent.

These days, of course, we have much more access to violent imagery and happily shell out for a movie ticket and snacks to go sit down in a crowded theatre and consume violence among strangers.

A 2006 study by Stefano DellaVigna and Gordon Dahl tried to take experimental evidence suggesting a link between violence in movies and patterns of human aggression and apply it to real-world contexts. To do this, they looked at trend levels of violence in blockbuster movies showing in theatres between 1995 and 2002 and compared them to same-day statistics for reports of violent assaults. What they found was interesting. Reports of violent crime *decreased* on days with higher theatre audience attendance for violent movies. In particular, the reduction was most apparent (a 1.5 to 2 percent decrease per million people attending the movies) during the movies' showtimes, suggesting that the people who might have been more likely to be engaging with violent crimes were instead passing that time engaging passively with violence on-screen. They also noted that there was still a detectable decrease in crimes in the hours after these movie showings, but acknowledged that even nonviolent movies seemed to have this post-movie crime-curbing effect. DellaVigna and Dahl propose a few possible interpretations for these results, including a possible catharsis effect, or the simple fact that, if would-be criminals are spending their time watching a movie, they can't be spending that time committing crimes.

Despite the lack of evidence for a direct link between on-screen violence and human aggression, violent incidents have turned accusing eyes back toward violent media again and again over time. In the United Kingdom, the James Bulger case inspired Elizabeth Newson from the Child Development Research Unit at Nottingham University to publish a paper titled "Video Violence and the Protection of Children" in 1994. Across the pond in the United States, the American Psychological Association (APA) held a commission on "Violence and Youth" in 1993 to look at factors influencing violent behavior in youth and to suggest solutions. Where mass media was involved, the Commission on Violence and Youth was quick to point to exposure to violence on TV and in movies as a factor steering young people toward aggression, especially if the youth in question already showed a propensity for aggressive behavior. Remember this conclusion—if it seems weird that the APA is placing blame on mass media for aggressive behaviors in children *who were already demonstrating aggressive behaviors,* that's because it is weird.

Around the same time, researchers at four universities collaborated on a three-year project known as the National Television Violence Study (1994 to 1997) to explore the extent to which violence saturated television media.

- The University of California, Santa Barbara assessed violence in all types of TV media, from comedies and dramas, to children's series and music videos.
- The University of Texas, Austin looked specifically at violence in reality-based shows like talk shows and nonfiction police shows.
- The University of Wisconsin, Madison focused on the role and effects of TV ratings on parents and children.
- And the University of North Carolina, Chapel Hill analyzed the effectiveness of anti-violence advertisements.

One of the conclusions of this study was that television violence contributes to harmful effects on viewers, which can include learning aggressive attitudes and behaviors, desensitization to violence, and fear of having violence enacted on them. They also concluded that these effects were particularly harmful to children under the age of ten.

These studies formed the foundations for societal views connecting media violence to real violence—views that still resonate decades later. The surreal dark comedy *Greener Grass* (2019, dirs. Jocelyn DeBoer and Dawn Luebbe) satirizes the idea that violent television begets violent children a good twenty years after the conclusion of the National Television Violence Study—a child left unattended while his parent naps watches part of a single episode of a (fictional) series called *Kids with Knives* and he is irreparably transformed into a delinquent.

It's easier to blame something visible and identifiable— bloody images on a screen—than it is to suggest exploring other social, structural, or psychological factors that might be at play. It's even easier if you can point to anecdotes as evidence. I watched *The Silence of the Lambs* (1991, dir. Jonathan Demme) when I was very young, and I got into trouble for repeating one of the especially offensive lines uttered by inmate Miggs (played by Stuart Rudin). For a while, I also wasn't allowed to watch *Mighty Morphin' Power Rangers* because I'd pretend to be the Pink Ranger and kick my sister. On paper this looks like a straight line drawn between violent language and violent acts on-screen and a child enacting violences in real life. But was I really being violent? Was I a serial killer in the making for reenacting what I saw on-screen?

Of course not. The first case was one of imitation (and completely clueless imitation at that) without the intent to cause harm, and the second is an example of playacting, a kid so riled up from the action on-screen that they wanted to kick and punch and wheel around in elaborate flips (uh, cartwheels, in my case) like a Power Ranger. But just as your relatives' shared memes on Facebook don't serve as evidence regarding the safety and efficacy of vaccines, someone's story linking a child's behavior to what TV shows they're consuming doesn't serve as proof. Anecdotes—and we'll see a few more in this section—are not evidence.

So, what does the evidence have to say?

Unfortunately, a lot of conflicting things.

To understand why, let's first take a look at some of the difficulties in running these studies.

Let's rewind a few decades to talk about Albert Bandura's famous (or perhaps infamous) Bobo doll experiment, which was first conducted in 1961. As part of the experiment, preschoolers were assembled into groups where they'd be in a room with an adult and a Bobo doll—an inflatable clown toy with a weighted bottom, designed to always wobble back to a vertical position when hit or knocked over. While kids played in the room, they were placed in conditions where an adult either behaved violently toward the doll, hitting it and speaking aggressively (given that this is an experiment involving kids, by "aggressive" I mean statements like "Pow!" and "Sock him on the nose!") or ignored the doll completely (a third, control group of kids got to play sans adult).

The kids who watched an adult demonstrate punching and kicking a Bobo doll were more likely to punch and kick the Bobo doll later. Like many people, I was taught in my first-year psychology class that this was a clear indicator of observed violent behavior inciting imitative violence. It seems like a pretty clear-cut cause and effect, right?

Other experiment design flaws aside, there are issues with how the experiment chose to measure aggression. Compare the behavior that we saw (kids hitting a toy designed specifically to be hit by kids) with the conclusion (if kids see violence, they will act violently). Something doesn't add up. It's a bit of a leap to define the act of bopping a Bobo doll around as an act of violence, or even aggression. The kids are playing with a toy in the exact way it's designed to be played with. As for the kids in the nonaggressive condition who didn't hit the Bobo doll? Well, if the Bobo doll were a novel toy and no adult or peer demonstrated how it was meant to be used, why would they intuit that the way to play with it was to hit it?

The problem with defining and measuring aggressive behaviors in children is not unique to Bandura's study. In fact, it's a recurrent theme in research that specifically seeks out relationships between violent media and how kids behave. Is it reasonable to conclude that kids playacting and play-fighting is equal to real-deal violent behaviors? It's unlikely.

So what *is* an adequate measure for aggression and violence in an experimental setting? Lab studies tell us very little about the actual effects of exposure to violent imagery. It's not like experimenters can ethically host a Fight Club in their lab, set their participants loose, and see what happens. Most of the studies don't observe actual aggression; rather they had to make do with analogues, or aggression proxies, like thoughts associated with aggression or violence, or loosely defined aggressive behaviors identified by adults watching children at play. Some, like in Bandura's experiment, measured the likelihood a kid will punch an inflatable clown that's literally built to be bopped. Another study in 1961, by researchers Paul Mussen and Eldred Rutherford, actually asked a child if he'd hypothetically pop a balloon if he were alone with it and called this metric a measure for aggression.

Classical measures for aggression in adults aren't much more precise. One experiment that has often been used as an analogue for measuring aggression involves placing the participant in a room with a button or dial after, for example, having the participant watch a violent or neutral video clip, instructing them to administer shocks to an unseen person and then observing how willingly they administer the shocks (or crank the dial to administer more aggressive shocks). This experiment, originally designed by Stanley Milgram in 1963—and controversial in its own right—was designed to look at participants' obedience to authority. Otherwise, self-reports of aggressive feelings and biometric tests, like blood pressure and brain scans, tend to be the main sources of data.

We can't be too hard on experimenters for struggling to find useful measures in their research. It's important to keep in mind how hard it is to pinpoint the causes of human behavior, especially complex behaviors. But it's equally important to keep in mind that we should probably take a lot of the research out there with a grain of salt because the measures aren't direct. Researching the correlation between violent movies and aggression is easier said than done. And at the end of the day, even if a correlative relationship is found, correlation is not causation.

What I'm saying is: researchers in this field have their work cut out for them. A lot of the studies looking at the effects of violent media are descriptive studies—they are trying to describe relationships between exposure to media violence and violent behavior among real people moving through their daily lives in the real world. In short, this is research where you can't exactly extrapolate from data measured in a controlled, experimental setting and call it real life. These aren't lab variables that can be easily isolated, measured, and compared. A lot of this research focuses on specific people—like a class of six-year-olds at a single school, or a group of people who demonstrate aggressive behaviors related to a diagnosed mood or mental disorder. The results from these studies are hard to generalize to whole populations of people like North America or the world.

Suspecting that, especially when taken in isolation, the conclusions drawn from a number of oft-cited experiments weren't painting an accurate picture of the relationships between media violence and violent behavior in children, psychologist Jonathan Freedman took it upon himself to do a comprehensive review of roughly two hundred studies published up until 1999. Of the studies that Freedman reviewed, once he controlled for experiments with poor measures for aggression, he suggested that 28 percent of the studies showed support for a causal relationship between violent media and aggressive behavior, 18 percent showed mixed findings, and 55 percent of the studies showed no support for a causal relationship. It's also worth mentioning that the bulk of the studies reviewed used really small sample sizes, so results either way should be interpreted with care. More recently, in 2012, researchers Christopher J. Ferguson and Joanne Savage performed an updated review of the body of research in this field and likewise found that there are major flaws and biases in how this research is conducted that has been muddying our ability to understand the phenomenon of violent media instigation of violent behaviors (or if the phenomenon even exists).

Now that we've established the difficulties of this area of research, let's look at some of the landmark studies, the ones that are often trotted out to highlight the potential harm of violent media. Are children who watch more horror and more violent media more aggressive than kids who stick to *Sesame Street* and Disney films?

One of the studies that was actually directly cited in the APA's commission report as evidence showing the harmful effects of violent television was one conducted by Lynette Friedrich and Aletha Huston-Stein in 1973. The study involved preschool kids between the ages of three and five and a half years old. They were divided into groups that either watched violent programming (six *Superman* cartoons and six *Batman* cartoons), prosocial programming (twelve episodes of *Mister Rogers' Neighborhood*), or neutral programming that had no violence and no significant prosocial messaging. Adult observers were tasked with watching the kids and making notes about their behaviors at various times throughout the school day.

When people reference this study, they claim that the children who watched the *Batman* and *Superman* cartoons scored higher on measures of aggression, which included physical aggression, verbal aggression, object aggression, fantasy aggression, and interpersonal aggression. Apparently they were more likely to disobey their teachers, argue, and hit their classmates. But in actuality, the initial study found that there were no effects, so the researchers performed an internal analysis to separate boys and girls into groups according to whether they tested as high aggression or low aggression *before* the television clips were shown (initially each condition had a mix of kids with varying levels of aggression) to see how individual kids changed.

They found that those who were low in aggression off the hop tended to score as somewhat more aggressive in every film clip condition, which means that Mister Rogers got them just as riled up as Batman. And those who tested as high aggression initially had a general tendency to score lower no matter the condition. These are what are known as regression effects—the tendency for extremely high and extremely low measures to become more moderate or closer to average with time and retesting—and probably would have occurred without any experimental manipulation.

Also, if you compare the results based on program type, the biggest increases in aggression for the low-aggression group happened from the neutral (a.k.a. the control) programming, and the biggest decrease in aggression for the high-aggression group—get this—also happened thanks to the neutral programming. As a field study without laboratory controls, we can't even be certain that any differences observed were thanks to the shows that the kids watched, but given that the biggest effects came from the controls, it's pretty darn unlikely that TV is at the root of kids' so-called aggression and disobedience. And even if there had been a small uptick in aggressive behavior after watching *Batman*, three-year-olds don't generally pull a Gage Creed from *Pet Sematary* (1989, dir. Mary Lambert) in real life. I wouldn't worry about it.

The ideal way to test the effects of violent media on aggression would be a longitudinal study in natural settings involving randomly assigning a large group of very young children to different television and film viewing groups (in terms of violent content) and then measuring their levels of aggression and criminal behavior as adults. But even this more ideal model has its flaws, as evidenced by the handful of longitudinal studies that were conducted in the 1970s, '80s, and '90s.

Most of these studies followed the same basic design: either ask children to report on their viewing habits or ask adults to monitor them, assess their aggression on various scales, and lather, rinse, and repeat every few years. Where the studies differed was in how they chose to measure exposure to violent media and aggression, and the lengths of time for which they followed their participants.

Probably the most influential of these studies was a twenty-two-year study conducted by Leonard Eron, Leopold Walder, Monroe Lefkowitz, and Rowell Huesmann. The study began in 1971. The researchers obtained information for third-grade students in Columbia County, New York. They interviewed the children, their parents, and their teachers for information about preferences for violent television and benchmark measures for aggressive behaviors. Ten years later, they interviewed the students again, using various measures for aggression, including psychological tests and personality inventories, self-rating surveys, and peer nomination (that is, asking their third-grade classmates, who may not even know each other anymore, to rate their aggression at age eighteen). Then, twelve years later, they conducted a final phase interview and collected data about the criminal activities of the third-graders (now adults) that they'd interviewed twenty-two years earlier.

When comparing results between phases one and two of the study, the researchers found a huge correlation between preference for violent media at age eight and aggression at age eighteen, but only for boys and only when looking at the peer-nomination measure for aggression (personality inventories and self-ratings didn't yield significant results).

As I mentioned, this study was not without its flaws. One that has been pointed out by other researchers is that the eighteen- and nineteen-year-olds being asked to report on their peers' behaviors weren't even necessarily in school together with these kids anymore. They were basically being asked to construct a memory of past behavior of others, rather than report on the present (the question was even phrased in past tense for phase two of this study). Another issue is that this study measured *preference* for violent media at a young age, but not necessarily how much exposure these kids were actually getting. So we're a step removed from any conclusion connecting the actual act of watching violent TV and movies to aggressive behavior.

One interesting conclusion that did come out of the final study was that aggressiveness seems to be a remarkably stable trait. The researchers identified that those children who scored high on aggression at eight years old tended to be the high scorers at age thirty.

At this point, you can see for yourself that results of research in this field have been inconsistent, but yet we continue to cling to this weird idea that violence and violent movies are connected.

With all of the issues with proxy measures for aggression, you would think that turning to neuroscience instead would be helpful. But, this is one realm where looking to neuroscience—specifically, interpreting brain activity—might actually muddy things more than it clarifies.

In 2014, Dr. Nelly Alia-Klein conducted a study to investigate whether there was a difference between how healthy viewers and those who displayed abnormally high physical aggression respond to violent media. The experiment took the form of three measures: blood pressure before, during, and after the viewing of violent film clips (with nonviolent, emotional clips acting as controls); self-reports of the participants' emotional states before, during, and after viewing; and FDG-PET imaging to highlight metabolic activity in different areas of the brain. FDG, or (18)F-fluorodeoxyglucose, is a radioactive tracer that is also a glucose analogue, which means that it chemically has a similar shape to glucose sugar molecules and so can "trick" glucose-metabolizing cells into taking it up as if it were glucose. A PET scan can use FDG to reveal parts of the brain that are functioning more actively at any given time according to how much the cells in those parts of the brain are metabolizing FDG molecules. More metabolic activity means a brighter spot on the scan.

I wish the study had indicated what violent media was sampled for this study, but all we're told is that the participants watched twenty scenes edited from R-rated movies and documentary films, and that these scenes depicted intentional acts of violence between people.

In terms of the results, the participants in the high-aggression group measured lower blood pressure rates, and lower activity in their right orbitofrontal cortex compared with their nonaggressive counterparts while watching violent scenes. The participants in the aggression group also self-reported that they felt less upset and nervous (compared with the nonaggressive viewers) when watching violent media, but instead felt "inspired" and "determined." In completely fictional terms, this calls to mind how Dr. Chilton (Anthony Heald) marvels over Hannibal Lecter's (Anthony Hopkins) relatively low pulse rate and blood pressure during violent acts in *The Silence of the Lambs*: "His pulse never got above 85, even when he ate her tongue."

The orbitofrontal cortex (OFC) mentioned above is a region of the frontal lobe responsible for impulse control and regulating emotional and social behavior. Basically, it's the part of your brain that keeps you in check, inhibiting you from externalizing emotions in ways that would be socially unacceptable. So, if there is lower activity in the OFC, as seen in Alia-Klein's research, then it suggests that the great social inhibitor is being inhibited and possibly not recognizing violent behaviors as unacceptable or taboo as readily as someone showing high OFC activity. Alia-Klein points to this as evidence for desensitization.

Other studies have connected low orbitofrontal cortex

activity while consuming violent media to desensitization. Further, they suggest that desensitization might disrupt how we morally process violent scenes in movies. It's worth noting, though, that for Alia-Klein's study, the researchers surveyed the participants and determined that the TV- and movie-viewing habits were pretty much the same across the board. So, at least in this case, exposure to film violence on its own doesn't seem a likely explanation for desensitization, which we'll talk about in more detail in the next section.

So, if your baseline state of being tends toward aggression, then watching a lot of graphic violence might reinforce aggressive traits that are already there—but it won't conjure new violent tendencies from nowhere. Otherwise, with the amount of violence—both real and fictional—available for us to access on small screens, big screens, and online, practically everyone everywhere would be living in nonstop *The Purge* (2013, dir. James DeMonaco) levels of violence.

Honestly, there is so much research out there looking at possible connections between media violence and real-life violence that it's hard to pick and choose which to highlight—and I don't want to spend this entire chapter talking strictly about this kind of research. Some of the studies that I chose to highlight aren't necessarily the most robust either way. Mostly I picked research that had a huge impact on shaping the biases that we have today (like the Bandura study and the Friedrich and Huston-Stein study) or because I found them experimentally interesting (because who wants to pore over the minutiae of hundreds of research papers if there isn't a degree in it for you at the end?).

Ultimately, though, what I want you to take away from this entire discussion is this: research continues to be interested in understanding humans' complex relationships with violent media, but we don't really understand what's going on yet. And with our current understanding of how we are influenced by film and television, claims that mass murders and serial killers have been spurred on by watching too many horror movies are grossly inflated, absolutely garbage takes.

DESENSITIZATION

As we touched on briefly in our discussion of Alia-Klein's study, the other major conversation point that comes up when violence is on the table is the idea that watching fictional violence makes us less responsive to real violence. When people witness real violence, we ideally want them to react in ways to stop it (or to take reasonable actions to protect themselves or others from it). So, if watching violent horror doesn't infect us like a zombifying RAGE virus, and we've established pretty thoroughly that it doesn't, is there a chance that it's actually having the complete opposite effect and making us complacent?

The desensitization hypothesis is different from the habituation effect that we discussed in the last chapter. Habituation in terms of horror movie violence refers to reduced responses to additional portrayals of movie violence—the first time you watch a violent sequence will be the time it packs the biggest punch. It will become less impressive or surprising the next time you watch it.

The desensitization hypothesis refers to reduced responsiveness to actual violence caused by exposure to media violence. So, the idea is that if you watched someone getting stabbed in a fictional horror movie context, the sensitivity of your emotional response to watching a person getting stabbed right in front of you for real becomes dulled. If the desensitization hypothesis is true, then it has horrible implications.

But is desensitization a proven phenomenon?

In 1988, researchers Daniel Linz, Edward Donnerstein, and Steven Penrod designed an experiment to investigate whether desensitization to real violence against women could occur from long-term exposure to violent or sexually degrading films. The idea was that young men (undergraduate students) who watched movies that associated violence with erotic scenes would be less sympathetic to female victims in real legal cases involving sexual violence. What the study classifies as "long-term" exposure involves watching two to five full-length films over multiple days, unlike most experiments, which just involve watching violent clips that have been excised from the context of their films. There were three types of movies in this study: R-rated slashers, including *Friday the 13th, Part 2* (1981, dir. Steve Miner), *Maniac* (1980, dir. William Lustig), and *The Toolbox Murders* (1978, dir. Dennis Donnelly); nonviolent R-rated teen sex comedies like *Porky's* (1981, dir. Bob Clark—the very same Bob Clark who directed the original *Black Christmas* in 1974) and *Fast Times at Ridgemont High* (1982, dir. Amy Heckerling); and X-rated pornographic movies, including *Debbie Does Dallas* (1978, dir. Jim Clark) and *Indecent Exposure* (1981, dir. Gary Graver).

The participants viewed either two or five films for their condition, one every other day. After they'd watched all of the movies assigned to them, they received a call notifying them that the final movie for the study hadn't arrived and that they'd been assigned to a second study being conducted by a law school. They were asked to sit in a courtroom and watch a videotape of a rape trial (where the victim and assailant were either acquainted or complete strangers), and then answer questions about the trial.

One clear conclusion from this study is that *habituation* definitely occurred: participants responded less strongly emotionally to subsequent films in their condition (especially in the case of the slasher films group). You've probably experienced this phenomenon yourself if you've ever sat through a horror movie marathon, especially a slasher marathon—once you've watched one, the next is still entertaining, but it doesn't necessarily pack the same experiential punch.

But what about the desensitization measure? Did participants in the violent movie groups perceive the rape trial differently? There was only a hint of evidence that the violent movie conditions produced slightly lower participant scores for victim sympathy and rape empathy when compared with participants in the nonviolent and control groups. There was no difference between the groups for the other measures relating to the trial, including verdicts and sentences, general acceptance of rape myths, and victim responsibility. It also didn't matter whether a participant had watched two films or five films in their category—watching more movies didn't produce greater effects. So, it appears that whatever effect occurred, desensitization wasn't the cause.

ARE HORROR FILMS MORE VIOLENT NOW?

Violent movies are not designed to convince anyone that violence is good and that we should all run outside and do harm to others. They don't even make us want to commit "good guy violence"—that is, violent acts committed by a character that we're supposed to identify with as the audience. Is the idea of a Final Girl posed with a weapon, face smeared with blood and hair matted with gore, a glamorous image of violence? For a horror fan, it could be! Sure! Does that mean that I want to be in that Final Girl's shoes? That would be a big nope.

The amount of violence hasn't appreciably changed. It's just changed its shape over time.

I guess the better question might be: Has the way that we access and consume horror movies changed?

Only until recent decades, if you missed a movie's theatrical release, you caught it when it aired on TV. And when you caught it on TV, unless you had a specialty channel, you were probably watching a modified version of the movie, cut down to fit into tidy programming time-slots and rinsed of anything too graphic or profane for the television network's standards. *This film has been modified from its original version. It has been edited for content.*

Nowadays, we have access to a slew of films at our fingertips. In 2019, streaming subscription services officially outstripped cable subscriptions worldwide as the go-to mode to access film and television media. Streaming services aren't necessarily beholden to the same content guidelines as television networks—they've been slowly adding content warnings, but without activating a "kid mode" setting, it's not hard for anyone to stumble from a family-friendly animated series onto a clip that looks startlingly like a snuff film.

When it comes to mainstream media, though, the images that we see aren't necessarily gorier. After all, the silent film *Un chien andalou* (1929, dir. Luis Buñuel) offers horrifying violence in the form of trick photography and sliced eyeballs that will still churn your stomach today. But some effects, including blood and digital effects, when applied masterfully, have greatly improved our sense of realism.

In terms of ratings, most horror films run the gamut from PG to NC-17. You might be surprised that a lot of horror classics, from *Jaws* to *Poltergeist*, are stamped with a relatively mild PG rating. These days, filmmakers often aim for a PG-13 or R rating to try to reach as wide an audience as possible.

There aren't a huge number of mainstream horror films that have clung to their NC-17 rating after it's been assigned by the MPAA, which seriously limits who can walk into the theatre and buy a ticket to see the film. Most will make edits to move the needle toward an R rating—gore sequences tend to be the first to get cut, or at least shortened. Showing an extra second or two of blood can sometimes mean the difference between a film being classified as R or NC-17. The R-rated theatrical version of *Saw* (2004, dir. James Wan) is apparently only about eight seconds shorter than the unrated (would-be NC-17) version. Similarly, the R-rated version of *Scream* (1996, dir. Wes Craven) was earned by shaving off bits and pieces of gore and blood here and there, for a total of seven seconds removed.

There are a few reasons for this. First, the NC-17 rating was first introduced in 1990 as an adults-only category for theatrical releases—the original intent of the X rating before it was co-opted by pornographic filmmakers in the '70s. The rating has been applied to some pre-1990 titles retroactively, usually to re-rate a film that was previously rated X for a wider audience, like *The Evil Dead* (1981, dir. Sam Raimi), which was re-rated from X (for "graphic horror violence and gore") to NC-17 in 1994. But, generally speaking, since getting your film rated in the first place is a voluntary move, the bulk of NC-17-rated horror films are post-1990, which gives the illusion that more movies these days merit the rating.

While the social implications of featuring—and let's face it, *glorifying*—violence in horror isn't as scary as concerned parents have made it out to be, it's undeniable that depictions of violence have been key to shaping horror as a genre. Horror has become a sandbox genre where storytellers can push for creative kills, design for shock value, and test just how permeable the barrier is between extremity and just plain bad taste. This is, after all, a genre that claims faux snuff films like *Guinea Pig 2: Flower of Flesh and Blood* (1985, dir. Hideshi Hino) and grotesque body horrors like *Tusk* (2014, dir. Kevin Smith) and *Taxidermia* (2007, dir. György Pálfi) alongside family-friendly fare like *Beetlejuice* (1988, dir. Tim Burton). Stomach-churning terrors might not be to every horror fan's taste, but as we'll see, (fictional) violence can broaden the horror movie palate in interesting ways.

CHAPTER 7

BLOOD, GORE, AND BODY HORROR

While it's not a requirement of the genre, very few horror movies—especially contemporary ones—skip out on mixing some form of violence into the story, whether it's a suggested threat or an unflinching shot of a body turned inside-out. When I did a casual search for recent examples of nonviolent horrors, the results put forth were surprising. It was immediately clear, from the breadth of films that made the cut, that people's individual tolerances for what is considered gory and violent differ wildly. At least one list even recommended *Funny Games* (1997 and 2007, dir. Michael Haneke) among the ranks of horrors stripped of shock-value violence, despite extended and gruesome torture sequences, simply because these acts were off-screen. We generally acknowledge that scary movies will contain violence, whether mild and implied or in-your-face and extreme. If so much of horror involves a sense of threat, as we've explored in previous chapters, then violence surely has a role to play in building a scare.

But what if we reversed the situation and stripped the horror away? Is violence on its own scary?

When we boil down horror movie violence to its barest essence, the scares spool from the experience of owning a human body, and the ways in which ownership can be threatened and wrested away. Those threats of violence can come from inside the body, or from an outside source.

VIOLENCE FROM WITHIN

The human body is an ideal site for horror: the body is personal, and even on a good day it's kinda gross. Fluids and squishy tissues aside, our bodies are the tools that allow us to exist in the world and experience it for all its pleasures and pains. But despite our marvelous complexity, at the end of the day, a human is just a fragile meat tube—a fact that movies like *The Human Centipede* (2009, dir. Tom Six) are quick to exploit—and physical existence is easily invaded, abused, and altered, even without an evil doctor helming the action.

Violence from within the body can take many shapes, including transformation and mutation (usually triggered by some sort of infection) and possession. While the tropes associated with each of these subgenres are distinct, they all lean into the idea of something getting under the skin or into the blood to make bodily changes.

Transformation horror takes many forms, ranging from classic werewolf flicks like *An American Werewolf in London* (1981, dir. John Landis) to non-lycanthropic transformations like *Afflicted* (2013, dirs. Derek Lee and Clif Prowse), which sees a tourist becoming a vampire in the aftermath of a one-night stand, and *Bite* (2015, dir. Chad Archibald), in which the consequences of a simple bug bite involve developing insectoid traits, spinning cocoons, and uncontrollably producing gloopy eggs. How do these fictionalized invasions play off real horrors? While thematically transformations speak to a loss of control—something that is already scary—the infection that leads to transformation speaks to common biological fears. While we can mitigate risks—we can wear condoms to help prevent STIs and use bug spray to stave off hungry bugs—nothing is ever 100 percent. For some of us, that leftover unpreventable *what-if?* can gnaw at our thoughts—especially if the worst-case *what-if* scenarios involve peeling flesh and drooling slime.

Even typically natural (and often welcomed) bodily invasions aren't safe from the genre. I'm talking, of course, about pregnancy horror. As a subgenre, pregnancy horror points out that the miracle of creating new life also entails an entire organism taking up residence within your body as a sort of parasite, pushing your organs around, siphoning off your blood and nutrients to grow, and causing not only change to your physical body, but lasting alterations to your neurochemistry.

The classic example of pregnancy horror is embodied by *Rosemary's Baby* (1968, dir. Roman Polanski), where the titular Rosemary (Mia Farrow) finds her pregnancy transforming her into something thin, weak, and sickly when she ought to be glowing. A ton of movies have since portrayed pregnancy as monstrous (or demonic, or alien) infections, and it continues to be an effective form of body horror, whether you have a uterus or not. Even the "Unprotected" segment of the anthology series *The Mortuary Collection* (2019, dir. Ryan Spindell) shows that uterus-less bodies don't necessarily get a free pass—a cocky frat boy who lies about condom use ends up gestating a monster and has no organs suitable to birth it. It ends in the only way it could: horribly.

On the neurochemical front, *Prevenge* (2015, dir. Alice

Lowe) is a great take on pregnancy directly messing with your brain. In the real world, what we commonly call "pregnancy brain" has been linked to a perfect cocktail of hormonal changes and exhaustion that causes pregnant people to feel more forgetful, unfocused, and out of sorts. Research is inconclusive about the extent to which pregnancy brain is more than anecdotal—one longitudinal study, led by Diane Farrar in 2014, compared pregnant women with nonpregnant women and did find that spatial recognition memory specifically was reduced in pregnancy—but other measured changes to the brain are even more interesting. One 2016 study found that pregnancy consistently pares down gray matter to make lasting efficiencies that are likely preparing the expectant parent's brain to form attachments to its baby; other studies have identified a phenomenon called fetal microchimerism, where a fetus's cells live on in its parent's body tissues, including the brain, like little souvenirs. These changes are natural and, as far as research can tell at this point, innocuous, if not beneficial. Horror would much rather take a sinister spin. In *Prevenge*, mother-to-be Ruth (Alice Lowe herself) can hear the voice of her unborn daughter whispering to her constantly, goading her to murder the people involved in a climbing accident that claimed her partner's life. The control that the whispering voice exerts is akin to a possession narrative.

In a sense, possession narratives can be thought of as a sort of spiritual infection. Instead of breaking through a body's physical barriers, possessing entities invade by exploiting weak points in a person's spirit, beliefs, emotions, or dreams. Instead of your cells breaking down and re-forming, or your own flesh turning against you, your experience of the world might become manipulated and your personality shoved aside. This isn't to say that a ghostly or demonic possession movie is devoid of body horror. It's quite the opposite: ghosts and demons aren't used to wearing a human meat suit and have no qualms about contorting it into joint-breaking positions, à la back-bending Nell Sweetzer (Ashley Bell) in *The Last Exorcism* (2010, dir. Daniel Stamm), or inflicting self-mutilation, as when a very possessed Mia Allen (Jane Levy) licks an X-Acto knife in *Evil Dead* (2013, dir. Fede Álvarez).

The body is terrifyingly fallible. It's all too easy for something—tangible or not—to germinate from deep within and wreak havoc. Of course, being so soft and fleshy, the human body is just as prone to violence at the hands of other people.

VIOLENCE FROM WITHOUT

Torture porn and extremity, especially, are among the most polarizing subgenres of horror. At one end there are the gorehounds who prefer their horror to be slick with blood and clotted with carnage, and at the other, there are atmospheric horror fans who claim to prefer "psychological" scares. (Yes, I'm totally being pedantic with my quotation marks because, as I've spent this whole book explaining, all scares are trying to leverage our psychology to a degree, not just the slow, creeping frights.) Many horror fans seem to have a pretty varied palate when it comes to what on-screen violence they'll tolerate (and I include myself among that bunch who will at least sample almost everything), but it's not uncommon for moviegoers to hit a limit when it comes to explicit, intense human suffering. Even among horror industry professionals, I'll often notice a similar pattern when the subject of torture comes up: they will grimace and say something like, "Oh, no, I'm not into that sort of stuff."

Or, to echo what Trudie (played by Shenae Grimes-Beech) in *Scream 4* (2011, dir. Wes Craven) poignantly observes where torture porn is concerned: "It's not scary—it's gross."

I do disagree with Trudie on one point: the concept of torture, any torture, but especially the seemingly meaningless *Why are you doing this?*-type torment featured in torture porn, is scary. It's horrifying. But it is also absolutely gross. That said, torture horror is hardly the only subgenre that qualifies as *gross*. Blood splatter, gore, and body horror are featured across horror's myriad subgenres, from slashers to revenge films to creature features. But what makes torture porn different is its approach.

According to Jeremy Morris, there are five basic elements that qualify a horror film as belonging to the torture porn subgenre, differentiating it from other ultraviolent horror films:

1. The torture is non-interrogational, so if the film violence is means to getting information, then it's disqualified.
2. The torture itself is the source of horror in the film, and not just added flavor.
3. At some point, the roles of the torturers and their victims are reversed and the victim has been transformed (for better or for worse) by their ordeal.
4. The victim's transformation into a torturer justifies the violence of the film. Sometimes it is a flimsy justification. Often it's the only one.
5. The torture is represented with realistic visuals. The torture shouldn't be of a magical, supernatural, or religious bent, at least not at first glance.

The realistic approach to torture porn in particular is what's so divisive to many audiences. While we typically have clear delineations between real life and horror, torture porn seems to approach blurring that line as a goal in order to have us connect directly to real bodies, and to feel the history that birthed this subgenre.

Torture porn has a specifically American flavor, mostly thanks to its emergence as a response to 9/11, as we discussed in chapter 2. Extreme horrors from other countries aren't a tidy fit with this category, and neither are exploitation films from other decades. Other types of films that are often mentioned in tandem with torture films, like French and Asian extremity movies, have extreme depictions of horror, even torture, but torture tends to be used as a tool for horror rather than being the strict source of horror itself. Take, for example, *Audition* (1999, dir. Takashi Miike): the final torture sequences of the film are certainly the climax of horror (and undeniably disturbing), but Asami's (Eihi Shiina) violent behaviors can be read as vengeance, rather than as torture for torture's sake. Through the violence, the film engages us to connect with the characters and their emotions, rather than to their bodily experiences.

We mention in chapter 1 that one of the brain regions that gets fired up during scare sequences is the insula. One of the insula's many functions includes interoception, or our awareness of what's going on within our own bodies. While individual interoceptive abilities differ (research points to dancers as having particularly incisive interoceptive powers), seeing a clip of a person being flayed in a torture sequence will light up your insula and make you very aware of your own skin. Narrative and visual techniques in torture films tend to divorce us from the characters and instead fill the screen with unflinching takes of bodies being injured. This forces us to connect with the body that we're seeing and builds upon that insular experience of mapping it to our own bodies.

Since I'm drawing a clear line between torture porn and other violent subgenres, let's also take a closer look at where lines can be drawn between torture and gore. While we often lump these two elements together, the most obvious distinction is that torture is a form of violence and gore is a possible outcome of violence. In fact, they can even be mutually exclusive: torture can be enacted without any guts or blood being spilled, while splatter and gore can absolutely wreck the upholstery without acts of torture. From a visual story-telling standpoint, adding gore to torture sequences serves to engage that connection to the body even more and stir up revulsion in addition to the horror of seeing characters being subjected to intentional suffering. Gore on its own has a broader palette: it can be fun and playful shorthand in the form of a splatter across a wall, an explosive kill, or a room saturated in the aftermath of some bloodbath. Gore on its own can also be an incredibly effective tool when it's used as part of a startle. One of the most stressful gore sequences I've ever experienced was from the genre-bending black comedy *Spontaneous* (2020, dir. Brian Duffield), in which scared students run through their school hallways, randomly exploding into a mess of death like blood-filled balloons. I think I spent the entire sequence with my hand clapped over my face in stress, even though most of the violence was only shown in fleeting glimpses. Sometimes the most powerful gore images end up being the ones that we barely see.

SIGHTS UNSEEN

If you've gone back to rewatch the first *Saw* movie (2004, dir. James Wan), you might have found yourself thinking *this isn't as violent as I remembered*. Habituation, as we talked about in chapter 5, accounts for only part of what's happening—the shock of Jigsaw's traps is bound to have less of an impact the second time you watch them. While not a torture-horror entry, a more famous example of this experience is the "Stuck in the Middle with You" ear-cutting torture scene in *Reservoir Dogs* (1992, dir. Quentin Tarantino). Audiences misremember seeing the moment when Mr. Blonde (Michael Madsen) tortures a captured cop (Kirk Baltz) and cuts his ear off, an action that never actually appears on-camera.

You might have heard of this referred to as the Mandela Effect. The term was coined by self-identified paranormal consultant Fiona Broome to describe the phenomenon where people tend to misremember that Nelson Mandela died while in prison during the 1980s—to the point where they claim to recall seeing his funeral when it aired on television. (Mandela was released in 1990, served as president of South Africa from 1994 until 1999, and died in his home, surrounded by family, in 2013.) Wildly, this collective misremembering happened around 2010, when Nelson Mandela was decidedly still alive. The term was solidified in public consciousness about five years later when people online misremembered the children's series *The Berenstain Bears* as "The Berenstein Bears" but could not find any evidence for this alternative spelling. Broome explains the effect using theories about parallel realities; others have blamed mischief and manipulation by time travelers, but neither of those concepts is something we can test scientifically. Instead, it is much more reasonable to propose a neuroscientific basis for the effect.

In the case of torture sequences where we cut away from the action, like in our *Reservoir Dogs* example, a similar phenomenon occurs, where we remember details of violence that weren't actually visible. So, what's actually going on in the brain when we fill in these gaps? The hippocampus seems to be the crucial component in creating this false memory by integrating sensory modalities into a "remembered" experience. The hippocampus specializes in consolidating long-term memories, but its main concern is what's known as episodic memory, or our life experiences and personal memories. It's also the part of the brain that can sift through your mental filing cabinet to pull really old memories up to integrate them into your present experience or imaginings of possible futures. So, the hippocampus calls up a memory of the last time we watched *Reservoir Dogs*, other areas of the brain, such as the ventromedial prefrontal cortex (vmPFC) and the dorsomedial prefrontal cortex (dmPFC), help to reconstruct the memory using present context clues and existing associations—an ear is cut off! That would make a bloody mess!—and now that we're done with remembering, the hippocampus reconsolidates the memory and puts it back into its cognitive file folder with the new info included. It's less like photocopying a photocopy—which would create a faded result over time—and more like making revisions every time the memory file is pulled up.

In a radio interview, neuroscientist Steve Ramirez explains one interpretation for why memories are so malleable: "the same machinery, for example, the hippocampus, that enables us to recall the past, is also the same machinery that enables us to reconstruct the past. It also happens to be largely the same machinery that helps us imagine ourselves in the future." To a degree, every consciously recalled memory can be considered a form of false-ish memory because the act of remembering activates pathways in the brain to *reconstruct* that memory experience. As we mentioned in chapter 5, memory consolidation can be disrupted really easily by new information—the same is true with memory *re*consolidation.

There are a few ways by which these false memories

might be built. One is that the template that we're using to rebuild the memory might be faulty, what are known as schema-driven errors. In psychological terms, schemas are conceptual knowledge templates that help to organize information. If I asked you to imagine a chair, for example, your basic schema for "chair" would probably be something like: "a structure with four legs, a seat, and a back," like a drawing of a basic wooden chair. This schema makes it easier for us to look at different pieces of furniture and quickly understand them as *chair* and *not-chair*.

The trouble with schemas comes when our memories distort new information in an effort to fit it into an existing schema in a process referred to as "effort after meaning." This means that it's easier for us to disregard and/or transform details that don't make sense or seem unfamiliar. In films, for example, this selective attention might be a factor in how the memory of a scene is encoded: if what we're seeing on-screen is not interesting, we'll instead pay attention to what's unfolding outside of the camera lens's field of view and integrate that information instead. And then of course our social, context-based understanding of what's going on in the scene helps shape how that memory is recalled and reconstructed.

So, when we remember the torture scene from *Reservoir Dogs*, we remember the context of Mr. Blonde dancing around with his straight razor, we remember the close-ups of the cop tied to the chair, his mouth duct-taped and blood dripping down his face, we remember the sounds of Mr. Blonde saying "hold still" while the cop grunts in pain, and we remember seeing the fleshy ear in Mr. Blonde's hand in the aftermath. Although we don't immediately get a glimpse of the gore that would be where the cop's ear used to be, our reconstruction of the memory of the scene fills in the logical missing step—the moment when the cop's ear was cut off while Mr. Blonde was straddling him on that chair—and readily conjures the missing visual for us. And if we hear from other people that they remember that image too, it serves as a reinforcement for the visual.

This lends support to the idea that whatever we imagine is going on in a narrative between cuts will be scarier than what we ultimately are shown. From context clues and our own past memories, our brains are able to construct and reconstruct events in ways that can be way more intense than what we see on-screen. And when it comes to torture horror, gore, and body horror, that reconstruction can feel very personal because it involves interpreting through the lens of our own experiences of having a body. Filmmakers recognize the power of that quick cut away *just* before a blade slices skin or *just* before the worst torture is about to take place on-screen. It's a clever way to exploit our brains into conjuring images possibly more intense than what can be accomplished with visual effects.

If you've come this far and thought to yourself, *Wait—my brain has never imagined any missing visuals for me. This definitely sounds fake,* you're not alone. The ability to visualize exists on a spectrum, and living at the extreme end of that spectrum is *aphantasia* or a complete inability to conjure mental images. It's not an easy phenomenon to measure, but existing research has estimated that anywhere from two to five percent of people might experience this absence of imagistic thought.

One 2021 study sought to explore the role of mental imagery in conjuring fear by placing electrodes onto the skin of participants, half of whom experienced aphantasia. The researchers sat them in a dark room, and then read them scary scenarios, like stories of the listener falling off a cliff, or being inside a plane that is crashing. The electrodes measured tiny changes in sweatiness associated with arousal, which changes your skin's electrical conductivity. While it's not a direct measure of fear (nor can it pinpoint an emotion as specific as fear), it's a good indicator that some sort of intense physiological reaction is happening. Participants who self-reported that they experience aphantasia showed no change in skin conductance while listening to the stories, while participants who did not experience aphantasia demonstrated spikes of arousal as they pictured themselves in the situations being described.

When the experiment was repeated using upsetting images instead of just stories, everyone showed the same amount of freaked-out skin conductivity, whether they experienced aphantasia or not. This result suggested that the lack of fear response in aphantasic participants when no images were presented boiled down to the power of visualization in heightening fear.

It's possible that people with aphantasia are the ultimate audience for the oft-cited "show, don't tell" rule of storytelling. Cutting away from gore won't, well, *cut it*: without actually seeing the scare on-screen, the aphantasic moviegoer just doesn't have enough information to experience the emotional wallop that the filmmakers are trying to conjure through implied violence. People with aphantasia can get spooked like everyone else, they just need to be presented with concrete visuals to get there.

When critics refer to horror as a "visual feast," it usually seems to refer to depictions of violence. While scares can be effective without any gore whatsoever, there can be something so appealing about the splashy violence and grotesque kills that only horror movies can achieve.

THE BLOODIER THE BETTER?

Blood Feast (1963, dir. Herschell Gordon Lewis) is often considered the first splatter film—or the first horror film to feature graphic on-screen gore. Merely three years earlier, *Psycho* (1960, dir. Alfred Hitchcock) had gone so far as to feature disembodied blood burbling down a shower drain in sterile black-and-white; *Blood Feast* feels like a response to *Psycho*, delivering buckets of blood, tongues, and body parts in raunchy Technicolor. It might seem schlocky and silly by today's standards, but it's undeniably bloody.

In real life, fear of blood, which is often rolled into the fear triad known as blood-injury-injection (BII) phobia, is common. It's estimated that up to 4 percent of people experience BII phobia, a high enough percentage that you've probably met someone at some point in your life who cannot handle the sight of blood, real or fake. While it's a common fear, it does have an unusual presentation. While all phobias trigger a fear response—that's a big part of what makes a phobia, well, a phobia—most fears don't cause people to faint. Fainting at the sight of blood is caused by a very specific physiological response called a vasovagal reaction. The vagus nerve controls involuntary "rest and digest"–type functions, like lowering your heart rate and telling your body to unleash gastric juices into your food-full stomach. When something triggers it to overreact, like a sudden scare, it might overshoot and cause heart and blood pressure to suddenly drop—basically the opposite of your typical scare responses, which usually send heart rates soaring. The sudden drops associated with the vasovagal reaction result in wooziness at best, and a dead faint at worst. Studies have proposed that blood fears might trigger a vasovagal reaction thanks to stimulating fear and disgust at the same time. Why blood, gory injuries, and hypodermic needles seem to be the only fears that consistently win the disgust-fear vasovagal lottery and not other gross-out fears remains a mystery.

As far as horror movie aesthetics are concerned, though, blood is a staple of the genre. It's hard to think of horror, especially the messier subgenres like splatter, revenge, and body horror, without liberal use of jets, drips, and splashes of blood. Too much blood, of course, will push a film into an R rating, or even the dreaded NC-17. Scorsese famously desaturated the blood to a brownish color in *Taxi Driver* (1976) when the MPAA was threatening an X rating. (He earned an R for his efforts.) As we've discussed in previous chapters, countless horror movies have also snipped away seconds from their bloodiest sequences to evade restrictive ratings.

Theatrical blood has seen a number of different formulas over time, from chocolate syrup to more complex concoctions containing dyes, syrups, and sometimes dangerously toxic chemicals (like Kodak Photo-Flo, a concentrated wetting agent for preventing water spots while processing photographic film, which was a key ingredient in the legendary fake blood recipe developed by Dick Smith). In terms of color, opacity, and viscosity, watch enough movies and it's obvious that some fake blood recipes look more realistic than others when captured on camera. This is partially due to changes in aesthetic trends over time, and partially due to which bloods were popular on the market. More recent bloods tend to be darker and less like the vibrant arterial bloods we've seen in the past. One quality is pretty consistent across fake bloods, though: most of them are sticky, cause stains, and are generally a pain to work with take after take.

SCARE SPOTLIGHT:
DEEP RED (1975, DIR. DARIO ARGENTO)

You can peep one of my favorite forms of movie blood in Dario Argento's aesthetically violent giallo films of the 1970s, like *Suspiria* (1977) and *Deep Red*. You can also see it in George Romero's *Dawn of the Dead* (1978), playing a nice, garish contrast to the grayish zombie makeup.

Consider the death scene of Helga (played by Macha Méril), near the beginning of Argento's *Deep Red*: Helga's just been struck from behind with a meat cleaver and has had her head smashed through a window. Marcus Daly (played by David Hemmings), who is on the street below, sees it happen and rushes up to the apartment to help her. As he pulls her back from the window, the blood on her throat looks dry and waxy, frozen into perfect drips around the piece of glass that's stuck into her neck. When she's laid out dead on the floor, more blood pours thickly from her mouth and pools on the floor like melted red crayon.

It's not one of the most realistic bloods—in fact, we could argue it's one of the *least* realistic. It's a garishly Technicolor red-orange and it looks suspiciously waxy or nail polish–like. The blood in question was known as Nextel Simulated Blood, which was developed by Phil Palmquist and Len Olson at 3M. The formula won a Technical Achievement Award at the 45th Academy Awards in 1972 and enjoyed a brief burst of popularity in the 1970s. What made it so innovative? It wouldn't stain skin, clothes, or sets.

It's a fun bit of science. You see, Nextel Simulated Blood didn't stain skin or clothing because no liquid dye or pigment was involved in the solution. The red color, and probably its plasticky appearance, came from microspheres—basically teeny-tiny red plastic spheres suspended in a colorless liquid thickener. Other recipes for blood include oily compounds that readily stain pretty much everything. So instead of soaking into surfaces like a stain, the Nextel blood just sits on top of the material that it's bloodying up and can be easily wiped away.

Unfortunately, while it was an attractive concept, and was popular for theatre productions and live shows (KISS used it for their concerts, and front-person Gene Simmons was once photographed pretending to drink a bottle of the stuff), Nextel Simulated Blood didn't exactly perform well on film sets. Tom Savini, who worked with Nextel Simulated Blood on *Dawn of the Dead,* reportedly wasn't a fan. As he describes in his book *Bizarro: A Learn-by-Example Guide to the Art & Technique of Special Make-up Effects* (1983), "At the time there wasn't a really great blood formula floating around. The blood I used in *Dawn* was 3M Brand Stage Blood which sometimes photographed terrifically—really deep, red blood—and other times looked like a tempera paint." He didn't recommend it for film productions based on how it was picked up by most film stock.

It isn't all that surprising that the Nextel blood didn't always behave as intended on camera. The structure of the near-microscopic spheres in suspension likely scatter light differently than the dissolved dyes of other fake bloods, giving the blood its unexpectedly crayon-like coloring. I don't have a patent for Nextel blood that I can read over, but it's possible that this inconsistent coloring comes from an effect known as structural color. For most objects, our perception of an object's color is dictated by light that is absorbed or reflected by a material. We perceive the pigment in red food coloring as red because the pigment's molecular structure absorbs light wavelengths that are not associated with our perception of the color red, but reflect the ones that are, and these reflected wavelengths of light then enter our eyes and excite the cones on our retinas that let us perceive that color.

But sometimes, the structural arrangement of a material, at micro-, but especially nanoscales, can actually affect how we perceive a color. If we take the iridescent blue morpho butterfly, for example, and zoom in on its wings until we're viewing them on a nanoscale, you'll see that the butterfly's wings aren't even blue at all—they're brown. The tiny brown scales that make up the blue morpho's wings are arranged in layered rows of structures that behave like a diffraction grating, scattering light and causing interference in the way the light is being reflected. The blue wavelengths experience constructive interference, amplifying the vibrant blue that we perceive, whereas other color wavelengths experience destructive interference. It's possible that the extremely small size and arrangement of the microspheres being used in the Nextel blood might have been similarly creating a structural color effect. So, just like how the color of the blue morpho's wing changes slightly as you tilt it, shooting Nextel Simulated Blood from different angles might produce small variations in color.

In any case, by the time he was working on *Friday the 13th* in 1980, Tom Savini was using a much more realistic-looking blood recipe, and Nextel Simulated Blood had more or less retired from Hollywood.

Is bloodier better? It's not a question that we can really answer. Blood is a tool—a bucket of it can ramp up the schlock factor and fun in a movie like *Evil Dead 2* (1987, dir. Sam Raimi); likewise, a bucket of blood can bring tension to the breaking point when it's dumped onto a traumatized and telekinetic prom queen's head in *Carrie* (1976, dir. Brian De Palma). Whether a wound seeps arterial red or "realistic" brownish blood, milky white fluid or, perhaps most frighteningly, nothing at all, blood can be used to conjure feelings of distress and disgust without too much effort (although I always imagine the bloodiest sets are a nightmare for sticky-coated actors and cleanup crew).

MORE THAN MEETS THE EYE

One of my first jobs out of university involved giving live organ dissections and demonstrations for visitors to a science center. People would gather around a table while I guided their gloved fingers through valves into the ventricles of pig hearts or pointed out different regions in a slice of a sheep's brain. My favorite demonstration, and the toughest sell to everyone else, was the cow eye dissection. Hearts, lungs, brains, or stomachs? Not a problem for most people. But pull out an eyeball and people start cringing, gagging, and backing away.

You might have noticed that the same squeamishness toward eyeballs translates to the screen. I know I see it. We all have different tolerances for gore and body horror, but seeing eyeballs pierced, punctured, or plucked out of their sockets tends to be where a lot of people find themselves squeezing their own eyes shut. But being vulnerably squishable vision-orbs filled with gelatinous goo (that's technically called *vitreous humor*), eye horror is making constant appearances in genre. And even if it's not featured in the movie itself, eyes have become synonymous enough with horror to grace all sorts of horror film posters (and book covers!).

When it comes to the people who can't handle seeing eye horror, I have a theory that the discomfort stems from the fact that eyes are intrinsically more personal, familiar organs. You don't see your liver in the mirror every morning while you're brushing your teeth. Probably you don't take selfies with your small intestine hanging out front and center. Our guts and gore live on the inside, and while it's gross when we see our insides exposed to open air, we don't have the same intimate attachment to our guts as we do to our eyes.

The external nature of eyeballs makes it easier to imagine having needles pushed into them while watching the same thing happen to Shigeharu (Ryo Ishibashi) in *Audition*, or having thumbs pressing them deep into your sockets like in *28 Days Later* (2002, dir. Danny Boyle), or even having them sliced with a straight razor like in *Un chien andalou* (1929, dir. Luis Buñuel) or *Would You Rather?* (2012, David Guy Levy). I know I squirmed and felt my own eyes water the first time I watched Alex's (Malcolm McDowell) eyes being propped open for aversion therapy in *A Clockwork Orange* (1971, dir. Stanley Kubrick), even if his character's eyes technically come out unscathed. And then I squirmed some more when I later read that, despite safety precautions, Malcolm McDowell's cornea got sliced on one of those eye clamps anyway.

It's not hard to extrapolate to a sympathetic reaction to seeing an eyeball getting speared or slashed. Seeing eyeballs get ruined so easily in movies is a painful reminder of how fragile and unprotected eyes are. Even I have a bizarrely specific preoccupation with the idea that I'll somehow accidentally slice my cornea open with a playing card whenever I'm playing a card game (even though this has never happened). While there isn't a wealth of research specifically on eyeball-related fears, studies have shown that eye mutilation occupies a similar fear dimension to blood, injection, and injury fears discussed earlier in terms of anxieties around loss of body integrity and bodily invasion. There's something about these fears specifically that have an especially large anxiety spike associated with anticipation (that good ol' amygdala-fueled fight-or-flight response) that switches quickly to insula-led disgust and interoception when we're actually confronted with visual imagery. Unlike other types of fears, blood-injection-injury (including eye injury) fears feel *personal*.

We love the spectacle that violence adds to horror more than the acts of violence themselves. We love the idea of a creative kill—limbs bent in ways that they shouldn't, and bodies taken apart in unusual ways. We love the visuals of blood raining down to soak our Final Girl from head to toe—or of a chopped limb sending an arc of blood splattering against a wall—but we love it because it's part of the horror experience, not because we love violence itself. Gore *is* gross; the threat of violence *is* stressful and scary, even when it's divorced from the context of horror. When violence becomes a part of horror, it becomes an emotional amplifier that connects us personally to the characters and to the action, because we all know the experience of owning a body. We may not always empathize with the violence we see on-screen, but we definitely recognize it.

IN CONVERSATION WITH JOHN FAWCETT

John Fawcett is a director and showrunner whose horror credits include cult werewolf film Ginger Snaps *(2000) and* Orphan Black *(2013).*

As a filmmaker, do you feel particularly drawn to horror compared to other genres?

I think horror for me was the real reason probably I became a filmmaker in the first place. My way of thinking about horror and my way into horror has always been from a very visceral, emotional point of view. It's never been particularly science-y; it's never been really, even really clearly thought through. It's only, I've only reacted to things in a really raw emotional kind of way.

I remember I was always very afraid as a kid. I was very fearful. I just remember being little, being like age five through, I don't know, like fifteen, and being really afraid of, like, the dark, of everything. It took a long time to kind of, like, develop myself away from that. It's funny, because I think that I started to look at horror almost as my own therapy. Because I was scared of it! I remember seeing *Black Christmas* [1974, dir. Bob Clark] on the television and it was really scary. And my parents shut it off before it got too intense, but it was too late! It had fully traumatized me.

I saw *Halloween* [1978, dir. John Carpenter] at a young age. I saw *American Werewolf in London* fairly young. I remember seeing parts of *The Exorcist* [1976, dir. William Friedkin] and *The Omen* [1976, dir. Richard Donner] really young and because I was so afraid, I was drawn to it. And it became this kind of thing where I would be . . . I would try and test myself and see how much I could stand and then back away again. It's funny because I started to get more understanding of how films were made and I used that as a way to conquer my fear of horror movies. And that was like, say, imagining what it would be like on set to make a movie.

Like taking yourself outside of the action?

So, imagine *Halloween*. *Halloween* was a movie that really, really scared me. I saw it in junior high. There's a lot of frightening images there, like Michael Myers with the mask and stabbing through someone into the door so they're up off the ground . . . and I was like, okay zoom back and now I'm inside a set, I might not even be in a real house. I've got lights at the windows, I've got a guy in a mask, I've got a microphone overhead, I've got people behind the camera, and, you know, if you've been on a set, it ain't scary. It's just not scary. So there was a part of me that conquered my fear of horror in that way, but I was always drawn to what frightened me in the first place as a kid. And I think that's where this "what scares you" kind of thing came from, really. As an understanding of horror films and what scared me in the first place.

And that came from really base, primal stuff. Like being a kid and being afraid.

How does that translate to how you see horror now?

Well, I think that part of what makes horror scary is when it takes real people, or what we perceive as real characters, and puts them in outlandish, scary situations. Which has been a sort of working theory of mine with regards to genre, not just horror, for a long time. That the way to make these things work, to make people go for the ride, to identify, you have to present them with characters that feel real. That their emotional journeys feel real. They don't feel like actors acting a script. There's always some kind of trope to a character, but there are always ways to circumvent the clichés. I think as long as we get presented with something that feels authentic, we buy into stories. Like stories of werewolves or clones or aliens, or whatever it is.

In the '70s, the style was very real. They weren't trying to do a kind of heightened comedic style. I don't know what your favorite movies of the '70s were. But there's a lot. A lot of my favorite horror movies came out of the '70s. I mentioned a few, but there was also: *Don't Look Now* [1973, dir. Nicolas Roeg], *Alien* [1979, dir. Ridley Scott], *Black Christmas, Dawn of the Dead*...*Jaws* [1975, dir. Steven Spielberg] was kind of one of the most successful horror films of all time. It's all very real approaches to the characters. So you buy in. As soon as you feel like a character is too stylized or not real, suddenly it's not scary.

You mention a lot of movies that are considered horror classics, which are sort of responsible for what audiences expect today when they go to see a horror movie. How much of your approach as a director involves navigating these audience expectations?

I think if you work in the genre, you become very aware of the tropes. And certainly as the filmmaker, you become very aware of what works and what doesn't work. And so some of this stuff works because it's easy. It's low-hanging fruit. And that doesn't mean don't do it. I think that...I love a good jump scare. I'll do it. There's a bunch of really simple little techniques that freak people out in the movies. Revealing someone standing behind them when you didn't think someone was back there, and leaving them out of focus. Having a suspense sequence leading to an area where there's a big empty space in the screen. And then not using that big empty space.

And the thing is, I like a lot of those old horror techniques.

And audiences do too!

I think they do! Listen: I think if you're presenting material that feels original—you still have to tell a story, you still have to cinematically tell a story. And there's not that many different ways to do it, to go about telling it. What makes something unique is, yes, a visual language can be...it doesn't have to be boring. But what makes it unique is the characters and the subject matter. That's what sets it apart from its tropes.

There are lots of these tropes that, if you present them in a way that feels fresh and original, in subject matter that is in a direction that people haven't seen before, then it's... I think that dipping your toe in some of these things is fun. It's like, when I was making *Ginger Snaps,* you become really aware there's a certain mythology behind the movie werewolf. I didn't actually want to make a werewolf movie at all. I wanted to make a metamorphosis movie. And so I wanted to make it about transformation, physical transformation—I wanted to make body horror and have it be comedic.

And the more I thought about it, the more I thought: this is the reason to do this. It's a genre that can be reinvented.

The way I looked at it was: here are the ten things that define a werewolf movie. And I would use them because people expect it! But I would use their expectations against them. I would reinvent the genre by taking their expectations and twisting them and bending them and subverting them. And sometimes to use them just for fun because it's fun. You're making a werewolf movie, let's have fun with it!

How do you feel about revisiting Ginger Snaps *twenty years later?*

It's really interesting to take that movie and update it. I think that it actually survived reasonably well over the last twenty years, but it's interesting to take it and go: let's put it in a contemporary setting now. Let's modernize it. Let's have it transcend people's expectations again, you know? And do something totally different with it.

That's been my theory of making movies and making stuff from the beginning. Just look for all of the tropes and try to avoid them and look for the things that you can take from the genre, that you can play with in the genre and make it unique and try and kind of either genre-mash or use unexpected elements to tell your story.

Because everything's been done! It's hard in horror. It's hard to make anything original these days.

What do you find scary?

I don't get frightened by fantasy creatures. I don't find that frightening. What I find frightening is things that actually could potentially exist or could affect me or could really attack me somehow in a dark alleyway. Or get in my bloodstream.

There are lots of different signposts of Canadian horror and body horror is definitely one of them. David Cronenberg was a big influence on *Ginger Snaps* and on just what I think is scary. I think things getting into your body or into your bloodstream is one of the more frightening genres in horror.

Audition really scared me. It was really, really creepy. I like *American Mary* [2012, dirs. Jen Soska and Sylvia Soska]. I liked, obviously *The Fly* [1986, dir. David Cronenberg] and *Dead Ringers* [1988, dir. David Cronenberg] were big influences on *Ginger Snaps*. *Alien* was another obviously big body horror movie. And *The Thing* [1982, dir. John Carpenter], which is probably one of my favorite body horror movies of all time. It's an amazing movie.

You do what feels frightening, right? You do what feels scary and that comes from an emotional place, and everyone is different. I think anything, if you want to make horror movies, body horror movies, thematically is a good starting spot for me. And another thematic starting piece for me always in horror is family. Those are the things that, to me, are big aspects that I like in horror. I like psychological horror. And, you know, if I think about psychological horror, I think about movies like, well, potentially starting with, say, *Repulsion* [1965, dir. Roman Polanski].

Do you find yourself drawn to horror more in your work? Or are you partial to any other genres?

I like humor, but often the two things go together well. More often than not I see things through a horror lens. Like not a super-serious horror lens, but through some kind of comedic horror lens.

Because for horror you have to be with a character. You have to be utterly with a character to be afraid. You can't be omniscient. If I'm going to make an audience fearful walking down a hallway, probably the most effective way to do that is to be with the person. To be right behind them. And so really, you could make a whole horror sequence out of two angles.

Like if someone is going into, say, an old barn. You could have one angle following behind them, so we see what they see, and one angle on their face to see how they feel. And you could probably construct the whole scene with those two angles and a flashlight.

It's been a common theme in my conversations that horror involves a lot of emotion, emotional intelligence, and empathy.

Well, I think that that makes sense. That is the kind of thing that makes a good story: there's two things for me. One is the believability of the characters, that you're presenting characters that the audience cares about, that they feel real. So, whatever the emotional story is, you need the audience to be able to get inside those characters. That's why I personally have a lot of issues with very stylized characters, because I can't . . . I feel like I'm being held at arm's length. I can watch it, but I can't emotionally engage with it because it feels like I'm just supposed to watch. There's something cold, there's something that's keeping me outside of it, and so it's very important with horror to be able to engage, to viscerally connect with characters, and that comes from emotion, that comes from empathy, but the other thing, for me, in terms of, you know, getting an audience to believe what is happening, is the way the actors are directed, the actors are in the scene and there is a kind of emotional landscape for the actors that is believable.

For example, the final scene in *Ginger Snaps*, after Ginger is lying dead on the floor there is a very emotional scene where Brigitte's tears are streaming down her face and this was a moment where I, making this movie on a shoestring budget, was terrified that people weren't going to believe for two seconds any of the effects that we were doing. It was just a guy in a rubber suit, right? And this thing that was lying on the ground was a big bunch of fur and . . . it's utterly fake. But what sells it is the totally authentic emotion on Emily [Perkins]'s face. And these tears. And you go *oh my god, her sister is dead.*

So, that makes me believe all of the makeup nonsense and absurdity of the concept that is *my sister has turned into a werewolf*—it's how much I believe the characters.

The second thing is also . . . and this is just my thing. It's not everyone's thing. My thing is: don't take yourself too seriously. I find that when movies are very earnest and there isn't a stitch of comedy anywhere, you can't laugh at anything, I find that I get disengaged a little bit. I find that when I can laugh, when I'm allowed to, I find myself much more invested in the characters and I find myself invested more in what's happening to them. I'm not saying make the horror elements funny, but I think allowing some humor through the eyes of the characters allows a larger bandwidth to accept the absurdity of the concept.

Because a lot of horror is kind of absurd.

Do you think it's possible to make something too novel that might alienate audiences?

I think as long as you're telling me a story about a character that I care about and they're real, and that story line is a character journey that is real—that's how stories are told and that's what generally works.

I think you can tell a weird story, a weird horror movie, as long as I believe in it and I give a shit about the characters. I have to believe in it. You have to make me believe in your content. So. Tell me some weird science. Tell me, make me believe in the mythology somehow, whatever it is that you're doing. Like, I haven't seen *Teeth* [2007, dir. Mitchell Lichtenstein]. I'm not sure how they're going to make me believe that a vagina has teeth.

CHAPTER 8

HORROR'S
LONG-LASTING APPEAL

No amount of understanding how horror engages our fear mechanisms manages to explain why we love it in the first place. Most theories of emotions suggest that humans are most motivated to seek out experiences that will increase pleasurable moods and emotions, and actively avoid anything that might be a downer. Obviously, horror, at least at a surface level, does not promise to make you happy or satisfied. If anything, horror qualifies as a downer genre. Even when the hero prevails, the narrative journey usually exposes us to an entire buffet of unpleasant experiences and images. This phenomenon—that people are drawn to horror despite its association with negative emotions like fear, anxiety, and disgust—is often referred to as the Horror Paradox.

The idea of recreational fear sounds counterintuitive. The concept extends beyond the world of horror cinema—there must be a good reason why we also love horror novels, video games, and haunted attractions.

Some researchers have gone so far as to describe paradoxical pleasures—like loving to feel scared—as a form of "benign masochism." This same line of thinking has been applied to explain why humans enjoy eating extremely hot peppers when we know that the compounds that make them so spicy activate our pain-sensation neural pathways. If the idea of benign masochism is a little muddy, Canadian cognitive psychologist Steven Pinker puts it in these terms:

> These paradoxical pleasures include consuming hot chili peppers, strong cheese, and dry wine, and partaking in extreme experiences like saunas, skydiving, car racing, and rock climbing. All of them are adult tastes, in which a neophyte must overcome a first reaction of pain, disgust, or fear on the way to becoming a connoisseur. And all are acquired by controlling one's exposure to the stressor in gradually increasing doses. What they have in common is a coupling of high potential gains (nutrition, medicinal benefits, speed, knowledge of new environments) with high potential dangers (poisoning, exposure, accidents). The pleasure in acquiring one of these tastes is the pleasure of pushing the outside of the envelope: of probing, in calibrated steps, how high, hot, strong, fast, or far one can go without bringing on disaster. The ultimate advantage is to open up beneficial regions in the space of local experiences that are closed off by default by innate fears and cautions.

When it comes to horror, very few of us entered into our love for the genre by plunging headfirst into a brutal entry like *Them* (2006, dirs. David Moreau and Xavier Palud) or maybe *Antichrist* (2009, dir. Lars von Trier); some of us never even make forays into these corners of the genre as a matter of personal preference. Most of us find our gateways into horror either by first watching horror-adjacent genres, like action movies or crime thrillers, by being introduced to older titles by parents, older siblings, or friends, or by starting with more family-friendly frights like *Beetlejuice* (1988, dir. Tim Burton), *Hocus Pocus* (1993, dir. Kenny Ortega), or *Coraline* (2009, dir. Henry Selick).

Neither of my parents is a fan of true horror movies (I'm the only horror fan in my immediate family, actually), and my main gateway into horror was crime procedurals like *CSI: Crime Scene Investigation* and psychological thrillers like *Kiss the Girls* (1997, dir. Gary Fleder), *Single White Female* (1992, dir. Barbet Schroeder), and *The Game* (1997, dir. David Fincher) until I was old enough to control my own viewing habits. I remember my younger sister coming home from a sleepover once when she was in middle school and reporting that she'd watched *The People Under the Stairs* (1991, dir. Wes Craven). She was braver than I was in middle school—I hid in another room at a birthday party while everyone else was watching *Children of the Corn* (1984, dir. Fritz Kiersch). Whatever your entry point into horror might have been, early film experiences help you to build up a tool kit of genre expectations, impressions, and tolerances that you carry with you every time you journey back into the genre.

HORROR IS FOR EVERYONE

Before we dig into possible biological, psychological, and even sociological reasons to love horror, let's banish one idea up front: loving horror is not a trait restricted to any individual gender. It might sound obvious to some of us, but it's a sticking point that still comes up in research circles.

Enjoying horror is not a niche phenomenon. Horror making its way into the mainstream over time has made it harder and harder to justify its supposed place as an underground genre.

One of the biggest limitations of research into responses toward horror films is that, while a variety of films are shown to study participants, the range of horror subgenres that these studies cover is relatively small. In reading over countless studies, some movie titles—like *The Texas Chain Saw Massacre* (1974, dir. Tobe Hooper), *Cannibal Holocaust* (1980, dir. Ruggero Deodato), and *Friday the 13th, Part III* (1982, dir. Steve Miner)—appear again and again. I can appreciate that these movies were selected either because they are classic entries (depending on when the study was conducted), because they demonstrate graphic violence, or both, but it strikes me as odd that so many studies loudly declare that women enjoy horror films less than men because they rated a five-minute clip from *Cannibal Holocaust* less favorably than their male peers. Not to mention that this area of study never even takes into account the horror preferences of trans men and women, nor nonbinary, genderfluid, or agender moviegoers.

The other big issue with this area of research—a limitation that is not limited to this specific area—is that it relies heavily on self-reported data to measure enjoyment. There are a few issues that tend to come up with self-reported data, but one of special interest is socially desirable response bias. This usually happens because we humans typically want to leave a good impression, even when filling in an anonymous survey, so we'll often consciously or subconsciously answer surveys with what we think is the desirable response rather than an honest reply. So, for example, if a man believes that it's socially desirable for men to enjoy horror movies, then he might be more likely to circle higher values on a scale measuring horror movie enjoyment than he really feels applies to him personally. I'm not saying that this means that all self-reported data is useless, far from it—self-reports are among the best ways we have to access individual insights—but be wary of any studies that rely solely on self-reports.

I've yet to see a horror study that looks at the horror genre globally, in terms of its many and varied subgenres, to see how different audience demographics are drawn to different flavors of horror narratives. It would be a huge undertaking, but I think it would be rewarding in terms of quashing the misconception that horror is meant exclusively for men, especially cisgender, white, able-bodied men.

Some researchers have attempted to understand what types of personalities might lead people to horror media, though. Matthias Clasen created a research survey to try to build profiles of different kinds of horror consumers. For example, what he called the "Enthusiastic Horror User" included participants who demonstrated high enjoyment of horror media, frequent use of horror media, and preference for intense horror. To a lesser degree, this profile was also associated with a tendency to report not being easily scared by horror movies. In terms of personality and motivations, Clasen's team identified four distinct profiles:

- The Enthusiastic Horror Users were the ones who tended to report that they turn to horror with the expectation that they will experience emotions of joy, anticipation, and surprise, and as people, they tend toward being imaginative and sensation-seeking (and maybe believe in paranormal phenomena).
- The Social Horror Users reported that they strongly prefer to consume horror with other people, tend to enjoy horror more when watching it with other people, and, fascinatingly, also tend to be more scared when consuming horror with other people. The Social Horror User scores

high on extraversion and agreeableness scales, and reports a similar affinity for belief in the paranormal in comparison to the Enthusiastic Horror User.

- The Supernatural Horror User strongly prefers horror media with a supernatural bent over natural horror, and also finds supernatural horror much scarier. This profile is *not* using horror to confront feelings of disgust or anger, and tends toward a belief in the supernatural.

- Lastly, the Fearful Horror User was defined as being easily scared by horror media and remaining scared after consuming horror media. Fearful Horror Users also found horror scarier if they watched it alone instead of with others. Unlike the other user profiles, Fearful Horror Users are not watching horror to experience joy. They are using the genre specifically to experience fear. Fearful Horror Users also tended to score high on scales of agreeableness and low on scales of emotional stability (which just means that they are more sensitive to experiencing negative emotions or being emotionally reactive).

According to Clasen, women who love horror tended to fall more often into the Social Horror User and Fearful Horror User categories. This tracks with past studies, which, when contrasting measures of horror enjoyment between men and women, tend to demonstrate that women report more feelings of fear than men. What is special about Clasen's profiles is that they classify this fear experience as a motivator for consuming horror, whereas past studies equated fear with dislike or avoidance. Although there have been pretty consistent findings in research that cisgender men report a higher tendency to enjoy horror and seek it out, the gap is not as big as you might think. And although cisgender men and women tend to be the only genders recorded in these sorts of studies, I feel confident in stating that all genders have strong representation in the horror family.

So, now that we have that out of the way, let's explore some actual possibilities at the root of our shared love for horror.

COULD A LOVE FOR HORROR LIVE IN YOUR GENES?

More than attraction to other movie genres like dramas or comedies, a love for horror film feels like something innate, a personality trait. If personality traits are generally accepted to be a cocktail mix of nature (inherited genetic effects) and nurture (environmental and epigenetic effects), is it possible that part of why we love to be scared is written in our DNA?

While we should always be wary of studies that claim that a complex human trait can be boiled down to whether a single gene is switched on or off in any given person's DNA blueprint, researchers have proposed a few gene candidates whose expression may contribute to how we experience horror.

The first of these suggested gene locations is FKBP5. This gene has been associated with abnormal stress responses, and possible contributions to depression and anxiety. It has been of particular interest to researchers studying post-traumatic stress disorder (PTSD) who have found that PTSD developed more often than average among people experiencing traumatic events if they possessed certain expressions of the gene.

A promoter region of the SLC6A4 gene, 5-HTTLPR controls levels of serotonin, an important mood-stabilizing hormone, during threatening experiences, and the gene region's function has been associated with our personal sensitivity to stress. Studies have suggested that people who are carriers of a variant allele for 5-HTTLPR, called the S-allele, or short-allele, might experience bigger emotional reactions when exposed to negative imagery, like scared or angry faces. The short 5-HTTLPR promoter group also seems to demonstrate a great vigilance, or bias for paying attention, toward negative or stressful images, whereas people with two L-alleles (the long variant for the promoter region) tend to selectively avoid stressful images and show bias for paying attention to positive images. There may even be a relationship between 5-HTTLPR and our ability to disengage from the emotional content of horror scenes, which might point to one genetic reason why people might enjoy and watch more horror.

And, of course, as we mentioned in chapter 1, variant expressions of the COMT gene might produce hyper-startlers, who are more primed than the average moviegoer to have bigger reactions during jump scares.

But while these genetic components might influence how we process fear and horror movie content, none of them comes close to touching the idea of *enjoying* horror as entertainment. You might be more likely to enjoy horror if your parents enjoy horror just as a result of being exposed to horror throughout your development more often than someone raised in a family where horror is verboten. A love for horror may be contagious, but it doesn't appear to be hereditary.

SENSATION-SEEKING

Since the horror experience is so often associated with the adrenaline rush of the fight-or-flight response, researchers have focused a lot of attention on measuring the correlation between a love for horror and a personality metric known as the Sensation-Seeking Scale.

High sensation-seeking scores are associated with personalities that are more likely to be drawn to experiences that highly engage different modalities, ranging from being very interested in trying unusual foods to being very interested in trying extreme activities (like free climbing or bungee jumping). Contrary to popular belief about so-called adrenaline junkies: extreme athletes have often reported feeling very calm and "in the zone" rather than screaming with a surge of chaotic energy, a feeling that psychologist Mihály Csikszentmihályi described as the "flow state." The flow experience is characterized by being present and focused on the present moment, feeling in control of the moment and whatever you're doing, feeling unselfconscious, like time is distorted or standing still, and feeling like the act of doing whatever it is that you're doing is rewarding in and of itself. In other words: it feels pretty great.

To some extent, we all crave new experiences and new sensations. Marvin Zuckerman identified four scales of sensation-seeking traits:

- thrill- or adventure-seeking, or the desire to engage in risky activities (at the extreme end of this scale, think free diving or base jumping), even if no one else has successfully done the activity before;
- experience-seeking, or a desire for experiences

that are arousing on the level of your senses or cognitive processes;

- disinhibition, or spontaneous and hedonistic behaviors, like being drawn to sex, partying, drugs, gambling, or social drinking as sources of sensation and pleasure; and
- susceptibility to boredom.

High sensation–seekers might be more motivated to watch horror movies, to satisfy morbid curiosity as much as to take in thrilling content and gore, than people who rank low on sensation-seeking scales.

Research has produced inconsistent results where the Sensation-Seeking Scale is concerned, though. Taken overall, the scale doesn't produce a significant relationship between thrill-seekers and horror consumption, but we do see small associations on some of the individual scales. For example, a slight tendency was found for people who rank high in experience-seeking to be scared more by the natural than the supernatural in horror, and for people who score high on boredom susceptibility to seek out and enjoy opportunities to watch horror with others. When looking specifically at graphic horror, other research has suggested that a preference for graphic horror correlated with high disinhibition scores, moderately for boredom susceptibility and experience-seeking, and not at all for thrill- or adventure-seeking. If you feel pretty certain that you don't watch horror films for the rush, perhaps you watch it for some sort of release.

CATHARSIS THEORY

The idea of consuming media for cathartic effects is probably the oldest concept that we're addressing in this book. The idea was first put forth by Aristotle, whose teachings suggested that consuming tragedies (in Aristotle's time, roughly 384 to 322 B.C.E., this would take the form of plays and not movies) gave their audience an emotional release, an opportunity to purge negative feelings like sadness, fear, or anger. We hear echoes of this idea over and over again emerging from the mouths of horror filmmakers. Alfred Hitchcock once said, "One of television's greatest contributions is that it brought murder back into the home where it belongs. Seeing a murder on television can be good therapy. It can help work off one's antagonism." More than one horror philosopher has suggested that horror might be a way of exploring the taboo in a relatively safe and harmless way—but how do you measure that?

I've often made a habit of watching horror movies—especially treating myself to a horror movie in a theatre with a friend—when I'm having a particularly bad day. I usually joke that I need it for catharsis, to distract myself from negative feelings by conjuring *different*, more immediate negative feelings up on a big screen. While I usually feel better after doing this, catharsis is not the most likely explanation for my mood improvement. The fact that I feel better probably comes from the shared time with a friend (including a requisite venting session over fast food before the movie) and the distraction of watching a movie, no matter its plot or genre.

In terms of self-reporting, people usually report feeling more scared, rather than less scared, after watching a horror movie. In general, there is no evidence to support that horror media has any real catharsis effect, but if watching horror makes you personally feel better, then there's no harm in watching horror to improve your mood.

In a similar vein, others have proposed that we enjoy horror because it's a relatively safe and controlled way to experience scary or stressful situations, kind of like experiencing a worst-case scenario with training wheels. In chapter 2, we saw an entire history of the genre reflecting real fears as hyperreal horrors. We deal with real fears of a global pandemic by tuning in to movies where the world's population is being demolished by even gnarlier viruses; we wade through our anxieties about climate change by watching movies that show us the world ending catastrophically. Admittedly, there isn't any research that I've found that tests this idea—besides, how would you go about measuring this feeling of safety?—but it circles back to that old refrain: unlike with real life, if you get scared, you can repeat to yourself, *It's only a movie. It's only a movie. It's only a movie.*

What if this catharsis theory could have applications beyond safely experiencing fear? In 2021, researchers Becky Millar and Jonny Lee suggested that horror films might be useful tools for processing grief. In part, they suggest that this is because the way the staple horror movie monster disrupts lives often parallels the way that grief can disrupt people's lives. On top of that, a huge number of horror movies are centered around grief, and Millar and Lee note that these movies tend to follow a set structure:

1. The main character loses a loved one during Act 1 (or the film opens just after such a loss). The main character's day-to-day life is disrupted by grief.
2. The monster appears to radically disrupt the main character's understanding of reality and mirrors the disruption in the world caused by bereavement.

3. The main character defeats, evades, or tames the monster and, in turn, restores some balance to their emotional life.

According to Millar and Lee, grief-filled horror movies that fit this mold include *Don't Look Now* (1973, dir. Nicolas Roeg), *The Changeling* (1980, dir. Peter Medak), *The Descent* (2005, dir. Neil Marshall), *Lake Mungo* (2008, dir. Joel Anderson), *The Babadook* (2014, dir. Jennifer Kent), *Hereditary* (2018, dir. Ari Aster), and *Midsommar* (2019, dir. Ari Aster). I'm sure many, many more also match up.

Following this structure, people working through grief can connect with bereavement depicted on-screen, as well as see an end in the eventual defeat of the disruptive monster that allows the main character to restore their life to post-grief, post-monster balance. While it can't be relied upon as a solution, it appears that horror can serve as a useful coping tool for viewers experiencing fear, stress, or sorrow.

SNUGGLE UP TO HORROR

As I've mentioned, I definitely have more fun watching horror movies with other people than I do watching them alone. Sitting through scares with a friend means sharing in an emotional experience—and often serves to heighten that experience. The feeling is likewise amplified when you're sitting among strangers in a crowded theatre. Being hit at the same time by a jump scare and by another audience member screaming amplifies the startle effect—not to mention that the inevitable laughter that happens in a movie theatre crowd works like a charm to diffuse tension. As Wes

Craven once said, "if you scream and everyone else in the audience screams, you realize that your fears are not just within yourself, they're in other people as well, and that's strangely releasing." Sharing a horror movie also often means having someone to process the emotional experience with as it happens, whether it's by someone diffusing tension with laughter, or by having someone to express your tensions or apprehensions to.

It's often been said that if you really want to bond on a romantic movie date, then opt for a horror movie rather than a romantic comedy or tearjerker. The idea is founded in what sociologists have termed the Snuggle Theory. Thanks to socialization differences, the theory—put forward by Dolf Zillmann and his team in 1986—suggests that the act of watching a horror movie with an opposite-gender date will reinforce desirable gender roles such as "fearless macho men." (I swear, these are the exact words that Zillmann's paper uses.) The study was conducted with a framework that excluded anyone who wasn't a cisgender man or woman who reported opposite-gender attraction. (The study notes that one male participant did report homosexual attraction, but since he also reported heterosexual attraction—I guess there wasn't a box to tick for bisexuality—he wasn't dismissed as a subject.) As a commentary on gender, sexuality, and horror movies, you can take this study with as little or big a grain of salt as you wish.

To test his theory, Zillmann paired up undergraduate students with an opposite-gender movie-watching partner who would either behave indifferently, distressed, or demonstrate "mastery" toward a fourteen-minute clip from *Friday the 13th, Part III*. The movie-watching partners were also categorized as being of high initial attractiveness or low initial attractiveness (although the study is unclear as to how the two men and two women who were acting as movie companions were assigned to these *high-appeal* and *low-appeal* roles).

According to the study, men enjoyed horror movies most when they were paired with a woman who was distressed by the movie, and least when they were paired with a woman who had mastered the material (unless that woman was also initially perceived as desirable). One of the reasons suggested for why men might have found horror less enjoyable when watching with a woman who demonstrated mastery was the fact that they would perceive the clip as intrinsically less scary if it failed to scare their partner—a comment that I find endlessly funny. Women, on the other hand, apparently enjoyed the movie the least when their male counterpart was distressed and tended to rate their companion as more sexually attractive if they demonstrated the "mastery" condition, and more attractive if they were initially in the low-appeal category. Fearlessness did not make women companions more attractive to male participants.

There are a lot of bold conclusions that have emerged from this tiny study that looked at the behaviors of only thirty-six female and thirty-six male undergraduate students (not exactly a diverse pool of participants). This study is interesting and continues to be cited in most meta-analyses involving gender and horror, but it's also thirty-five years old and hasn't, to my knowledge, seen replication in more recent decades. Also, not to be nitpicky, but this claim is also based on responses to one single clip from *Friday the 13th, Part III*, not the full film, and not contrasting with other types of video clips, or even other types of horror. Other studies from that era suggested that slashers were favored less by women, so it's odd that a subgenre thought to be favored by men was selected for the study.

A more likely reason than antique stances on gender roles for why a horror movie might be a good choice for your next date might be *excitation-transfer theory* (coincidentally, a theory also first described by Zillmann). We mentioned excitation-transfer theory in chapter 1 as a possible explanation for why we laugh after we catch ourselves screaming at a jump scare, and, while I didn't mention it chapter 6, excitation-transfer theory is also often cited as a possible mechanism for transforming the pent-up arousal of seeing a horror movie into aggressive behaviors. Consider that pent-up arousal could instead be transformed into sexual arousal—not in a *horror makes you horny* kind of way, but in a way by which sharing a high arousal state with someone makes you feel closer to that person. Some studies have suggested that sharing unpleasant or painful experiences—on the milder end, eating extremely hot peppers together or having to do a strenuous, uncomfortable exercise; on the extreme end, surviving a traumatic event or fighting in a war together—can act as a sort of "social glue" to reinforce bonding and cooperation with another person. We've established throughout this book that horror movies contain stressful and uncomfortable moments by design. So, maybe sitting down to a scary movie with your crush might actually help you become a little bit closer.

This idea is also supported by Shelley Taylor's "tend and befriend" metaphor for social affiliation during times of stress, which suggests that humans are just as likely to turn toward social interactions, like seeking protection or comfort, as a stress response as they are to respond with a fight-or-flight reaction. This is based on the idea that some stressful experiences (watching a horror movie counts!) can promote the release of the hormone oxytocin. This release of oxytocin will also make you more sensitive to the effects of dopaminergic and opioid pathways in the brain, also known as the brain's reward systems, which will reinforce the whole ordeal as a positive experience if you have a positive social experience to couple it with. Be forewarned, though: Taylor also proposes that the converse is true: if your movie-watching buddy isn't very supportive, then that oxytocin surge might actually serve to deepen negative feelings toward them. This idea is reinforced by other studies that report that oxytocin can reinforce negative social feelings like schadenfreude, gloating, or envy.

Oxytocin has gotten a lot of hype in both the science world and in the media. Mainstream reporting channels often refer to oxytocin as the "hug hormone" or the "cuddle hormone" because it's been heavily implicated in social bonding, intimate bonding during sex, trust, and empathy. Experiments have reported that oxytocin release can have calming effects and make us more likely to open up about our emotions, even to strangers. But oxytocin is a bit more complicated than that.

Rather than being a miracle hormone that can make us all trust and love each other a little more if only we hug each other more, recent research suggests that oxytocin is more or less a regulatory hormone, doing its best to keep our brain and body in check by mediating a bunch of physiological processes, a state of relative equilibrium known as *homeostasis*. It definitely does *something* in our brains when we're sharing social experiences, but it's more likely that oxytocin's role is in anticipatory effects, or pulling our attention toward our interpersonal relationships and so making our feelings about those relationships feel amplified because we are focused on them, than it is in conjuring up our feelings toward those relationships, whether they be warm and fuzzy or uncomfortable.

In my time spent as a horror writer and in my time spent researching this book, I've met horror fans whose love for horror takes on countless shapes and spans horror's myriad subgenres to various degrees. Some horror fans will unabashedly consume any form of horror, from low-budget schlock to big studio oeuvres, with equal relish. Others will hyperfocus on their favorite skinny pie slices of the genre, reserving their energy exclusively for found footage or giallo. Some are casually obsessed fans who love horror in a way that consistently gets their butts into a cinema seat for every new horror release but doesn't demand engagement outside of the movie theatre; others are encyclopedic in their passion, able to draw from startlingly deep wells of horror trivia. While it appears that there might be some personality traits that might make some of us more likely to find horror sooner, it strikes me that our reasons and motivations for consuming horror are as nuanced and varied as the ways in which we love it. Whatever the shape of your love for horror, as long as it is in good faith toward other horror fans, it's a valid love for horror.

IN CONVERSATION WITH
ALEXANDRA HELLER-NICHOLAS

Dr. Alexandra Heller-Nicholas is a film critic, author, and academic from Melbourne, Australia, who writes about cult, horror, and exploitation film with an emphasis on gender politics, representations of sexual violence, and women's filmmaking.

Can you talk about what exactly makes a cult film? In what ways does the cult film overlap with horror?

As the name implies, cult films are films that—for better or for worse—conjure up a cult following. The magic to cult film is that it can't really be faked; cult film is about taste and reception, and as many fine scholars and critics have noted, there's a certain (sub)cultural cachet in having oppositional taste to that of the mainstream. It's this, in cult film terms, that leads to films that fall under the supposedly "so bad it's good" umbrella. What I love about cult film is that it really is not possible to set out to say "oh, I'm going to make a cult film"; cult audiences are much too savvy for such cynicism, and when people try, it's actually quite cringeworthy. And there are huge cult films that might have been meant for a mainstream audience and, although effectively tanking at the time, have through the years developed an enormous cult following—Paul Verhoeven's *Showgirls* (1995) and Elaine May's *Ishtar* (1987) are two big studio films that were very poorly received at the time to the point that they became punch lines to jokes, but in the decades since their original releases have garnered enormously passionate cult audiences.

As these films indicate, cult films and horror films are not synonymous, but that being said, of course, many horror films are cult films. Largely, I think, because there is from a cult film fan perspective something almost precious in finding pleasure in what academic Jeffrey Sconce once called "cultural detritus." In horror, this terrain of trash connoisseurship and cult fandom intersect frequently in lowbrow body horror terrain—stuff like Troma films or things like J. Michael Muro's *Street Trash* (1987). But again, cult films can also emerge (often over time) from the bigger studios; Karyn Kusama's initially widely disparaged *Jennifer's Body* (2009), for example, has been recently embraced by a huge cult audience who celebrate its feminist horror credentials, and we need look no further than Stanley Kubrick's *The Shining* (1980) for a case of what in the orthodox sense might be considered highbrow or auteurs cult film.

What makes a horror film stand out as a cult film?

Cult film is about reception. There are cases where you can see someone trying to make a cult film, and it almost verges on embarrassing; there's a process of reception when it comes to cult film that has no time for such commercial cynicism, as it really goes against the grain of what cult film is. What I find so fascinating about cult horror especially, however, is that taste categories such as "good" and "bad" and "highbrow" and "low-brow" ultimately fall by the wayside with cult film reception—there is, instead, something much closer to fascination, and that sense is held on a communal, discursive level (for example, have a look for how many think pieces there are on *Jennifer's Body* marking its ten-year anniversary which fall under the "this is a feminist masterpiece, how did we get it so wrong at the time?"). Again, we come back to that quite literal meaning of cult—there has to be a sort of critical mass of like-minded fans who approach a given text in a certain way, be it horror or otherwise, who share a perspective or an experience of a film that unites them. And in horror, that it's such a broadly dismissed, lowbrow form to begin with grants it a little more danger, makes it a little more subversive as a cult text.

In your work you've often discussed sensation/sensory experience; where horror is concerned, the sensory seems to be the thread that connects its various subgenres together. Am I way off in this remark?

I talk a lot about the sensory experience of horror because as a horror fan first and foremost, it's really how I am most rewarded by the genre. This is more than being frightened or scared—in fact, for me, they are the least interesting things perhaps a horror movie can do, because they too often are linked to overdone clichés like jump scares. My favorite horror films are those that overwhelm, confuse, disorient, and—through my eyes and ears—provoke other sensory responses. Laura U. Marks famously talked about the concept of "haptic visuality," and while horror was not something she was particularly interested in, for me that sense of feeling horror in a haptic or tactile way is always a precious, rare joy—it's more than goose bumps, almost a kind of visceral, bodily reaction.

That being said, while I think all horror subgenres are capable of provoking a sensory response—indeed some, like body horror, really speak for themselves—others might be more broadly intellectual, but still have the capacity to cause this sensory reaction. When I think of my own favorite horror films, on one hand we have things like Dario Argento's *Suspiria* (1977) and Andrzej Żuławski's *Possession* (1981) which in their own ways are aggressively focused on triggering a sensory response. But then something like Brad Anderson's *Session 9* (2001), which—on the surface at least—should be a typical haunted house movie, transcends that entirely and in ways that are still practically unfathomable to me, also becomes a primarily sensory experience rather than an intellectual riddle or mystery. Then again, in cult film, we also can't deny the "so bad it's good school"—I loathe this mode of reception as I think it's fundamentally snobbish, but there is certainly a joy that many audiences of cult horror film have which hinges on the "badness," and the lack of a film to fully capture or provoke a genuine sensory response.

Can you elaborate on the sensory as it connects to different forms of screen violence?

This very much changes from category to category. In giallo, for example, screen violence is almost baroque (as are the films themselves), and—like their descendant, the slasher film—scenes of violence are presented as spectacular vignettes where the sensory provocation is both tied frequently to sex, and also contained within certain narrative sections of the film. Body horror is less structured, perhaps, and it is the danger of that sense that the body horror can appear at any time that renders these films so exciting and, at the same time, extremely potent for subversive or transgressive themes—David

Cronenberg and Julia Ducournau are, of course, both masters of the form here. Rape-revenge is entirely different because it is such an enormously diverse category—there were rape-revenge films in westerns before they really became synonymous with horror, and it is still a trope that transcends genre. Absolutely scenes of sexual violence in these films can, have, and will continue to be used as a bad-taste titillating sexual spectacle, but as the post-#MeToo wake-up call to women-directed rape-revenge films has indicated (a tradition, by the way, that is not recent and goes back many, many decades), depictions of rape in the rape-revenge film can also, again, be used for subversive, ideological reasons rather than just providing a sensory provocation.

What aspect of horror are you currently digging into with your own work?

I'm someone who always has many fingers in many research pies; my work on women's horror filmmaking is still continuing, as is my work on rape-revenge film (I recently published a second edition of my book *Rape-Revenge Films: A Critical Study* to mark its tenth anniversary which has an entirely new chapter on women-directed rape-revenge films). I have a fascination with filmmakers who consciously seek to evoke powerful sensory responses in their audiences by using the language of genre in often abstract ways—rather than necessarily making genre films per se—and this has resulted in my co-editing books with John Edmond on Peter Strickland, Hélène Cattet, and Bruno Forzani, and a forthcoming collection on Lucile Hadžihalilović.

AFTERWORD

A horror movie is more than a sequence of frame after frame, in the same way that a painting is more than just paint on a canvas. Our experience in viewing a painting is shaped by the artist's use of light and shadow, by brushstrokes and textures, not to mention the past experiences and present emotional states that we bring into the viewing. While a horror film might not be considered fine art, it's no less complex in how it delivers on its experience. In researching this book, I got to pick apart the elements that form the parts of a horror movie experience that are shared across audiences, whether that audience is made up of casual horror fans, genre diehards, or the squeamish ones who got dragged along for the show. Monster design, soundscaping, and editing are the brushstrokes, the technique. Cultural anxieties and personal fear responses bring in the context and nuance.

I don't necessarily hope that this book changes how you watch horror movies. That's like wishing for a distracting cinematic experience (as someone who once had a stranger light a butane lighter under my theatre seat while I was just trying to mind my own business and watch *The Witch*, I wish anyone who reads this only the best when sharing a movie with a roomful of strangers). I do hope that for some people *Nightmare Fuel* might deepen their appreciation for the genre, provide new points of interest with which to engage with horror, or maybe inspire them to dip their toes into a subgenre that they previously swore was off-limits.

One of the most exciting things about this book is that, while it's finished, science isn't done with learning about fear, human emotions, and horror movies. The body of research can only grow, and maybe someday we'll uncover exactly why it is that we humans love to get scared.

ACKNOWLEDGMENTS

Huge thanks to my editor, Kristin Temple, for bringing her talents, perspective, and enthusiasm for horror to our collaboration. Thanks also to the folks at Tor Nightfire for producing *Nightmare Fuel*. Thank you to Jamie Stafford-Hill for designing killer cover art.

This book wouldn't exist without Maria Vicente, who is key for taking my *wouldn't these be cool?* ideas and transforming them into the beginnings of a book. I'm forever grateful.

Thank you to those who generously gave their time to answer my questions and support with research: Christopher Bloom, John Fawcett, Alexandra Heller-Nicholas, Jamie Kirkpatrick, Ronen Landa, Mary Beth McAndrews, Terry Mesnard, Rachel Reeves, and Alexandra West.

Writing a book about horror movies means watching a lot of horror movies, and this research was much more fun when I didn't have to watch them alone. A hearty thanks to my main horror movie–watching buddies, Cam Cope and Katrina Tisdale, as well as Brittany Baker, Joshua Osika, Natalie Eisen, and Grayson McNamara.

Thank you to my family, who continue to support me

even though no one quite gets how I ended up being the only one of us who likes horror. I don't get it either.

And last, but never least, to my wife, Cora Eckert. Thank you for watching *The Faculty* with me more times than is reasonable. I love you.

MOVIES WATCHED

I watched *a lot* of horror films to write this book. Some I'd seen before, but many I watched for the first time. This isn't the full list of movies that I watched; but rather every horror and horror-adjacent movie that got a mention in this book. If you ever need an excuse to finally visit your horror blind spots (not that you ever *need* an excuse), I highly recommend writing a book on the subject.

INTRODUCTION

Black Sunday (1960, dir. Mario Bava)
Final Destination (2000, dir. James Wong)
Get Out (2017, dir. Jordan Peele)
Hell Night (1981, dir. Tom DeSimone)
Hereditary (2018, dir. Ari Aster)
It Follows (2014, dir. David Robert Mitchell)
Jaws (1977, dir. Steven Spielberg)
Peeping Tom (1960, dir. Michael Powell)
Psycho (1960, dir. Alfred Hitchcock)
Scream (1996, dir. Wes Craven)
The Exorcist (1976, dir. William Friedkin)
The Silence of the Lambs (1991, dir. Jonathan Demme)
The Witch (2015, dir. Robert Eggers)

CHAPTER 1. THIS IS YOUR BRAIN ON HORROR

10 Cloverfield Lane (2016, dir. Dan Trachtenberg)

Aliens (1986, dir. James Cameron)

A Nightmare on Elm Street (1984, dir. Wes Craven)

Cat People (1942, dir. Jacques Tourneur)

Friday the 13th (1980, dir. Sean S. Cunningham)

Halloween (1978, dir. John Carpenter)

Hereditary (2018, dir. Ari Aster)

Jurassic Park (1993, dir. Steven Spielberg)

Lights Out (2013, dir. David F. Sandberg)

Lights Out (2016, dir. David F. Sandberg)

Martyrs (2008, dir. Pascal Laugier)

My Friend Dahmer (2017, dir. Marc Meyers)

Rabid (1977, dir. David Cronenberg)

Raw (2016, dir. Julia Ducournau)

Scream (1996, dir. Wes Craven)

Shivers (1975, dir. David Cronenberg)

Sinister (2012, dir. Scott Derrickson)

Split (2016, dir. M. Night Shyamalan)

Suspiria (1977, dir. Dario Argento)

The Blair Witch Project (1999, dirs. Eduardo Sánchez and Daniel Myrick)

The Brood (1979, dir. David Cronenberg)

The Exorcist III (1990, dir. William Peter Blatty)

The Fly (1986, dir. David Cronenberg)

The Others (2001, dir. Alejandro Amenábar)

The Poughkeepsie Tapes (2007, dir. John Erick Dowdle)

The Shining (1980, dir. Stanley Kubrick)

The Silence of the Lambs (1991, dir. Jonathan Demme)

The Texas Chain Saw Massacre (1974, dir. Tobe Hooper)

Videodrome (1983, dir. David Cronenberg)

We Summon the Darkness (2019, Marc Meyers)

You're Next (2011, dir. Adam Wingard)

CHAPTER 2. A BRIEF HISTORY OF HORROR

13 Ghosts (1960, dir. William Castle)

A Nightmare on Elm Street (1984, dir. Wes Craven)

Battle Royale (2000, dir. Kinji Fukasaku)

Beginning of the End (1957, dir. Bert I. Gordon)

Black Christmas (1974, dir. Bob Clark)

Black Christmas (2019, dir. Sophia Takal)

Black Devil Doll from Hell (1984, dir. Chester Novell
Turner)

Blackenstein (1973, dir. William A. Levey)

Black Xmas (2006, dir. Glen Morgan)

Blacula (1972, dir. William Crain)

Blood and Black Lace (1964, dir. Mario Bava)

Blood Cult (1985, dir. Christopher Lewis)

Blood Feast (1963, dir. Herschell Gordon Lewis)

Candyman (1992, dir. Bernard Rose)

Candyman (2021, dir. Nia DaCosta)

Cannibal Holocaust (1980, dir. Ruggero Deodato)

Contagion (2011, dir. Steven Soderbergh)

Critters (1986, dir. Stephen Herek)

Dark Water (2002, dir. Hideo Nakata)

Dark Water (2005, dir. Walter Salles)

Dracula (1931, dirs. Tod Browning and Karl Freund)

Fatal Attraction (1987, dir. Adrian Lyne)

Faust et Méphistophélès (1903, dir. Alice Guy)

Fear in the Dark (1991, dir. Dominic Murphy)

Final Destination (2000, dir. James Wong)

Frankenstein (1910, dir. J. Searle Dawley)

Frankenstein (1931, dir. James Whale)

Freaks (1932, dir. Tod Browning)

Friday the 13th (1980, dir. Sean S. Cunningham)

Ganja and Hess (1973, dir. Bill Gunn)

Get Out (2017, dir. Jordan Peele)

Ginger Snaps (2000, dir. John Fawcett)

Godzilla (1954, dir. Ishirō Honda)

Gremlins (1984, dir. Joe Dante)

Gremlins 2: The New Batch (1990, dir. Joe Dante)

Halloween (1978, dir. John Carpenter)

Hereditary (2018, dir. Ari Aster)

High Tension (2003, dir. Alexandre Aja)

Host (2020, dir. Rob Savage)

Hostel (2005, dir. Eli Roth)

House of Wax (1953, dir. André De Toth)

House of Wax (2005, dir. Jaume Collet-Serra)

I Drink Your Blood (1970, dir. David E. Durston)

Invasion of the Body Snatchers (1956, dir. Don Siegel)

It (1990, dir. Tommy Lee Wallace)

It's Alive (1974, dir. Larry Cohen)

Jizo the Spook (1898, dir. unknown)*

Kiss the Girls (1997, dir. Gary Fleder)

Le château hanté (1897, dir. Georges Méliès)

Le manoir du diable (1896, dir. Georges Méliès)

M (1931, dir. Fritz Lang)

Martyrs (2008, dir. Pascal Laugier)

Matango (1963, dir. Ishirō Honda)

Night of the Living Dead (1968, dir. George A. Romero)

Nosferatu (1922, dir. Friedrich Wilhelm Murnau)

Parasite (2019, dir. Bong Joon-ho)

Parents (1989, dir. Bob Balaban)

Peeping Tom (1960, dir. Michael Powell)

Photographing a Ghost (1898, dir. G. A. Smith)

Psycho (1960, dir. Alfred Hitchcock)

Pulse (2001, dir. Kiyoshi Kurosawa)

Rabid (1977, dir. David Cronenberg)

Raw (2016, dir. Julia Ducournau)

Resurrection of a Corpse (1898, dir. unknown)*

Ringu (1998, dir. Hideo Nakata)

Rosemary's Baby (1976, dir. Roman Polanski)

Saw (2004, dir. James Wan)

Scream (1996, dir. Wes Craven)

Scream 3 (2000, dir. Wes Craven)

Se7en (1996, dir. David Fincher)

Shivers (1975, dir. David Cronenberg)

Single White Female (1992, dir. Barbet Schroeder)

Society (1989, dir. Brian Yuzna)

Squirm (1976, Jeff Lieberman)

Straw Dogs (1971, dir. Sam Peckinpah)

Sugar Hill (1974, dir. Paul Maslansky)

Suicide Club (2001, dir. Sion Sono)

Tarantula! (1955, dir. Jack Arnold)

The Bird with the Crystal Plumage (1970, dir. Dario Argento)

The Black Scorpion (1957, dir. Edward Ludwig)

The Blob (1958, dirs. Irvin S. Yeaworth, Jr., and Russell S. Doughten, Jr., uncredited)

The Blood on Satan's Claw (1971, dir. Piers Haggard)

The Brood (1979, dir. David Cronenberg)

The Cabinet of Dr. Caligari (1920, dir. Robert Wiene)

The Craft (1996, dir. Andrew Fleming)

The Creature from the Black Lagoon (1954, dir. Jack Arnold)

The Driller Killer (1979, dir. Abel Ferrara)

The Exorcist (1973, dir. William Friedkin)

The Faculty (1997, dir. Robert Rodriguez)

The Gate (1987, dir. Tibor Takács)

The Girl Who Knew Too Much (1963, dir. Mario Bava)

The Grudge (2004, dir. Takashi Shimizu)

The Hand That Rocks the Cradle (1992, dir. Curtis Hanson)

The Hunchback of Notre Dame (1923, dir. Wallace Worsley)

The Invisible Man (1933, dir. James Whale)

The Last House on the Left (1972, dir. Wes Craven)

The Lawnmower Man (1992, dir. Brett Leonard)

Them! (1954, dir. Gordon Douglas)

The Matrix (1999, dirs. Lilly Wachowski and Lana Wachowski)

The Mummy (1932, dir. Karl Freund)

The Omen (1976, dir. Richard Donner)

The Phantom of the Opera (1925, dir. Rupert Julian)

The Platform (2020, dir. Galder Gaztelu-Urrutia)

The Ring (2002, dir. Gore Verbinski)

The Silence of the Lambs (1991, dir. Jonathan Demme)

The Slumber Party Massacre (1981, dir. Amy Holden Jones)

The Slumber Party Massacre II (1987, dir. Deborah Brock)

The Stepford Wives (1975, dir. Bryan Forbes)

The Texas Chain Saw Massacre (1974, dir. Tobe Hooper)

The Thing from Another World (1951, dir. Christian Nyby)

The Town That Dreaded Sundown (1976, dir. Charles B. Pierce)

The Trollenberg Terror (1958, dir. Quentin Lawrence)

The War of the Worlds (1953, dir. Byron Haskin)

The Wicker Man (1973, dir. Robin Hardy)

The Witch (2015, dir. Robert Eggers)

The Wolf Man (1941, dir. George Waggner)

They Live (1988, dir. John Carpenter)

Thir13en Ghosts (2001, dir. Steve Beck)

Turistas (2006, dir. John Stockwell)

Us (2019, dir. Jordan Peele)

Uzumaki (2000, dir. Higuchinsky)

Videodrome (1982, dir. David Cronenberg)

X-Ray Fiend (1897, dir. G. A. Smith)

CHAPTER 3. HOW TO MAKE A MONSTER

28 Weeks Later (2007, dir. Juan Carlos Fresnadillo)

Alien (1979, dir. Ridley Scott)

Aliens (1986, dir. James Cameron)

Annabelle: Creation (2017, dir. David F. Sandberg)

Attack the Block (2011, dir. Joe Cornish)

Bird Box (2018, dir. Susanne Bier)

Blade II (2002, dir. Guillermo del Toro)

Cloverfield (2008, dir. Matt Reeves)

Crawl (2019, dir. Alexandre Aja)

Dark Star (1974, dir. John Carpenter)

Dawn of the Dead (1978, dir. George A. Romero)

Dawn of the Dead (2004, dir. Zack Snyder)

Dog Soldiers (2002, dir. Neil Marshall)

Eight-Legged Freaks (2002, dir. Ellory Elkayem)

Gremlins (1984, dir. Joe Dante)

Halloween (1978, dir. John Carpenter)

Hatchet (2006, dir. Adam Green)

In the Mouth of Madness (1995, dir. John Carpenter)

Invasion of the Body Snatchers (1978, dir. Philip Kaufman)

It (2017, dir. Andrés Muschietti)

It: Chapter Two (2019, dir. Andrés Muschietti)

It Follows (2014, dir. David Robert Mitchell)

Jurassic Park (1993, dir. Steven Spielberg)

Lake Placid (1999, dir. Steve Miner)

Mimic (1997, dir. Guillermo del Toro)

Night of the Creeps (1986, dir. Fred Dekker)

Orphan (2009, dir. Jaume Collet-Serra)

Ouija: Origin of Evil (2016, dir. Mike Flanagan)

Pan's Labyrinth (2006, dir. Guillermo del Toro)

Phenomena (1985, dir. Dario Argento)

Poltergeist (1982, dir. Tobe Hooper)

Red Dragon (2002, dir. Brett Ratner)

Rosemary's Baby (1967, dir. Roman Polanski)

Silent Hill (2006, dir. Christophe Gans)

Slither (2006, dir. James Gunn)

Tales of Halloween (2015, dir. Axelle Carolyn)

Terminator 2: Judgment Day (1991, dir. James Cameron)

The Amityville Horror (1979, dir. Stuart Rosenberg)

The Babadook (2014, dir. Jennifer Kent)

The Beast Within: The Making of Alien (2003, dir. Charles de Lauzirika)

The Blob (1958, dirs. Irvin S. Yeaworth, Jr., and Russell S. Doughten, Jr., uncredited)

The Brood (1979, dir. David Cronenberg)

The Descent (2005, dir. Neil Marshall)

The Exorcist (1973, dir. William Friedkin)

The Haunting of Bly Manor (2020, showrunner Mike Flanagan)

The Host (2006, dir. Bong Joon-ho)

The Howling (1981, dir. Joe Dante)

The Invisible Man (2020, dir. Leigh Whannell)

The Mist (2007, dir. Frank Darabont)

The Phantom of the Opera (1925, dir. Rupert Julian)

The Poughkeepsie Tapes (2007, dir. John Erick Dowdle)

The Ritual (2017, dir. David Bruckner)

The Shape of Water (2017, dir. Guillermo del Toro)

The Silence (2019, dir. John R. Leonetti)

The Stuff (1985, dir. Larry Cohen)

The Terminator (1984, dir. James Cameron)

The Thing (1982, dir. John Carpenter)

Total Recall (1990, dir. Paul Verhoeven)

Tremors (1990, dir. Ron Underwood)

Trick 'r Treat (2007, dir. Michael Dougherty)

Twilight (2008, dir. Catherine Hardwicke)

Us (2019, dir. Jordan Peele)

CHAPTER 4. PUTTING FEAR IN YOUR EARS

1BR (2019, dir. David Marmor)

28 Days Later (2002, dir. Danny Boyle)

A Quiet Place (2018, dir. John Krasinski)

At the Devil's Door (2014, dir. Nicholas McCarthy)

Blair Witch (2016, dir. Adam Wingard)

Book of Shadows: Blair Witch 2 (2000, dir. Joe Berlinger)

Eloise (2016, dir. Robert Legato)

Halloween (1978, dir. John Carpenter)

Irréversible (2002, dir. Gaspar Noé)

Jaws (1975, dir. Steven Spielberg)

Paranormal Activity (2007, dir. Oren Peli)

Psycho (1960, dir. Alfred Hitchcock)

Shaun of the Dead (2004, dir. Edgar Wright)

The Blair Witch Project (1999, dirs. Eduardo Sánchez and Daniel Myrick)

The Innocents (1961, dir. Jack Clayton)

The Pact (2012, dir. Nicholas McCarthy)

The Shining (1980, dir. Stanley Kubrick)

CHAPTER 5. WHY SOME SCARES STICK WITH YOU

Alien (1979, dir. Ridley Scott)

Aliens (1986, dir. James Cameron)

Arachnophobia (1990, dir. Frank Marshall)

A Tale of Two Sisters (2003, dir. Kim Jee-woon)

Carved (2007, dir. Kōji Shiraishi)

Child's Play (1988, dir. Tom Holland)

Deep Star Six (1989, dir. Sean S. Cunningham)

E.T.: The Extra-Terrestrial (1982, dir. Steven Spielberg)

Friday the 13th (1980, dir. Sean S. Cunningham)

Ginger Snaps (2000, dir. John Fawcett)

Gremlins (1984, dir. Joe Dante)

It (1990, dir. Tommy Lee Wallace)

It (2017, dir. Andrés Muschietti)

Jaws (1975, dir. Steven Spielberg)

Little Shop of Horrors (1986, dir. Frank Oz)

Night of the Living Dead (1968, dir. George A. Romero)

Poltergeist (1982, dir. Tobe Hooper)

Psycho (1960, dir. Alfred Hitchcock)

Psycho 2 (1983, dir. Richard Franklin)

Raiders of the Lost Ark (1981, dir. Steven Spielberg)

Scream (1996, dir. Wes Craven)

Suspiria (1977, dir. Dario Argento)

Suspiria (2018, dir. Luca Guadagnino)

The Blair Witch Project (1999, dirs. Eduardo Sánchez and Daniel Myrick)

The Day the Earth Stood Still (1951, dir. Robert Wise)

The Last House on the Left (1972, dir. Wes Craven)

The Mangler (1995, dir. Tobe Hooper)

The Ring (2002, dir. Gore Verbinski)

The Texas Chain Saw Massacre (1974, dir. Tobe Hooper)

CHAPTER 6. VIOLENCE AND MAYHEM

American Psycho (2000, dir. Mary Harron)

Beetlejuice (1988, dir. Tim Burton)

Black Christmas (1974, dir. Bob Clark)

Child's Play 2 (1990, dir. John Lafia)

Child's Play 3 (1991, dir. Jack Bender)

Exorcist II: The Heretic (1977, dir. John Boorman)

Friday the 13th, Part 2 (1981, dir. Steve Miner)

Greener Grass (2019, dirs. Jocelyn DeBoer and Dawn Luebbe)

Guinea Pig 2: Flower of Flesh and Blood (1985, dir. Hideshi Hino)

Maniac (1980, dir. William Lustig)

Marble Hornets (2009–2014, dirs. Joseph DeLage and Troy Wagner)

Mercy Black (2019, dir. Owen Egerton)

Natural Born Killers (1994, dir. Oliver Stone)

Oldboy (2003, dir. Park Chan-wook)

Pet Sematary (1989, dir. Mary Lambert)

Saw (2004, dir. James Wan)

Scream (1996, dir. Wes Craven)

Slender Man (2018, dir. Sylvain White)

Taxidermia (2007, dir. György Pálfi)

The Evil Dead (1981, dir. Sam Raimi)

The Exorcist III (1990, dir. William Peter Blatty)

The Killers (1964, dir. Don Siegel)

The Purge (2013, dir. James DeMonaco)

The Silence of the Lambs (1991, dir. Jonathan Demme)

The Toolbox Murders (1978, dir. Dennis Donnelly)

Tusk (2014, dir. Kevin Smith)

Un chien andalou (1929, dir. Luis Buñuel)

CHAPTER 7. BLOOD, GORE, AND BODY HORROR

28 Days Later (2002, dir. Danny Boyle)

A Clockwork Orange (1971, dir. Stanley Kubrick)

Afflicted (2013, dirs. Derek Lee and Clif Prowse)

Alien (1979, dir. Ridley Scott)

American Mary (2012, dirs. Jen Soska and Sylvia Soska)

An American Werewolf in London (1981, dir. John Landis)

Audition (1999, dir. Takashi Miike)

Bite (2015, dir. Chad Archibald)

Black Christmas (1974, dir. Bob Clark)

Blood Feast (1963, dir. Herschell Gordon Lewis)

Carrie (1976, dir. Brian De Palma)

Dawn of the Dead (1978, dir. George A. Romero)

Dead Ringers (1988, dir. David Cronenberg)

Deep Red (1975, dir. Dario Argento)

Don't Look Now (1973, dir. Nicolas Roeg)

Evil Dead (2013, dir. Fede Álvarez)

Evil Dead 2 (1987, dir. Sam Raimi)

Friday the 13th (1980, dir. Sean S. Cunningham)

Funny Games (1997, dir. Michael Haneke)

Funny Games (2007, dir. Michael Haneke)

Ginger Snaps (2000, dir. John Fawcett)

Halloween (1978, dir. John Carpenter)

Jaws (1975, dir. Steven Spielberg)

Orphan Black (2013, showrunners John Fawcett and Graeme Manson)

Prevenge (2015, dir. Alice Lowe)

Psycho (1960, dir. Alfred Hitchcock)

Reservoir Dogs (1992, dir. Quentin Tarantino)

Rosemary's Baby (1968, dir. Roman Polanski)

Saw (2004, dir. James Wan)

Scream 4 (2011, dir. Wes Craven)

Spontaneous (2020, dir. Brian Duffield)

Suspiria (1977, dir. Dario Argento)

Teeth (2007, dir. Mitchell Lichtenstein)

The Exorcist (1976, dir. William Friedkin)

The Fly (1986, dir. David Cronenberg)

The Human Centipede (2009, dir. Tom Six)

The Last Exorcism (2010, dir. Daniel Stamm)

The Mortuary Collection (2019, dir. Ryan Spindell)

The Omen (1976, dir. Richard Donner)

The Thing (1982, dir. John Carpenter)

Un chien andalou (1929, dir. Luis Buñuel)

Would You Rather? (2012, David Guy Levy)

CHAPTER 8. HORROR'S LONG-LASTING APPEAL

Antichrist (2009, dir. Lars von Trier)

Beetlejuice (1988, dir. Tim Burton)

Cannibal Holocaust (1980, dir. Ruggero Deodato)

Children of the Corn (1984, dir. Fritz Kiersch)

Coraline (2009, dir. Henry Selick)

Don't Look Now (1973, dir. Nicolas Roeg)

Friday the 13th, Part III (1982, dir. Steve Miner)

Hereditary (2018, dir. Ari Aster)

Hocus Pocus (1993, dir. Kenny Ortega)

Jennifer's Body (2009, dir. Karyn Kusama)

Kiss the Girls (1997, dir. Gary Fleder)

Lake Mungo (2008, dir. Joel Anderson)

Midsommar (2019, dir. Ari Aster)

Possession (1980, dir. Andrzej Żuławski)

Session 9 (2001, dir. Brad Anderson)

Single White Female (1992, dir. Barbet Schroeder)

Street Trash (1987, dir. J. Michael Munro)

Suspiria (1977, dir. Dario Argento)

The Babadook (2014, dir. Jennifer Kent)

The Changeling (1980, dir. Peter Medak)

The Descent (2005, dir. Neil Marshall)

The Game (1997, dir. David Fincher)

Them (2006, dirs. David Moreau and Xavier Palud)

The People Under the Stairs (1991, dir. Wes Craven)

The Shining (1980, dir. Stanley Kubrick)

The Texas Chain Saw Massacre (1974, dir. Tobe Hooper)

* Okay, I couldn't actually watch these two because they are considered to be lost films, but both are mentioned in the text and deserve to be featured here.

FURTHER READING

Nightmare Fuel is the product of years of swimming through existing research ranging from human fear responses, to human interactions with scary and violent media, and back again. This reference list isn't exhaustive, but it will give you a good snapshot of what informed the making of this book.

INTRODUCTION

Carroll, Noël. "The nature of horror." *The Journal of Aesthetics and Art Criticism* 46, no. 1 (1987): 51–59. https://doi.org/10.2307/431308.

Clover, Carol J. *Men, Women, and Chain Saws: Gender in the Modern Horror Film.* Princeton University Press, 1992.

CHAPTER 1. THIS IS YOUR BRAIN ON HORROR

Acharya, S., and S. Shukla. "Mirror neurons: Enigma of the metaphysical modular brain." *Journal of Natural Science, Biology, and Medicine* 3, no. 2 (2012): 118–24. https://doi.org/10.4103/0976-9668.101878.

Baird, Robert. "The startle effect: Implications for spectator cognition and media theory." *Film Quarterly* 53, no. 3 (2000): 12–24. https://doi.org/10.2307/1213732.

Bastos, Aline, et al. "Stop or move: Defensive strategies in humans." *Behavioural Brain Research* 302 (2015): S48-S48. https://doi.org/10.1016/j.bbr.2016.01.043.

Bayle, D. J., M. A. Henaff, and P. Krolak-Salmon. "Unconsciously perceived fear in peripheral vision alerts the limbic system: A MEG study." *PLOS One* 4, no. 12 (2009): e8207. https://doi.org/10.1371/journal.pone.0008207.

Gallup, G. G. "Tonic immobility: The role of fear and predation." *The Psychological Record* 27 (1977): 41–61. https://doi.org/10.1007/BF03394432.

Hagenaars, Muriel A., Karin Roelofs, and John F. Stins. "Human freezing in response to affective films." *Anxiety, Stress & Coping* 27, no. 1 (2014): 27–37. https://doi.org/:10.1080/10615806.2013.809420.

Kilner, J. M., and R. N. Lemon. "What we know currently about mirror neurons." *Current Biology* 23, no. 23 (2013): R1057-R1062. https://doi.org/10.1016/J.CUB.2013.10.051.

Maier, S., et al. "Clarifying the role of the rostral dmPFC/dACC in fear/anxiety: Learning, appraisal or expression?" *PLOS One* 7, no. 11 (2012): e50120. https://doi.org/10.1371/journal.pone.0050120.

Morales, Andrea C., Eugenia C. Wu, and Gavan J. Fitzsimons. "How Disgust Enhances the Effectiveness of Fear Appeals." *Journal of Marketing Research* 49, no. 3 (2012): 383–93. https://doi.org/10.1509/jmr.07.0364.

Straube, T., et al. "Neural representation of anxiety and personality during exposure to anxiety-provoking and neutral scenes from scary movies." *Human Brain Mapping* 31 (2010): 36–47.

Volchan, Eliane, et al. "Is there tonic immobility in humans? Biological evidence from victims of traumatic stress." *Biological Psychology* 88 (2011): 13–19. https://doi.org/10.1016/j.biopsycho.2011.06.002.

CHAPTER 2. A BRIEF HISTORY OF HORROR

Allmer, P., D. Huxley, and E. Brick (Eds.). *European Nightmares: Horror Cinema in Europe Since 1945*. Wallflower Press, 2012.

Balmain, Colette. *Introduction to Japanese Horror Film*. Edinburgh University Press, 2008.

Clover, Carol J. *Men, Women, and Chain Saws: Gender in the Modern Horror Film*. Princeton University Press, 1992.

Cowan, D. E. *Sacred Terror: Religion and Horror on the Silver Screen*. Baylor University Press, 2016.

"Fright Exclusive Interview: Bob Clark." Icons of Fright, 2005. http://www.iconsoffright.com/IV_BClark.htm.

Grant, B. K. *The Dread of Difference: Gender and the Horror Film*. University of Texas Press, 1996.

Jones, D. *Horror: A Thematic History in Fiction and Film*. Bloomsbury Academic, 2002.

Keesey, Douglas. *Twenty First Century Horror Films*. Kamera Books, 2017.

Kerner, A. M. *Torture Porn in the Wake of 9/11: Horror, Exploitation, and the Cinema of Sensation.* Rutgers University Press, 2015.

Mallory, Michael. *Universal Studios Monsters: A Legacy of Horror.* Universe Publishing, 2009.

McRoy, Jay. *Nightmare Japan: Contemporary Japanese Horror Cinema,* Ernest Mathijs and Steven Jay Schneider (Eds.). Rodopi, 2008.

West, Alexandra. *The 1990s Teen Horror Cycle: Final Girls and a New Hollywood Formula.* McFarland, 2018.

Zinoman, J. *Shock Value: How a Few Eccentric Outsiders Gave Us Nightmares, Conquered Hollywood, and Invented Modern Horror.* Penguin Press, 2011.

CHAPTER 3. HOW TO MAKE A MONSTER

Adolphs, R. "What does the amygdala contribute to social cognition?" *Annals of the New York Academy of Sciences* 1191 (2010): 42–61. https://doi.org/10.1111/j.1749-6632.2010.05445.x; pmid: 20392275.

Apicella, C. L., et al. "Facial averageness and attractiveness in an isolated population of hunter-gatherers." *Perception* 36 (2007): 1813. https://doi.org/10.1068/p5601.

Bonhommeau, S., et al. "Eating up the world's food web and the human trophic level." *PNAS* 110, no. 51 (2013): 20617–20. https://doi.org/10.1073/pnas.1305827110.

Cheetham, M., P. Suter, and L. Jäncke. "The human likeness dimension of the 'uncanny valley hypothesis': Behavioral and functional MRI findings." *Frontiers in Human Neuroscience* 5, no. 126 (2011). https://doi.org/10.3389/fnhum.2011.00126.

Chien-Chung Chen, Kai-Ling C. Kao, and Christopher W. Tyler. "Face configuration processing in the human brain: The role of symmetry." *Cerebral Cortex* 17, no. 6 (2007): 1423–32. https://doi.org/10.1093/cercor/bhl054.

Crawfurd, J. "On the physical and mental characteristics of the Negro." *Transactions of the Ethnological Society of London* 4 (1866): 212–39. https://doi.org/:10.2307/3014290.

Davey, G. C. L. "Characteristics of individuals with fear of spiders." *Anxiety Research* 4, no. 4 (1991): 299–314. https://doi.org/10.1080/08917779208248798.

Feeley, K. J., and B. Machovina. "Increasing preference for beef magnifies human impact on world's food web." *PNAS* 111, no. 9 (2014): E794. https://doi.org/10.1073/pnas.1323071111.

Fischoff, Stuart, et al. "Favorite movie monsters and their psychological appeal." *Imagination, Cognition and Personality* 22, no. 4 (2003): 401–26. https://doi.org/10.2190/CJ94-83FR-7HQW-2JK4.

Fischoff, S., et al. "The psychological appeal of movie monsters." *Journal of Media Psychology* 10 (2005): 1–33.

Freud, S. "The uncanny." In J. Strachey (Ed.), *Standard Edition of the Complete Psychological Works of Sigmund Freud* (pp. 219–56). Hogarth Press, 1919/1955.

Greenberg, Jeff, Sheldon Solomon, and Tom Pyszczynski. "Terror management theory of self-esteem and cultural worldviews: Empirical assessments and conceptual refinements." *Advances in Experimental Social Psychology* 29 (1997): 61–139. https://doi.org/10.1016/S0065-2601(08)60016-7.

Griffin, A. M., and J. H. Langlois. "Stereotype directionality and attractiveness stereotyping: Is beauty good or is ugly bad?" *Social Cognition* 24 (2006): 187. https://doi.org/10.1521/soco.2006.24.2.187.

Hanson, David, et al. "Upending the uncanny valley." *Proceedings of the National Conference on Artificial Intelligence* 4 (2005): 1728–29.

Hayakawa, S., N. Kawai, and N. Masataka. "The influence of color on snake detection in visual search in human children." *Scientific Reports* 1, no. 80 (2011). https://doi.org/10.1038/srep00080.

Heberlein, A. S., and R. Adolphs. "Impaired spontaneous anthropomorphizing despite intact perception and social knowledge." *PNAS* 101 (2004): 7487–91. https://doi.org/10.1073/pnas.0308220101; pmid: 15123799.

Ho, C.-C., K. F. MacDorman, and Z. A. Pramono. "Human emotion and the uncanny valley: A GLM, MDS, and Isomap analysis of robot video ratings." *Proceedings of the 3rd ACM/IEEE International Conference on Human Robot Interaction, HRI '08* (2008): 169–76. https://doi.org/10.1145/1349822.1349845.

Kawai, N., and H. He. "Breaking snake camouflage: Humans detect snakes more accurately than other animals under less discernible visual conditions." *PLOS One* 11, no. 10 (2016): e0164342. https://doi.org/10.1371/journal.pone.0164342.

Ketelaar, T. "Lions, tigers, and bears, oh God! How the ancient problem of predator detection may lie beneath the modern link between religion and horror." *Behavioural and Brain Sciences* 27 (2004): 740–41.

Lovett, Laura L. "'Fitter families for future firesides': Florence Sherbon and popular eugenics." *The Public Historian* 29, no. 3 (2007): 69–85. www.jstor.org/stable/10.1525/tph.2007.29.3.69.

Masataka, N., S. Hayakawa, and N. Kawai. "Human young children as well as adults demonstrate 'superior' rapid snake detection when typical striking posture is displayed by the snake." *PLOS One* 5 (2010): e15122.

Mori, M. "The uncanny valley." *Energy* 7 (1970): 33–35.

Mormann, F., et al. "A category-specific response to animals in the right human amygdala." *Nature Neuroscience* 14 (2011): 1247–49.

Morris, M. R., et al. "Fluctuating asymmetry indicates the optimization of growth rate over developmental stability." *Functional Ecology* 26 (2012): 723. https://doi.org/10.1111/j.1365-2435.2012.01983.x.

Pallett, P. M., et al. "New 'golden' ratios for facial beauty." *Vision Research* 50 (2009): 149. https://doi.org/10.1016/j.visres.2009.11.003.

Richerson, P. J., and R. Boyd. *Not by Genes Alone: How Culture Transformed Human Evolution*. University of Chicago Press, 2005.

Roopnarine, P. D. "Humans are apex predators." *PNAS* 111, no. 9 (2014): e796. https://doi.org/10.1073/pnas.1323645111.

Rosenthal-von der Pütten, A. M., et al. "Neural mechanisms for accepting and rejecting artificial social partners in the uncanny valley." *Journal of Neuroscience* 39, no. 33 (2019): 6555–70. https://doi.org/10.1523/JNEUROSCI.2956-18.2019.

Saxe, R., and A. Wexler. "Making sense of another mind: The role of the right temporo-parietal junction." *Neuropsychologia* 43, no.10 (2005): 1391–99. https://doi.org/10.1016/j.neuropsychologia.2005.02.013.

Schiller, D., et al. "A neural mechanism of first impressions." *Nature Neuroscience* 12 (2009): 508–14. https://doi.org/10.1038/nn.2278; pmid: 19270690.

Selden, Steven. "Transforming better babies into fitter families: Archival resources and the history of the American eugenics movement, 1908–1930." *Proceedings of the American Philosophical Society* 149, no. 2 (2005): 199. EBSCO host.

Seligman, M. E. "Phobias and preparedness." *Behavior Therapy* 2, no. 3 (1971): 307–20. https://doi.org/10.1016/S0005-7894(71)80064-3.

Sipos, Thomas M. *Horror Film Aesthetics: Creating the Visual Language of Fear*. McFarland, 2010.

Steckenfinger, S. A. and A. A. Ghazanfar. "Monkey visual behaviour falls into the uncanny valley." *PNAS* 106 (2009): 18362–66.

Vermeij, G. J. "The limits of adaptation: Humans and the predator-prey arms race." *Evolution* 66 (2012): 2007–14. https://doi.org/10.1111/j.1558-5646.2012.01592.x.

Wang, S., S. O. Lilienfeld, and P. Rochat. "The uncanny valley: Existence and explanations." *Review of General Psychology* 19, no. 4 (2015): 393–407. https://doi.org/10.1037/gpr0000056.

Winston, J. S., et al. "Automatic and intentional brain responses during evaluation of trustworthiness of faces." *Nature Neuroscience* 5 (2002): 277–83. https://doi.org/10.1038/nn816; pmid: 11850635.

CHAPTER 4. PUTTING FEAR IN YOUR EARS

Arnal, L. H., et al. "Human screams occupy a privileged niche in the communication soundscape." *Current Biology* 25, no. 15 (2015): 2051–56. https://doi.org/10.1016/j.cub.2015.06.043.

Beckerman, J. *The Sonic Boom: How Sound Transforms the Way We Think, Feel, and Buy*. Houghton Mifflin Harcourt, 2014.

French, C. C., et al. "The 'Haunt' project: An attempt to build a 'haunted' room by manipulating complex electromagnetic fields and infrasound." *Cortex* 45, no. 5 (2009): 619–29.

Lerner, N. (Ed.). *Music in the Horror Film: Listening to Fear*. Routledge, 2009.

Novak, Colin. "Summary of the 'Windsor Hum Study.'" GAC, May 23, 2014. https://www.international.gc.ca/department-ministere/windsor_hum_results-bourdonnement_windsor_resultats.aspx?lang=eng.

Raphael, Amy. *Danny Boyle: Authorised Edition*. Faber & Faber, 2013.

Singer, N., et al. "Common modulation of limbic network activation underlies musical emotions as they unfold." *NeuroImage* 141 (2016): 517–29. https://doi.org/10.1016/j.neuroimage.2016.07.002.

Tandy, Vic, and Tony Lawrence. "The ghost in the machine." *Journal of the Society for Psychical Research* 62, no. 851 (1998): 360–64.

Wiseman, R., et al. "An investigation into alleged 'hauntings.'" *British Journal of Psychology* 94 (2003): 195–211. https://doi.org/10.1348/000712603321661886.

CHAPTER 5. WHY SOME SCARES STICK WITH YOU

Brown, R., and J. Kulik. "Flashbulb memories." *Cognition* 5, no. 1 (1977): 73–99. https://doi.org/10.1016/0010-0277(77)90018-X.

Burgess, A. W., and L. L. Holmstrom. *Rape: Victims of crisis.* Robert J. Brady, 1974.

Cantor, J. (2006, May) Long-term memories of frightening media often include lingering trauma symptoms. *Association for Psychological Science.* Presented at the Association for Psychological Science convention, New York, USA.

Cantor, J. "Why Horror Doesn't Die: The Enduring and Paradoxical Effects of Frightening Entertainment." In J. Bryant & P. Vorderer (Eds.), *Psychology of Entertainment* (pp. 315–27). Lawrence Erlbaum Associates Publishers, 2006.

Cantor, Joanne, Dean Ziemke, and Glenn Sparks. "Effect of forewarning on emotional responses to horror film." *Journal of Broadcasting* 28 (2009). https://doi.org/10.1080/08838158409386512.

Clasen, M. "'Can't sleep, clowns will eat me': Telling scary stories." In C. Gansel & D. Vanderbeke (Eds.), *Telling Stories: Literature and Evolution.* De Gruyter, 2012.

Fanselow, M. S., and Z. T. Pennington. "A return to the psychiatric dark ages with a two-system framework for fear." *Behaviour Research and Therapy* 100 (2018): 24–29. https://doi.org/10.1016/j.brat.2017.10.012.

Holmes, E. A., et al. "Can playing the computer game 'Tetris' reduce the build-up of flashbacks for trauma? A proposal from cognitive science." *PLOS One* 4, no. 1 (2009): e4153. https://doi.org/10.1371/journal.pone.0004153.

Kerr, Margee. *Scream: Chilling Adventures in the Science of Fear.* Public Affairs, 2015.

LeDoux, Joseph E. "Coming to Terms with Fear." *Proceedings of the National Academy of Sciences* 111, no. 8 (2014): 2871–78. https://doi.org/10.1073/pnas.1400335111.

Neuendorf, Kimberly, and Glenn Sparks. "Predicting emotional responses to horror films from cue-specific affect." *Communication Quarterly* 36 (1988): 16–27. https://doi.org/10.1080/01463378809369704.

Piaget, J. *The Child's Conception of the World.* Littlefield Adams, 1990.

Piaget, J. *The Psychology of the Child.* Basic Books, 1972.

Watson, J. B., and R. Rayner. "Conditioned emotional reactions." *Journal of Experimental Psychology* 3, no. 1 (1920): 1–14. https://doi.org/10.1037/h0069608.

Wilson, B. J., and J. Cantor. "Reducing fear reactions to mass media: Effects of visual exposure and verbal explanation." In M. McLaughlin (Ed.), *Communication Yearbook* 10 (pp. 553–73). Sage, 1987.

CHAPTER 6. VIOLENCE AND MAYHEM

Alia-Klein, N., et al. "Reactions to media violence: It's in the brain of the beholder." *PLOS One* 9, no. 9 (2014): e107260. https://doi.org/10.1371/journal.pone.0107260.

American Psychological Association. *Report of the APA Commission on Violence and Youth*, January 1, 1993. http://www.apa.org/pubs/info/reports/violence-youth.

Bandura, A., D. Ross, and S. A. Ross. "Transmission of aggressions through imitation of aggressive models." *Journal of Abnormal and Social Psychology* 63, no. 3 (1961): 575–82.

Chaffee, Steven. "National Television Violence Study 3." *Journal of Communication* 49, no. 3 (1999): 194–96.

Chaffee, Steven. "The National Television Violence Studies." *Journal of Communication* 47, no. 4 (1997): 170–73. https://doi.org/10.1093/jcom/47.4.170.

Dahl, Gordon, and Stefano DellaVigna. "Does Movie Violence Increase Violent Crime?" SITE Conference Archive—Spotlight at Stanford. Stanford University, 2006. https://exhibits.stanford.edu/site-archive/catalog/pb218gw7580.

Eron, L. D., et al. "Does television violence cause aggression?" *The American Psychologist* 27, no. 4 (1972): 253–63. https://doi.org/10.1037/h0033721.

Ferguson, C., and J. Savage. "Have recent studies addressed methodological issues raised by five decades of television violence research? A critical review." *Aggression and Violent Behavior* 17 (2012): 129–39.

Freedman, Jonathan L. *Media Violence and Its Effect on Aggression: Assessing the Scientific Evidence.* University of Toronto Press, 2002. http://www.jstor.org/stable/10.3138/j.ctt1287sxj.

Friedrich, L. K., and A. H. Stein. "Aggressive and prosocial television programs and the natural behavior of preschool children." *Mono-*

graphs of the Society for Research in Child Development 38, no. 4, Serial No. 151 (1973): 63. https://doi.org/10.2307/1165725.

Hennigan, K. M., et al. "Impact of the introduction of television on crime in the United States: Empirical findings and theoretical implications." *Journal of Personality and Social Psychology* 42 (1982): 461–77. https://doi.org/10.1037/0022-3514.42.3.461.

Huston-Stein, Aletha, et al. "The effects of TV action and violence on children's social behavior." *Journal of Genetic Psychology* 138, no. 2 (1981): 183–91. https://doi.org/10.1080/00221325.1981.10534133.

Kendrick, J. *Film Violence: History, Ideology, Genre.* Wallflower Press, 2010.

Linz, Daniel, Edward Donnerstein, and Steve Penrod. "The effects of long-term exposure to violent and sexually degrading depictions of women." *Journal of Personality and Social Psychology* 55 (1988): 758–68. https://doi.org/10.1037/0022-3514.55.5.758.

Milgram, S. "Behavioral study of obedience." *Journal of Abnormal and Social Psychology* 67, no. 4 (1963): 371–78. https://doi.org/10.1037/h0040525.

Mussen, P., and E. Rutherford. "Effects of aggressive cartoons on children's aggressive play." *Journal of Abnormal and Social Psychology* 62 (1961): 461–64. https://doi.org/10.1037/h0045672.

Newson, Elizabeth. "Video violence and the protection of children." *Journal of Mental Health* 3, no. 2 (1994): 221–27. https://doi.org/10.3109/09638239409003802.

Oliver, M. B. "Adolescents' enjoyment of graphic horror: Effects of viewers' attitudes and portrayals of victim." *Communication Research* 20 (1993): 30–50.

Sharrett, C. (Ed.). *Mythologies of Violence in Postmodern Media.* Wayne State University Press, 1999.

CHAPTER 7. BLOOD, GORE, AND BODY HORROR

Eichenbaum, H. "Prefrontal–hippocampal interactions in episodic memory." *Nature Reviews Neuroscience* 18 (2017): 547–58. https://doi.org/10.1038/nrn.2017.74.

Gagnepain, P., et al. "Collective memory shapes the organization of individual memories in the medial prefrontal cortex." *Nature Human Behaviour* 4 (2020): 189–200.

Morris, Jeremy. "The Justification of Torture-Horror: Retribution and Sadism in Saw, Hostel, and The Devil's Rejects." In Thomas Fahy (Ed.), *The Philosophy of Horror* (pp. 42–56). University Press of Kentucky, 2010.

Ramirez, S., et al. "Creating a false memory in the hippocampus." *Science* 341, no. 6144 (July 26, 2013): 387–91. https://doi.org/10.1126/science.1239073.

Ramirez, Steve, and Mark Mayford. "Melding Two Memories into One." Interview by Flora Lichtman. NPR: Science Friday, July 26, 2013.

Ritz, Thomas, Alicia E. Meuret, and Erica S. Ayala. "The psychophysiology of blood-injection-injury phobia: Looking beyond the diphasic response paradigm." *International Journal of Psychophysiology* 78, no. 1 (2010): 50–67. https://doi.org/10.1016/j.ijpsycho.2010.05.007.

Savini, Tom. *Bizarro: A Learn-by-Example Guide to the Art & Technique of Special Make-up Effects.* Harmony Books, 1983.

Wicken, Marcus, Rebecca Keogh, and Joel Pearson. "The critical role of mental imagery in human emotion: Insights from fear-based imagery and aphantasia." *Proceedings of the Royal Society Biological Sciences* 288, no. 1946 (2021). https://doi.org/10.1098/rspb.2021.0267.

CHAPTER 8. HORROR'S LONG-LASTING APPEAL

Andersen, Marc Malmdorf, et al. "Playing with fear: A field study in recreational horror." *Psychological Science* 31, no. 12 (2020): 1497–510. https://doi.org/10.1177/0956797620972116.

Anthony Lane, et al. "Oxytocin increases willingness to socially share one's emotions." *International Journal of Psychology* 48, no. 4 (2013): 676–81. https://doi.org/10.1080/00207594.2012.677540.

Bantinaki, Katerina. "The paradox of horror: Fear as a positive emotion." *Journal of Aesthetics and Art Criticism* 70, no. 4 (2012): 383–92. https://doi.org/10.1111/j.1540-6245.2012.01530.x.

Bartsch, Anne, Markus Appel, and Dennis Storch. "Predicting emotions and meta-emotions at the movies: The role of the need for affect in audiences' experience of horror and drama." *Communication Research* 37, no. 2 (2010): 167–90. https://doi.org/10.1177/0093650209356441.

Beevers, C. G., et al. "Association of the serotonin transporter gene promoter region (5-HTTLPR) polymorphism with biased attention for emotional stimuli." *Journal of Abnormal Psychology* 118, no. 3 (2009): 670–81. https://doi.org/10.1037/a0016198.

Clasen, Mathias. "Monsters evolve: A biocultural approach to horror stories." *Review of General Psychology* 16 (2012): 222–29. https://doi.org/10.1037/a0027918.

Clasen, Mathias, Jens Kjeldgaard-Christiansen, and John A. Johnson. "Horror, personality, and threat simulation: A survey on the psychology of scary media." *Evolutionary Behavioral Sciences* 14, no. 3 (2020): 213–30.

Fox, E., A. Ridgewell, and C. Ashwin. "Looking on the bright side: Biased attention and the human serotonin transporter gene." *PRSB* 276, no.1663 (2009): 1747–51. https://doi.org/10.1098/rspb.2008.1788.

Harari, H., N. Perach-Bloom, and Y. Levkovitz. "Intranasal administration of oxytocin increases envy and schadenfreude (gloating)." *Biological Psychiatry* 66, no. 9 (2009): 864–70. https://doi.org/10.1016/j.biopsych.2009.06.009.

Hoffner, C. A., and K. J. Levine. "Enjoyment of mediated fright and violence: A meta-analysis." *Media Psychology* 7 (2005): 207–37.

Johnston, D. D. "Adolescents' motivations for viewing graphic horror." *Human Communication Research* 21 (1995): 522–52. https://doi.org/10.1111/j.1468-2958.1995.tb00357.x.

Millar, B., and J. Lee. "Horror films and grief." *Emotion Review* 13, no. 3 (2021): 171–82. https://doi.org/10.1177/17540739211022815.

Nakamura, J., and M. Csikszentmihályi. "The Concept of Flow." In *Flow and the Foundations of Positive Psychology.* Springer, 2014. https://doi.org/10.1007/978-94-017-9088-8_16.

Pinker, Steven. *The Better Angels of Our Nature: Why Violence Has Declined.* Penguin Publishing Group, 2012.

Quintana, D. S., et al. "Oxytocin pathway gene networks in the human brain." *Nature Communications* 10 (2019), Article No. 668. https://doi.org/10.1038/s41467-019-08503-8.

Rozin, Paul, et al. "Glad to be sad, and other examples of benign masochism." *Judgment and Decision Making* 8 (2013): 439–47.

Sparks, Glenn G., and Cheri W. Sparks. "Violence, mayhem, and horror." *Media Entertainment: The Psychology of Its Appeal* 4, no. 2 (2000): 73–92.

Tamborini, Ron. "Enjoyment and social functions of horror." In *Communication and Emotion* (pp. 425–52). Routledge, 2003.

Tamborini, Ron, and James Stiff. "Predictors of horror film attendance and appeal: An analysis of the audience for frightening films." *Communication Research* 14, no. 4 (August 1987): 415–36. https://doi.org /10.1177/009365087014004003.

Taylor, Shelley E. "Tend and befriend: Biobehavioral bases of affiliation under stress." *Current Directions in Psychological Science: A Journal of the American Psychological Society* 15, no. 6 (2006): 273–77.

Tudor, A. "Why horror? The peculiar pleasures of a popular genre." *Cultural Studies* 11 (1997): 443–63.

Welsh, A., and L. Brantford. "Sex and violence in the slasher horror film: A content analysis of gender differences in the depiction of violence." *Journal of Criminal Justice and Popular Culture* 16 (2009): 1–25.

Zillmann, D., et al. "Effects of an opposite-gender companion's affect to horror on distress, delight, and attraction." *Journal of Personality and Social Psychology* 51 (1986): 586–94.

Zuckerman, Marvin. "Behavior and biology: Research on sensation seeking and reactions to the media." In *Communication, Social Cognition, and Affect.* Psychology Press, 1988.